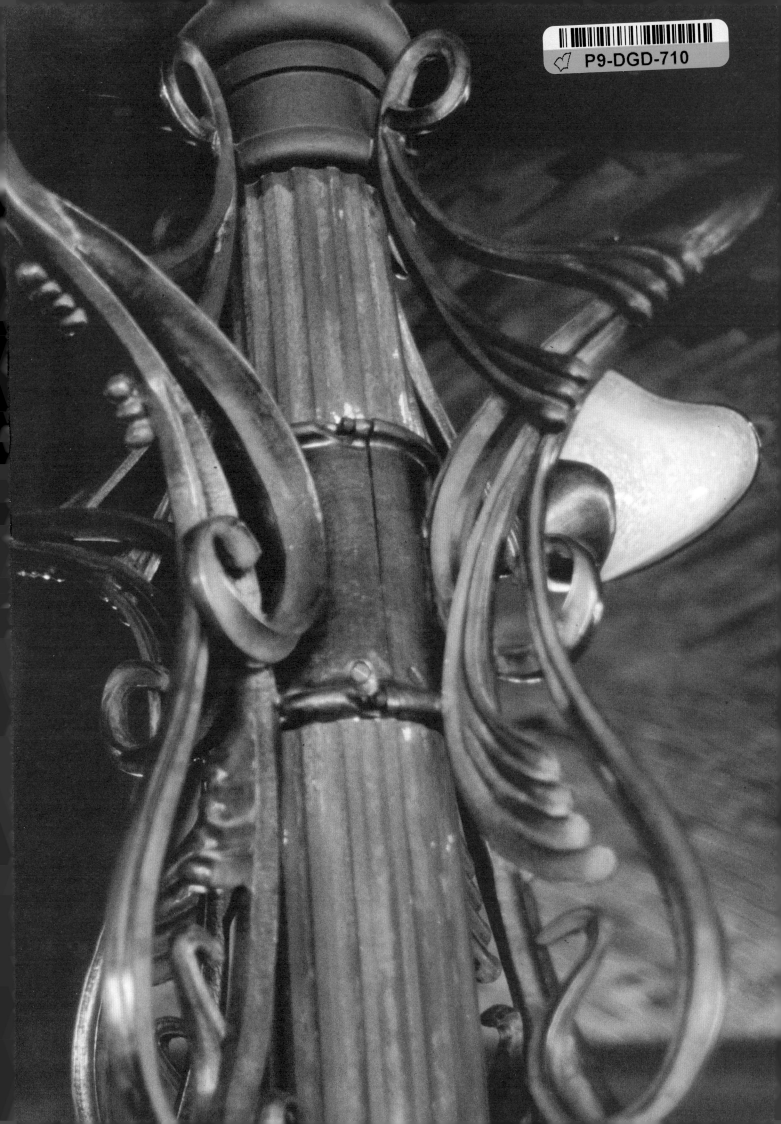

BOULEVARD

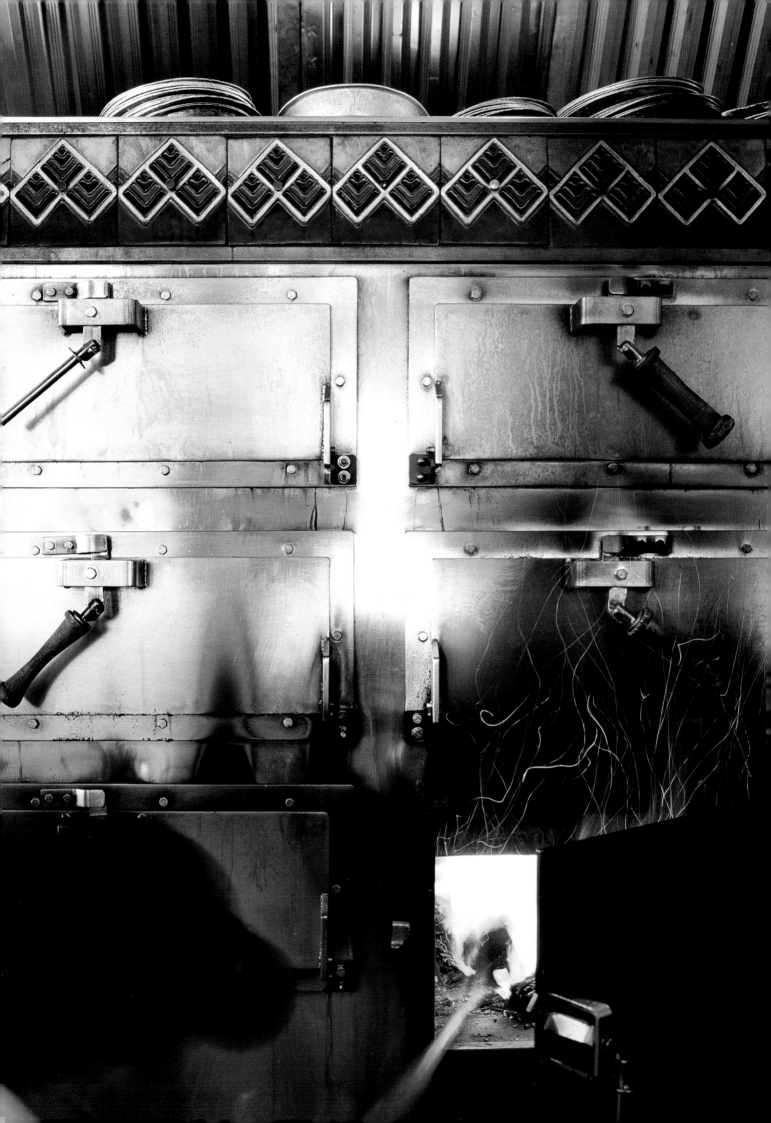

BOULEVARD

THE COOKBOOK

NANCY OAKES AND **PAMELA MAZZOLA**

WITH LISA WEISS

FOOD PHOTOGRAPHS

MAREN CARUSO

LOCATION AND TECHNIQUE PHOTOGRAPHS

ED ANDERSON

TEN SPEED PRESS

BERKELEY / TORONTO

Ten Speed Press
P.O. Box 7123
Berkeley, California
94707

Distributed in Australia by Simon and Schuster Australia, in Canada by
Ten Speed Press Canada, in New Zealand by Southern Publishers Group,
in South Africa by Real Books, and in the United Kingdom and Europe by
Airlift Book Company.

Cover and Interior Design by Ed Anderson
Food Styling by Kim Konecny and Erin Quon
Photography Assistance by Faiza Ali
Digital Imaging and Prepress by Mark Rutherford

Library of Congress Cataloging-in-Publication Data

Oakes, Nancy.
    Boulevard : the cookbook / Nancy Oakes and Pam Mazzola, with Lisa Weiss.
        p. cm.
    Includes index.
    ISBN-13: 978-1-58008-553-3
    ISBN-10: 1-58008-553-9
1. Cookery. 2. Cookery—California—San Francisco. I. Mazzola, Pam.
II. Weiss, Lisa, 1951- III. Boulevard (Restaurant) IV. Title.
    TX714.O23 2005
    641.5'09794'61--dc22
                                2005014661*

First printing, 2005

Printed in China
2 3 4 5 6 7 8 9 10 – 09 08 07 06 05

For my talented and loving husband, Bruce Aidells, who encouraged us
to write this book.

In memory of my parents, Fletcher and Audrey Oakes, who brought me to
San Francisco and taught me about delicious food.

To my husband, Charles, and my children, Maria, Mason, and Maddy—
my favorite people to feed.

ACKNOWLEDGMENTS

. . . .

THANK YOU

. . . .

To date, about 1,940,000 people have joined us for lunch and dinner and 1,100 people have come to work with their hearts, hands and minds and all have left their mark. Every day these two forces come together to create the lively environment and ambiance that is Boulevard. Without them, it's just an empty space.

That said, we start our thanks with Pat Kuleto, whose design is an inspiration every day and has certainly stood the test of time.

To the investors, thank you for believing in us.

Lisa Weiss, thank you for organizing our thoughts, all of your wonderful research, the use of your home as a test kitchen and writers studio. Special thanks to Dan Weiss our taster and commentator who never forgot to offer us a glass of wine after a long day of cooking and writing.

Ed Anderson, the designer who helped us see Boulevard with fresh eyes and kept us inspired through his design, artistry, and his incredible location shots.

To Doe Coover, who led us to Ten Speed Press.

Our editors, Lorena Jones, who brought all the right people to the team and helped us turn our ideas into a book, and Annie Nelson, who showed us how to finish the project and stayed by our side to see it through.

To Deborah Mintcheff, for her superb copy editing. And to Sharon Silva. We stand corrected.

Kathy King, the general manager, for her humor, intelligence, friendship, energy, and patience. We wouldn't want to run this place without you.

Richard Miyashiro, our opening general manager, thank you for watching over us.

Pamela McGee, for getting us open, for being a great cook who has become a great event manager and for making us laugh every day and reminding us what girlfriends are all about.

Nancy Pitta, Boulevard's pastry chef for developing recipes, testing recipes, writing recipes, and making sure these recipes work. You are a treasure.

Romney Steele, for organizing the dessert recipes and turning them into a manuscript.

A special thanks to Brian Martinez, Jacob Kenedy, Ravi Kapur, Tim Quaintance, Susan Bussiere, Richard Crocker, and John Desmond for all your support, contributions, and diligent work getting these recipes on paper.

Maren Caruso, the food photographer, and her fabulous crew, thank you for the enthusiasm you brought to the project, you were a pleasure to work with. Thank you for the gorgeous food shots.

We can't complete these acknowledgments without thanking the people who came from L'Avenue to open Boulevard: Gaines Dobbins, Alex Padilla, Susan Bussiere, John Desmond, Richie Rosen, Jennifer Holbrook, Pam Barnett, Carmen (Melo) Alvarez, Len Van Ho, Phil Barton, Patty Evans, Jay Altobelli, Carrie Bridgers, Raphael Morales, Patrick Boyle, and David Touye.

Thank you to all our purveyors, who go above and beyond and are always excited about introducing us to new products.

The artisans and crafts people, who created the beautiful tile, glass, wood, and metal work that brought Boulevard to life, your creations bring us joy every day.

Thank you to the fabulous staff at Boulevard, past and present, with a special thanks to all of our sous chefs, managers, sommeliers, hosts, waitstaff, bussers, bartenders, controller, reservationists, sauciers, pastry cooks and our executive prep crew. We are so fortunate.

Special thank you to my parents, Stan and Lois, who supported my move from college to cooking with encouragement and great pride.

. . . .

In addition to the talented staff at Boulevard, I would personally like to thank my agent, Jane Dystel, for her unwavering support and integrity; Lorena Jones, Annie Nelson, and the staff at Ten Speed for their guidance and unbelievable patience throughout this project; Ed Anderson and Maren Caruso for giving this book its stunningly beautiful visual "voice," and Bruce Aidells, who gets a special thank you for encouraging me from the beginning to do this project. Finally I thank Nancy and Pam, brilliant chefs of course, but also two of the most dedicated, funny, and generous people I've ever had the good fortune to work with.

Lisa Weiss

1   A Quest for What's Delicious

2   Cooking from This Book

4   The Boulevard Pantry

SALADS

9   **Endive and Heirloom Apple Salad,** Applewood-
Smoked Bacon, Candied Pecans, and Creamy
Montgomery Cheddar Dressing

11 **White Asparagus Salad with "Crunchy" Poached
Farm Egg,** Fresh Porcini, Parmesan Fonduta, and
Serrano Ham

14 **Mediterranean Mussels with Panzanella and
Arugula,** Fennel Confit and Soft Saffron Aioli

19 **Warm Medjool Dates Stuffed with Goat Cheese,**
Blood Oranges, Pistachios, Pomegranate, Bitter
Greens, and Blood Orange Vinaigrette

21 **Carpaccio of Fresh Hearts of Palm, Cucumbers,
and Summer Truffles,** Ricotta Salata and Banyuls
Vinaigrette

23 **Salt-Roasted Bosc Pear and Roquefort Salad,**
Toasted Walnut Relish, Port Vinaigrette, and Lollo
Rossa Lettuce

SOUPS

29 **Cauliflower Soup with Maine Lobster**

31 **White Corn Soup,** Little Crab Cake "Soufflés"

33 **Roasted Ratatouille Soup with White Beans and
Serrano Ham**

35 **Braised Chestnut Soup,** Apple Cream and Crispy
Duck Confit

37 **Provençal Fish Soup,** Herb-Roasted Jumbo Prawns,
Bouillabaisse Relish, and Aioli

41 **Artichoke Soup,** Artichoke Hearts, Marcona Almond
and Mint Pesto

STARTERS

46 **Dungeness Crab Cakes,** Asparagus, Lemon Vinaigrette, and Crab Salad

51 **Black Truffle Pappardelle,** Shaved Black Truffles and Parmesan Beurre Fondue

54 **Pan-Seared Monterey Calamari,** Fresh Dungeness Crab Legs and Oven-Roasted Tomatoes

57 **Fried Green Tomato and Crispy Hama Hama Oyster "BLT,"** Tartar Sauce and Green Tomato Vinaigrette

60 **Goat Cheese and Truffle Ravioli,** Pine Nut Pesto, Basil and Tiny Fava Pesto, Roasted Tomatoes, White Asparagus and Truffles

64 **Trio of Tuna Tartares,** Jalapeño and Ginger, Spicy Red Chile, Shiitake, and White Soy

67 **Seared Sea Scallop,** Fresh Shelling Beans, Lomo Embuchado, Smoked Spanish Paprika

70 **Sand Dabs Stuffed with Lobster,** Artichoke Confit, Parsley Beurre Fondue

73 **Maine Lobster Tail with John Desmond's Black Pudding,** Potato Mousseline, Fennel and Leek Relish, Blood Orange Jus

76 **Pan-Seared Foie Gras,** Bosc Pear Confit, Almond *Pain Perdu,* Sherry Vinegar Reduction, and Assorted Salts and Peppers

80 **Quail Stuffed with Foie Gras and Roasted Porcini Mushrooms,** Kabocha Squash Puree and Asian Pear, Thyme and Spanish Sherry Relish

86 **Glazed Sweetbreads in Potato Crust,** Chanterelle Mushrooms and Red Wine Reduction

91 **Pan-Roasted Mediterranean Rouget Barbet,** Melted Eggplant, Shrimp and Basil Beignets, Heirloom Tomato Carpaccio

FISH

96 **California White Sea Bass Roasted with Olives and Basil,** Potatoes Crushed With Garlic, Chiles, and Arugula, Tomato Vinaigrette

98 **Pan-Roasted Halibut Fillets and Cheeks,** Fresh Morel Mushrooms, Spring Vegetables, Green Garlic Pesto, and Morel Mushroom Jus

103 **Pan-Roasted Wild King or Ivory Salmon,** Potato, Bacon, and Watercress Cake, Shaved Apple and Fennel Salad, Cider Sauce, and Mustard Vinaigrette

106 **Roasted True Cod,** Tomato Gratin, Pancetta and Baby Spinach Salad, Pine Nut Relish

110 **Pan-Roasted Black Bass,** Santa Barbara Spot Prawns, Cauliflower "Risotto"

113 **Crispy-Skinned Onaga,** Braised Shellfish Mushrooms and Fresh Hearts of Palm

116 **Bacon-Wrapped Maine Monkfish Stuffed with Lobster and Avocado,** Fresh Coriander Risotto and Green Almonds

121 **Spiny Lobster Paella** with a Pot of Steamed Clams and Chorizo

POULTRY AND GAME

127   **Buttermilk-Brined Fried Little Chickens,** Mashed
      Potatoes, Gravy, and Cream Biscuits

131   **Roasted Poussin with Spicy Corn Bread Stuffing,**
      Andouille Gumbo Sauce

134   **Pot-Roasted Guinea Hens,** Twice-Cooked Potatoes
      with Garlic Mousseline, Warm Arugula and Olive Salad
      with Glazed Walnuts

139   **Pan-Roasted California Pheasant Breast,** Spring
      Onions, Prunes in Armagnac, Braised Bacon, Savoy
      Spinach, and Lisa's Potato Pancakes

143   **Duck Breast Stuffed with Apples and Chestnuts
      and Roasted in Bacon,** Celery Root Puree and
      Calvados Sauce

146   **Pan-Roasted Squab,** Hazelnut Pancakes, Grape and
      Kumquat Relish, Foie Gras Sauce

153   **Rabbit Two Ways:** Legs Fried in a Parmesan Crust
      and Roasted Loins Wrapped in Smithfield County
      "Prosciutto," Fava Beans, English Peas, and Mint

MEAT

158   **Fennel-Roasted Pork Tenderloin and Porcini-Pork
      Sausage Wrapped in Pancetta,** White and Green
      Beans with Garlic Confit, Pork-Porcini Jus

161   **Cider-Brined Berkshire Pork Loin Chop,** Bacon,
      Pomegranate, and Pistachio Relish, Shaved Brussels
      Sprouts, and Cider Jus

164   **Lamb Porterhouse Chop Stuffed with Broccoli Rabe
      and Melted Garlic,** Potato "Risotto"

168   **Veal Chops Stuffed with Porcini Mushrooms and
      Asiago Cheese,** Roasted Fingerling Potatoes,
      Tomatoes, Sage, Pancetta, and Arugula

171   **Veal, Veal, Veal** Roasted Tenderloin, Veal Osso Buco,
      and Veal Cheek Ravioli

177   **Fire-Roasted Angus Beef Filet,** Sweet White
      Corn and Chanterelles, Blue Cheese Fritters,
      Heirloom Tomatoes

180   **New York Strip Roasted in an Herbed Salt Crust,**
      Creamed Morels with Aged Madeira on Toast

185   **"Steamship" Short Ribs Bourguignon**

193   **New Year's Eve Venison Chop "Rossini":** Venison,
      Foie Gras, Toast, Creamed Spinach, Truffle Sauce,
      and Shaved Black Truffles

DESSERTS

198   **Whole-Apple Crisp,** Rum Raisin Ice Cream, Cider
      Caramel Sauce

200   **Chocolate Cherry Shortcakes,** Old-fashioned Vanilla
      Ice Cream and Cherries Jubilee

203   **Manjari Chocolate Truffle Tart with Salted Caramel
      Ice Cream**

206   **White Chocolate-Banana Cream Pie**

208   **Carrot Cake with Cream Cheese Filling,** Candied
      Walnut Ice Cream, Cream Cheese Ice Cream,
      Carrot Sorbet

212   **Heather Ho's Lemon Meringue Icebox Cake**

215   **Bittersweet Chocolate Cake,** Caramel Corn Ice
      Cream and Caramel Sauce

218   **Chocolate Temptation:** Chocolate Panna Cotta,
      Chocolate Toffee Crunch

223   **Vanilla, Vanilla, Vanilla** Crème Brûlée, Bavarian
      Timbale, Ice Cream Sandwich

226   Boulevard Basics
236   Sources
238   Index

A QUEST FOR WHAT'S DELICIOUS

NANCY OAKES AND **PAM MAZZOLA**

For years we've successfully avoided writing a cookbook. In fact, if certain people hadn't continued to encourage and pester us, it probably wouldn't have happened. Our work has never been static or at a point where we're certain of it because our thoughts about food are always evolving. Our biggest hurdle has been to assemble a collection of recipes that we feel represents the food that we've done to date, as well as alludes to the work that we'll do in the future. Most of these recipes have appeared in one form or another at L'Avenue or Boulevard and actually encompass bits and pieces of how we cook at home. All of the recipes we've included have withstood the test of time, and we continue to cook them. After having looked through all the recipes in the book, we've probably included too many with bacon but in the words of our friend Frank Everette, "Everything is better with bacon." (Thank goodness we decided to omit the recipe for bacon ice cream).

This book has been organized in a fairly traditional manner except for the omission of a side dish chapter. To some extent, Boulevard food has become defined by the accompanying side dishes, and we've decided to remain true to our menu writing style and include the side dishes as accessories to the center of the plate. We know that people are very intrigued by the side dishes and plan their meals around them. Hopefully you will do the same and see that there are infinite possibilities and combinations for all of the dishes and that they can be rearranged like furniture.

We cook because we love to feed people and also because we love the process of cooking. From the first glimpse of the raw ingredients, through all the stages of their transformation, we still get extraordinarily excited by the prospect of developing new dishes. We don't think for a minute that we've invented a new cuisine or discovered a new approach to cooking—only a never-ending quest for what's delicious.

People are often surprised to hear that we have been cooking together for seventeen years. We both realize that this is an unusual partnership considering we aren't bound by any legal documents. Our work together has forged a friendship that has certainly withstood the heat of the kitchen and has transcended the restaurant. It is our most valuable asset.

There are days we suspect we are turning into the same person and can often be found completing each other's sentences or saying the same thing at the same exact moment. In case this is sounding too syrupy, we don't always share the same opinion, and we do disagree, but our secret is as follows: don't hold grudges, be liberal with apologies (they're free), admit your mistakes, and it's OK to let someone else be right. Let's not understate the importance of mutual respect, but the greatest bond of all is that we appreciate each other's sense of humor and think that we are hysterically funny.

Even for us there is a difference between home and restaurant cooking. We are fortunate to work with a group of extremely talented people and we have easy access to amazing ingredients, so with this being said, you might find some of the recipes challenging to produce in the home kitchen without our experienced crew. Hopefully the *Kitchen and Shopping Notes* will help you successfully reproduce these recipes at home.

Reading and writing about food is only a fraction of the pleasure. For us, the true gratification is in choosing and preparing the ingredients, getting our hands and minds involved in the process, maybe making a mistake and figuring out how to fix it, but ultimately making a lot of people happy with our efforts. We hope this book finds a home in your kitchen and soon will bear the marks of an often-used cookbook: grease spots and gravy stains.

COOKING FROM THIS BOOK

LISA WEISS

There's an inherent difficulty in writing recipes for chefs, beyond the obvious fact that their recipes are often technically difficult, have many components, and call for unusual or hard-to-find ingredients. After working with many chefs and coauthoring several chef cookbooks, the biggest challenge I've encountered has been that most chefs—Nancy and Pam in particular—are reluctant to commit any recipe to paper. That is, chefs never view a dish as "done" and always seem to be experimenting with new ingredients, combinations, or presentations, much in the same way as an artist always sees something that needs to be changed in his or her work.

From a writer's point of view, this freewheeling creative attitude can be frustrating, but from a cook's point of view it can be inspiring. Of course, all great chefs accrue a lot of tricks of the trade that can be useful to home cooks, and Nancy and Pam are no exception. For instance, now I know that—with help from the microwave—I can make a mellow garlic confit in a couple of minutes, or that a lean piece of meat, like a rabbit loin, can be wrapped in a thin slice of pancetta or bacon to protect it and give it flavor. Now my freezer always has dark chicken stock made with readily purchased, on-sale chicken wings, rather than homemade veal demi-glace made from expensive and hard-to-find veal bones. I learned to keep aged artisanal balsamic vinegar on hand for last-minute drizzling over meats and salads, and I use my small kitchen torch not just for caramelizing, but also for warming the sides of a metal mold to release a dessert.

In order to ensure that the recipes in this book would accurately reflect the dishes served at Boulevard, Nancy and Pam (with Nancy Pitta on desserts) set about with their characteristic dedication, personally testing each recipe themselves, either in my home kitchen or at the restaurant.

Of course, I learned a great deal from them, though not in the way I expected. Yes indeed, I picked up a lot of professional tips that you'll find scattered throughout the book. But the first thing that struck me as I watched them, their movements seemingly choreographed and their thoughts telegraphed almost telepathically from one to the other, was that there's a joy they share in the process and how much fun they have. Although Nancy and Pam are serious about their craft, and there's a perfectionism driving their work, it was also obvious to me just how much they love what they do. They truly enjoy the act of cooking.

As the two of them hustled about the kitchen, chopping, pureeing, sautéing, I kept noticing how they're forever tasting. This tasting thing is not new to me; I was taught long ago that to be a good cook, you need to taste as you go along, but Nancy and Pam are obsessive about making sure their food tastes good. And although their plated food is beautiful to look at, their ultimate goal is not about precious ingredients with architecturally precarious arrangements. Their food cries out to be eaten—devoured—each bone licked clean and every last morsel consumed.

But at every turn in this project, the recipes kept changing. Ingredients as well as recipes kept being omitted or added, even at the very end as we were shooting final photos. It was then that I came to the realization that most truly inspired cooks never view the act of cooking simply as a means to an end. Nancy and Pam are two professionals who love what they do and are constantly striving to make their food taste better, so it's no wonder that their dishes continued to evolve even as we were writing them down for the book. Recipes after all are only meant to be guides. And although Nancy and Pam approached the writing of each recipe as if they were teaching a class, trying to answer questions and anticipate problems, it's impossible to take into account all the variables, such as the expertise of the cook, the quality of ingredients, or the even the variations between electric or gas, or oven and stove top temperatures. Yes, the recipes in this book had their genesis in a restaurant kitchen, made with wonderful ingredients, lots of kitchen help, and cutting-edge culinary equipment. But Nancy and Pam, as they tested their own recipes with the home cook in mind, never hesitated to substitute an ingredient if they couldn't find the one they initially wanted to use, or to eliminate a step if it would be one too many.

That's why it's important to remember, as you read and cook your way through this book, above all to be flexible, because a recipe can capture a dish at only one moment in the time of its evolution. The real lesson to be learned from this book—or any other cookbook for that matter—is that at the end of the day, it still all comes down to trusting your own instincts and taste buds.

So as you cook from this book, keep in mind the following:

Ingredients can be substituted; search out the best you can find and then experiment with them.

Many dishes in this book can be challenging, so consider making just one part of a dish, say the Lamb Porterhouse Stuffed with Broccoli Rabe and Melted Garlic, without the potato risotto. Or, just try the potato risotto the next time you broil some lamb chops.

If it's the first time you're making a recipe, read it through carefully, find out if there is any special equipment called for, gather your ingredients, and follow it closely. The second time you make the recipe, approach it the way a chef would: think about how you might change it to make it your own.

There's a great deal of kitchen wisdom in these pages. Even if you're not interested in preparing a particular dish, read its *Kitchen and Shopping Notes,* because you'll learn a little something that you may be able to use another time.

Cook the recipes in this book with the same spirit in which they were created: with joy.

THE BOULEVARD PANTRY

With a basic pantry, one that at the very least contains some really good extra-virgin olive oil, aged balsamic vinegar, a few kinds of salt along with a pepper grinder, a couple of homemade stocks, plus some fresh vegetables and some meat from a good butcher, you'll not only be able to prepare many of the dishes in this book, but you'll always be prepared to throw together a simple and sophisticated dish on short notice. Here's an overview of the ingredients we frequently refer to throughout this book.

OIL

Generally pure olive oil (called simply olive oil in the recipes) is used for cooking and extra-virgin olive oil for salads. Occasionally, canola oil is called for, for which you can substitute any flavorless vegetable oil, or grape seed oil, which is also flavorless and great for sautéing because of its high smoking point. In some recipes, you'll see that a "special" or artisanal extra-virgin olive oil is specified, which means that it's time to use the best oil you can afford, because its flavor will be discernable in the finished dish. The number of specialty oils available today can make choosing difficult. They come from Italy, France, Greece, Spain, and the United States, and range from mild and delicate, fruity and fragrant, and olivy and peppery to leafy green and grassy. Which one you prefer is a matter of personal taste and how it will be used.

VINEGAR

The production of good-quality vinegar, like olive oil, has exploded in the last few years and shelves of specialty markets often carry a dizzying and confusing array. Three vinegars are always on the restaurant's pantry shelves: Aged sherry vinegar from Spain, Banyuls from France, and *aceto balsamico tradizionale di Modena,* or artisanal balsamic, from Italy, which is used only very, very sparingly. When larger quantities of balsamic are required, such as for salad dressings, a good-quality commercial brand will work. Again, let your own taste buds be the judge.

STOCK

Primarily Dark Chicken Stock is used as a base for all sauces, and then flavor is added with browned bones and trimmings from various meats and poultry. While you'll need to devote some time and attention (and maybe a Saturday and Sunday) to making this stock, it's worth its weight in gold in your fridge or freezer, and can be used to transform quick pan sauces from simple to sublime. The recipes for this and other stocks are in Boulevard Basics (page 226).

GARLIC

Nancy and Pam are fanatics about using fresh garlic—never stooping to the prepeeled or chopped and preserved stuff in a jar. At Boulevard, cooks take no shortcuts where garlic is concerned and peel and chop fresh garlic several times a day as part of their *mise en place.*

SALT AND PEPPER

Diamond Crystal kosher salt was used for testing the recipes in this book and is the all-purpose salt used at the restaurant. Sometimes it's sea salt, particularly in fish dishes, and some dishes get a sprinkling of *fleur de sel* or flaky Maldon salt before serving. Specialty salts and peppers can also be used in a mini-tasting, where several salts and peppers are served on the plate.

BUTTER

Only unsalted (sweet) butter is used at the restaurant for cooking and serving. In cooking, unsalted butter lets you control the amount of salt in a finished dish, which in pastry is particularly important. Though butter flavor varies according to what the cows are fed, no matter which brand you prefer, keep in mind that unsalted butter goes bad quickly (salt is a preservative), so make sure it smells fresh and store it well wrapped in the refrigerator.

CHOCOLATE

Over the past few years we have seen an explosion of artisan chocolate producers. Fine baking chocolates from both Europe and America are now widely available in grocery stores across the country. Cocoa beans are grown in many tropical regions of the world, and the chocolate they produce will vary according to the how they've been roasted and the amount of sugar or other flavors such as vanilla that are added. Terms such as *semi-sweet, bittersweet* and *extra-bitter* can be confusing and many chocolate manufacturers are now adding cocoa percentages to their labels. The ratio of cocoa to sugar determines the chocolate to sweet flavor. For example, 100% would have no added sugar, and anything with less than 50% cocoa would be on the sweet side. Most high-quality semi-sweet and bittersweet chocolate fall within the 50% to 70% range and have a rich, deep chocolate profile. Where the depth of chocolate flavor is important in a recipe, we've specified a percentage for you to look for when you're shopping. All of the dessert recipes in this book were tested using French Valrhona chocolate, which is available in many supermarkets and by mail-order (see Sources, page 237).

SHALLOTS 4/25/05

SHALLOTS 4/25/05

CHY   HOUS   BALSAMIC

SALADS

ENDIVE AND HEIRLOOM APPLE SALAD

**APPLEWOOD-SMOKED BACON, CANDIED PECANS, AND
CREAMY MONTGOMERY CHEDDAR DRESSING**

SERVES 4

**CREAMY CHEDDAR
DRESSING**

¾ cup heavy cream
5 ounces Montgomery Cheddar or
    other high-quality Cheddar,
    grated (see Kitchen and
    Shopping Notes)
1 tablespoon whole-grain mustard
1 tablespoon Dijon mustard
1 cup crème fraîche
Kosher salt and freshly ground
    black pepper

CANDIED PECANS

1 cup Candied Pecans (see Basics,
    page 228), chopped

SALAD

8 thin slices bacon
8 Belgian endive
1 Pink Pearl apple or other heirloom
    variety (see Kitchen and
    Shopping Notes)

Can any one salad contain all our favorite things? Crisp, tart apples, smoky bacon, sharp Cheddar, candied pecans, and crunchy endive—this salad really has it all. Taste, texture, and, best of all, our muse, bacon. We like to serve this salad in the autumn and early winter when locally grown apples are at their peak. And though red-skinned apples make a prettier salad, we love it with all kinds of heirloom apples that appear in our farmers' markets, especially the pink-fleshed Pink Pearl apples from Oz Farms in Mendocino County. Try to search out specialty apple varieties in your area and support your local growers.

KITCHEN AND SHOPPING NOTES

Most of the commercially grown apples that consumers are familiar with have been developed for a long storage life that meets the demands of worldwide shipping. Unfortunately, most supermarket apples, while readily available, lack complex flavor and character. In the last few years, however, we've been encouraged by the number of growers producing heirloom varieties that have robust flavor, texture, and beauty.

We've become addicted to the wonderful award-winning Montgomery Cheddar from Neal's Yard in England but are really excited by the renewed interest in artisanal cheese production in the United States. This salad presents a perfect opportunity to search out some excellent sharp American Cheddar, such as Dan Carter's Black Diamond or the aged Cheddars from Widmer's Cheese Cellars and Shelburne Farms. For this salad to be extraordinary, choose each ingredient as if it were to be savored on its own.

continued

METHOD

FOR THE CHEDDAR DRESSING: Heat the heavy cream in a small saucepan over low heat until bubbles appear around the edge. Whisk in the cheese and continue to whisk for about 2 minutes, or until melted, then strain through a fine-mesh sieve into a bowl. Whisk in the mustards and crème fraîche until combined. You will have about 2 cups of dressing. Chill the dressing in the refrigerator for at least 1 hour, or until thickened, or refrigerate for up to 3 days. Season to taste with salt and pepper just before serving.

TO SERVE

Cook the bacon in a skillet until golden but not too crisp. Set aside on paper towels to drain. While the bacon is cooking, cut off about ½ inch from the bottoms of the endives and separate into individual leaves. Put the leaves into a bowl and toss with enough of the dressing to coat them lightly. On each of 4 dinner plates, reassemble the endive leaves to form a loose "head." Quarter the apple lengthwise and cut out the core with a paring knife. Using a mandoline, thinly shave the apple on top of the endive. Drizzle more dressing (you may not use all of it) around the endive and sprinkle with the candied pecans. Finish each salad by draping 2 strips of warm bacon on top.

WHITE ASPARAGUS SALAD WITH "CRUNCHY" POACHED FARM EGG

FRESH PORCINI, PARMESAN FONDUTA, AND SERRANO HAM

SERVES 4

ASPARAGUS
12 white asparagus spears

PORCINI MUSHROOMS
½ pound fresh porcini mushrooms, cleaned
2 tablespoons olive oil
4 peeled cloves garlic
6 thyme sprigs
Kosher salt and freshly ground black pepper

POACHED EGGS
1 tablespoon distilled white or cider vinegar
4 very fresh extra-large "farm" eggs
1 cup panko (Japanese bread crumbs)
1 teaspoon kosher salt
½ teaspoon chopped fresh thyme
2 extra-large egg whites, lightly beaten

¾ cup olive oil
Kosher salt

PARMESAN FONDUTA
½ to ¾ cup heavy cream
½ cup Parmigiano-Reggiano cheese
Freshly ground black pepper

GARNISH
4 slices serrano ham or prosciutto
Fresh flat-leaf parsley leaves
Porcini powder (see Basics, page 234)
Smoked salt (optional, see Sources, page 237)
Grains of paradise (optional, see Sources, page 237)

Few things are more satisfying than poached eggs; we think they are an almost perfect food. But when eggs are coated in bread crumbs and then fried in olive oil, satisfying turns into sublime. It would be difficult to choose the star of this dish: the earthy porcini; elegant white asparagus; poached eggs textured with crunchy bread crumbs; the rich, slightly salty serrano ham; or the tangy Parmesan fonduta. Combined they create a soulful but sophisticated warm salad that we enjoy as a generous first course or all by itself as a light supper or brunch.

KITCHEN AND SHOPPING NOTES

There are several ways to achieve neatly poached eggs, and you can find simple instructions in many basic cookbooks. The key, however, to getting perfectly cooked yolks suspended in a compact white pouch has little to do with technique. Simply make sure your eggs are fresh. The whites of less-than-fresh eggs turn into wisps as soon as they hit the water. Check the dates on the egg cartons at your grocer or, better yet, look for farm eggs at your local farmers' market, where you can often find local sources for eggs that are very fresh. Because the quality of the eggs is so important to this dish, a bonus to farm eggs is that they're often from hens that are fed on grass as well as grain, so their yolks can be vivid yellow to orange.

Many years ago, Julia Child suggested using egg holders—perforated oval molds on legs with handles to remove them from the water—to guarantee "handsomely" poached eggs. Luckily these inexpensive little gadgets are still available in many better cookware shops (see Sources, page 237). We like to use the holders for the eggs in this dish because they turn out perfect ovals that make a great presentation after they've been fried in their bread-crumb coating. Eggs poached without the holders, however, will still be perfectly fine.

continued

The time for cooking asparagus can vary, depending on the kind and size of the stalks (white asparagus takes longer). We recommend that you cook the asparagus in a wide skillet so that you can easily check the asparagus. Begin checking after 3 minutes for medium-size asparagus.

METHOD

FOR THE ASPARAGUS: Bring a wide, deep skillet of salted water to a boil. Snap off the woody ends of the asparagus where they break naturally, then peel the stalks. With a paring knife, trim the end of each stalk to form a ¾-inch-long point. Cook the asparagus in the boiling water until just tender (see Kitchen and Shopping Notes), then remove and set aside.

FOR THE PORCINI: Separate the mushroom caps from the stems and set aside. Peel the stems and cut in half or slice in thirds if they're particularly large. Heat the oil in a skillet over medium-high heat. Add the porcini caps and stems and sauté for 5 minutes. Decrease the heat to medium-low, add the garlic and thyme, and cook for 10 minutes more, or until the porcini are tender. Season with salt and pepper and set aside.

TO POACH THE EGGS: Bring 2 inches of water to a boil in a large sauté pan or skillet. Decrease the heat to maintain a low simmer and add the vinegar. You want to see bubbles just slowly breaking the surface. Break 1 of the eggs into a small cup or ramekin. Working clockwise and starting at the 12 o'clock position, partially immerse the cup in the water and quickly slide in the egg. Repeat with the remaining 3 eggs. Cook for 3 to 5 minutes, or until the yolks feel medium-firm to the touch. Using a slotted spoon, remove the eggs and drain on a clean kitchen towel. Using a paring knife, trim away any ragged edges. Alternatively, if you're using "Julia's" oval molds, place them in a pan of simmering water and, using the clockwise method, slide the eggs from the cups into the molds. (If the molds aren't nonstick, first give them a little spritz of nonstick cooking spray.) When the eggs are done, remove the molds from the water and gently scoop the eggs out onto a towel with a spoon. The poached eggs can be stored in a bowl of cold water in the refrigerator for up to 1 day.

Combine the panko, salt, and thyme in a small bowl. Gently roll 1 of the poached eggs in the egg whites until it's coated on all sides, then roll in the panko mixture. Don't worry if there are some bare spots on the eggs. Set aside on a plate and repeat with the other eggs.

FOR THE FONDUTA: Bring ½ cup of the heavy cream to a bare simmer in shallow skillet or small saucepan. Whisk in the Parmesan for about 2 minutes, or until it's melted. Add the salt and season to taste with pepper. Set aside for up to 2 hours and gently reheat until warm just before serving, adding more cream if the fonduta has become too thick.

TO SERVE

About 10 minutes before serving, heat the olive oil in a 10-inch sauté pan or skillet over medium heat until the oil just begins to shimmer. Working clockwise, starting at 12 o'clock, gently slide 1 of the eggs into the oil, yolk-side down. Continue with the other 3 eggs. When the last egg goes in, flip the first egg, and cook on the bottom side for 30 seconds. Remove the 12 o'clock egg and place on a paper towel to drain. Repeat this sequence with the remaining eggs and remove them in the same order. Season with a little salt.

Place 3 asparagus spears on each of 4 dinner plates. Spoon some of the warm fonduta over the asparagus and top with an egg. Arrange the mushrooms alongside (leaving the garlic and thyme in the pan) and drape each dish with the ham. Top with parsley leaves and sprinkle some porcini powder, smoked salt, and grains of paradise around the edge.

MEDITERRANEAN MUSSELS WITH PANZANELLA AND ARUGULA

FENNEL CONFIT AND SOFT SAFFRON AIOLI

SERVES 4

PANZANELLA

1 cup (¼-inch) diced good-quality well-textured French bread, such as *pain levain* or sourdough

6 tablespoons olive oil

2 teaspoons minced shallots

1 teaspoon minced garlic

¼ cup julienned dry-packed sun-dried tomatoes

½ cup julienned Oven-Dried Tomatoes (see Basics, page 232)

2 tablespoons rinsed capers

1 tablespoon julienned fresh basil leaves

MEDITERRANEAN MUSSELS

1 tablespoon olive oil

2 tablespoons thinly sliced shallots

1 clove garlic, thinly sliced

2 thyme sprigs

¾ cup dry white wine

2 pounds large Mediterranean mussels (see Kitchen and Shopping Notes)

FENNEL CONFIT

2 cups (½-inch) diced fennel

1 cup olive oil

3 thyme sprigs, tied together

SAFFRON SAUCE

1 teaspoon olive oil

1 shallot, diced

1 clove garlic, chopped

Pinch of saffron threads

1 cup reserved mussel cooking liquid

½ cup heavy cream

¼ cup Aioli (see Basics, page 228)

1 large egg yolk

ARUGULA SALAD

2 teaspoons sherry vinegar, red wine vinegar, champagne vinegar, or freshly squeezed lemon juice

Pinch of kosher salt

2 tablespoons extra-virgin olive oil

4 cups loosely packed cleaned arugula

Freshly ground black pepper

Extra-virgin olive oil, for drizzling

1 tablespoon chopped fresh flat-leaf parsley leaves

1 teaspoon freshly squeezed lemon juice

Julienned fresh basil leaves, for garnish

Much of what we find appealing to our palates is captured in this salad: it's briny, creamy, crunchy, peppery, fresh, and tart—qualities that renew our interest with every bite. Assembled on one plate are actually three salads: a warm confited fennel salad, panzanella, the Italian bread salad, and a fresh, peppery arugula salad. This stretches the boundaries of what is traditionally considered a salad, but we've come to love this way of eating.

If all this seems like a bit of a bother to prepare, the dish is easily deconstructed. The stuffed mussels make tempting hors d'oeuvres served on individual spoons or stuffed back into their shells and dressed with the warm aioli. Or they can be layered in a casserole and served family style with arugula and aioli on the side. The fennel confit is a wonderful condiment for grilled meats, fish, or poultry and, as you may notice if you've read through this book, arugula seems to be the appropriate garnish for most everything.

KITCHEN AND SHOPPING NOTES

Mediterranean mussels are a large variety (the key word here is *large,* since they need to be stuffed) cultivated in the Pacific Northwest and available year-round, even during the summer months when other mussels are on the undesirable list (see Sources, page 236). In fact, any large mussel will work in this recipe. If, however, the only mussels you can get are too small to stuff, toss them together in a shallow casserole or baking dish and top with the panzanella, then bake until everything is warmed through.

Store the raw mussels in a bowl in the refrigerator covered with a damp towel. Before cooking, scrub them clean with a stiff brush and pull out the beard if necessary. If any are open slightly, tap them on the kitchen counter, let sit for 30 seconds to see if they close, then throw away any that don't.

METHOD

FOR THE MUSSELS WITH PANZANELLA: Preheat the oven to 350°F. To make the stuffing, toss the diced bread with 2 tablespoons of the olive oil in a medium bowl and spread out on a rimmed baking sheet. Set the bowl aside. Bake, turning with a spatula once or twice, for about 6 minutes. Sprinkle the shallot and garlic over the bread, stir with the spatula, and bake for 2 minutes more, or until the bread is crisp and golden. Return the bread to the bowl, add the tomatoes, capers, and the remaining 4 tablespoons olive oil, and toss until well mixed. Set aside to let the bread cubes absorb the juices.

continued

To cook the mussels, heat the olive oil in a large sauté pan or saucepan, add the shallot, garlic, and thyme and cook, stirring, for 2 minutes. Add the mussels, stirring to coat with the oil, then add the wine. Cover and cook for 3 to 5 minutes, or just until the mussels have opened, shaking the pan or stirring a couple of times to make sure the mussels cook evenly. Using a slotted spoon, transfer the mussels to a bowl. Discard any unopened mussels. Strain the mussel liquid through a fine-mesh sieve and reserve. The mussels can be cooked up to 1 day ahead, but they should be stuffed no more than 1 hour before you plan to serve them. Stuff the mussels with $\frac{1}{2}$ to 1 teaspoon of the tomato-bread mixture, depending on the size of the mussels, place on a small rimmed baking sheet, and cover loosely with plastic wrap.

FOR THE FENNEL CONFIT: Combine the fennel with the oil and thyme in a small casserole or saucepan. Bring to a low simmer on top of the stove. Cover and bake in a 350°F oven for about 20 minutes, or until the fennel is very soft. Strain through a sieve into a bowl and reserve the oil for another use. An alternative method we often use at home is to cook the fennel in the microwave on HIGH for 6 to 8 minutes. The fennel can be cooked and refrigerated up to 2 days ahead.

FOR THE SAFFRON SAUCE: Heat the oil in a saucepan over medium-high heat. Add the shallot, garlic, and saffron and cook for 30 seconds or so. Add the mussel cooking liquid and heavy cream, raise the heat, and bring to a boil (watch that it doesn't boil over). Lower the heat to medium and simmer until the liquid has reduced to $\frac{1}{2}$ cup. Strain the sauce through a fine-mesh sieve into a small saucepan and whisk in the aioli and egg yolk. Set the sauce aside for up to 1 hour before serving. The sauce can be gently reheated over low heat, but be very careful because reheating can cause it to break or separate.

FOR THE ARUGULA SALAD: Whisk the vinegar and salt together in a medium bowl, then whisk in the olive oil until blended. Add the arugula and toss until the leaves are coated. Season to taste with pepper.

TO SERVE

Drizzle the mussels with a little olive oil and rewarm in the oven for 5 to 8 minutes. Rewarm the fennel in a saucepan on top of the stove or in a microwave and toss with the parsley and lemon juice in a small bowl. Place a 4-inch ring mold in the center of a dinner plate and pack it with one-quarter of the fennel salad. Carefully remove the ring mold and repeat with 3 more plates. Place 5 or 6 mussels on top of the fennel and drizzle with any liquid left in the warming pan. Spoon the sauce around the plates, sprinkle with the basil, and top with the arugula salad.

If you've read through this book, arugula seems to be the appropriate garnish for most everything.

WARM MEDJOOL DATES STUFFED WITH GOAT CHEESE

BLOOD ORANGES, PISTACHIOS, POMEGRANATE, BITTER GREENS, AND BLOOD ORANGE VINAIGRETTE

SERVES 4

BLOOD ORANGE VINAIGRETTE

6 blood oranges

3 tablespoons light corn syrup

2 tablespoons rice wine vinegar

1 teaspoon kosher salt

1 cup grape seed oil

½ cup pistachios

MIXED GREENS SALAD

1 small head radicchio

2 cups loosely packed
    cleaned mizuna

2 cups loosely packed
    cleaned arugula

2 cups loosely packed torn
    cleaned frisée

DATES

12 Medjool dates

4 ounces fresh goat cheese

GARNISH

Pomegranate seeds (see Cider-
    Brined Berkshire Pork Loin
    Chop, page 161)

Pistachio oil

If ever there was a seasonal salad that proves "What grows together goes together," this is it. We eagerly wait for the later months of the year, just before the holidays, when the California Medjool date, blood orange, pistachio, and pomegranate seasons all converge. There are few things as soft and rich as Medjool dates, and stuffing them with tangy goat cheese creates a nice contrast, as well as an explosion of flavor when you bite into them while warm.

Slightly bitter, peppery, and crisp greens are essential to balance the sweet richness of the oranges and dates. Don't be tempted to substitute milder greens, even if someone at your table claims to be a "super-taster" (a person who cannot bear bitter flavors.) Super-tasters complain bitterly when confronted with the likes of endive, arugula, and radicchio, but we prefer to think that acquiring a taste for these greens is a sign of a mature and well-rounded palate. If you sense your argument will fall on deaf ears, try this Italian technique for tempering the bitterness: core the radicchio and endive and soak the cut leaves in cold water for 10 minutes. Drain and discard the water, then repeat the procedure 2 more times.

KITCHEN AND SHOPPING NOTES

Originally from Morocco, Medjool dates are grown almost exclusively in the Coachella Valley in California. (In fact, California produces 90 percent of the dates in the United States.) If you've never tried these luscious, meaty, plump, dark dates, you're in for a treat. They're most plentiful from November to March and are usually sold loose in the produce section of supermarkets. It's widely assumed that dates are dried, but they are actually fresh fruits. Other date varieties, such as Barhi or Khadrawi, make adequate—but not equal—substitutes here.

Blood oranges come to market from December to April, depending on the variety, the Moro and Tarocco being the two most common. We love their ruby red flesh and slightly tart, orange-raspberry-like flavor.

continued

METHOD

FOR THE BLOOD ORANGE VINAIGRETTE: With a swivel-bladed vegetable peeler, remove the zest from the oranges, then peel away and discard all the white pith. Pull the oranges apart into segments and put segments from 2 of the oranges into a blender with the zest. Reserve the remaining segments for garnish. Add the corn syrup, rice vinegar, and salt and puree. With the machine running slowly, gradually add the oil and blend until thickened. Set aside at room temperature for up to 6 hours or refrigerate for up to 2 days.

FOR THE PISTACHIOS: Preheat the oven to 350°F. Put the pistachios in a small baking pan and toast for 8 to 10 minutes, or until they take on color, stirring once or twice. Remove from the oven and put the nuts on a clean kitchen towel. Fold the towel over the nuts, then rub the nuts together and roll them around to remove some of the skins. Set the nuts aside on a plate to cool.

FOR THE SALAD: Cut the radicchio in half and cut out the core. Cut the radicchio into ½-inch pieces and put into a large bowl. Add the rest of the greens and refrigerate loosely covered with a damp towel for up to 8 hours.

FOR THE DATES: Make a lengthwise slit in each date and pull out the pit. Roughly divide the goat cheese into 12 pieces, stuff into the dates, and press them closed. Place, seam side down, on a small sheet pan or baking pan. Set aside or refrigerate until ready to serve. Just before serving, heat the dates in a 350°F oven for 1 to 2 minutes (if the dates have been refrigerated, they will take longer to reheat), or until warm.

TO SERVE

Toss the greens with some of the vinaigrette (you may not need all of it) until lightly coated. Place a mound of greens on each of 4 dinner plates and arrange 3 warm dates around the salad with alternating piles of the reserved orange segments. Sprinkle the pistachios and pomegranate seeds around the plate and drizzle pistachio oil over all.

CARPACCIO OF FRESH HEARTS OF PALM, CUCUMBERS, AND SUMMER TRUFFLES

RICOTTA SALATA AND BANYULS VINAIGRETTE

SERVES 4

BANYULS VINAIGRETTE
2 tablespoons Banyuls vinegar (see Sources, page 237)

1 cup extra-virgin olive oil

SALAD
1 (10-inch) English cucumber

1 (9-ounce) piece fresh heart of palm

3 ounces summer truffles

Coarse sea salt

Freshly ground black pepper

4 teaspoons finely sliced fresh chives

¼ pound fresh ricotta salata cheese

Extra-virgin olive oil (optional)

This is an elegantly simple salad composed of some pretty hard-to-find ingredients. We've included this recipe—in spite of its "energetic" shopping list—because it never fails to delight us or our guests. At a Parisian wine bar, we were served an equally simple and delicious salad of shaved cucumbers, fresh goat cheese, chives, and fruity extra-virgin olive oil. It was memorable, even with just those ingredients.

KITCHEN AND SHOPPING NOTES

Italian summer truffles, available from late spring through summer, are cousins to the regal white Italian and black French truffles that are eagerly anticipated in the winter. With their nutty flavor, black skin, and beautiful almost-white interior, summer truffles offer flavor, as well as eye appeal and, of course, they're much more affordable than their winter kin. Like white truffles, they should only be eaten raw. Combined simply with extra-virgin olive oil and sea salt, summer truffles make a wonderful salad or pizza topping.

Fresh hearts of palm are often available in Latin markets, shipped fresh from Costa Rica and Hawaii; seek them out or leave them out. Fresh hearts of palm have a clean, slightly sweet flavor and light crunchy texture that bear no resemblance to their cooked, canned, and brined counterparts. If fresh hearts of palm and fresh summer truffles are out of your reach, just revert to the simpler Parisian wine-bar version; though different, it's delicious.

Banyuls, made from Grenache and Muscat grapes, is a fortified dessert wine from a seaside town in southern France of the same name. Aged vinegar made from Banyuls wine is complex and smooth and makes an excellent vinaigrette.

continued

METHOD

FOR THE BANYULS VINAIGRETTE: Whisk the vinegar with the oil in a bowl until combined. Set aside.

TO SERVE

Using a mandoline, thinly slice the cucumber onto 4 dinner plates; it is not supposed to be perfectly arranged. Again with the mandoline, thinly slice the heart of palm randomly over the cucumber. Repeat in the same manner with the truffle. Season to taste with the sea salt and pepper. Shave the ricotta salata with a cheese plane or crumble over the salad, sprinkle with the chives, and drizzle with the vinaigrette (you'll have extra) or, if you prefer, just a little extra-virgin olive oil

SALT-ROASTED BOSC PEAR AND ROQUEFORT SALAD

TOASTED WALNUT RELISH, PORT VINAIGRETTE, AND LOLLO ROSSA LETTUCE

SERVES 4

WALNUT RELISH

½ cup walnuts

½ cup extra-virgin olive oil

¼ cup finely diced shallots

1 tablespoon chopped fresh
   flat-leaf parsley leaves

SALT-ROASTED PEARS

1 (4-pound) box rock salt

2 firm Bosc pears
   (about ½ pound each)

PORT VINAIGRETTE

2 cups ruby port

2 tablespoons red wine vinegar

1 tablespoon aged balsamic vinegar

¾ cup extra-virgin olive oil

Kosher salt and freshly ground
   black pepper

SALAD

4 cups loosely packed, cleaned Lollo
   Rossa lettuce leaves

4 ounces Roquefort cheese
   (about 1 cup crumbled)

It may sound like an odd technique—salt-roasting fruit—but when Bosc pears are roasted in a cloak of salt, all their perfume and flavor becomes concentrated, and their naturally crisp, crunchy flesh is transformed into velvet. Of course, once we discovered how fabulously the pears turned out, we went on to roast all the fruit we could get our hands on. To our dismay, we found that only Bosc pears succumb to this technique. In this dish, the trio of pears, Roquefort, and port is a sweet, salty, and savory combination that seems to make everyone happy.

KITCHEN AND SHOPPING NOTES

We must confess to employing the microwave for a few culinary tasks, such as melting garlic, making vegetable purees, roasting lemons, and heating tortillas for family meals. But we've also discovered that the microwave yields meltingly soft salt-roasted pears quickly and easily. Microwave instructions are offered in this recipe as an alternative to using a conventional oven. The rock salt can be saved and reused 4 or 5 times before it gets saturated with moisture and starts to solidify.

Lollo Rossa is one of our favorite red lettuces. Its ruffled leaves are beautiful as well as tasty, and it lofts into a nice high pile when dressed with vinaigrette, but oak leaf or plain red lettuce is just fine too.

continued

METHOD

FOR THE WALNUT RELISH: Preheat the oven to 325°F. Bring salted water to a boil in a small saucepan and add the walnuts. Boil for 3 minutes. (This removes their bitterness.) Drain the walnuts and spread out on a small sheet pan or baking pan. Toast for 15 minutes, or until dry and crisp but not browned. Remove from the oven and, when cool, chop into pea-size pieces. While the walnuts are toasting, heat the olive oil in a small skillet over medium heat and add the shallots. Cook for about 4 minutes, or until translucent, then remove from the heat and let cool. Set aside in a small bowl for up to 4 hours.

FOR THE PEARS: Raise the oven temperature to 350°F. Spread a 1-inch-deep layer of salt in a high-sided baking or casserole dish. Lay the pears on their sides and nestle into the salt with the stems facing in opposite directions. Pour enough salt on top of the pears so that they are completely buried. Roast the pears for 40 minutes, then remove the pan from the oven and let the pears rest in the salt for 15 to 25 minutes, or until they're easily pierced with a thin wooden skewer or paring knife. Transfer the pears to a plate and brush off the clinging salt with a pastry brush. Halve the pears lengthwise and let cool to room temperature.

To roast the pears in the microwave, spread a 1-inch-deep layer of salt in a small, high-sided microwave-safe container. Lay the pears on their sides and nestle into the salt with the stems facing in opposite directions. Pour more salt over so that the pears are completely buried. Microwave on HIGH for 6 minutes. Remove the container and let the pears sit in the salt for 5 to 10 minutes, or until they can be easily pierced with a thin wooden skewer or paring knife.

Once the roasted pears have cooled, peel them using a serrated peeler. Cut each pear half lengthwise. Cut in half again to form wedges. Using a melon baller, scoop out the core and pull out the center strings and stems. Set aside or refrigerate overnight. Let come to room temperature before serving.

FOR THE PORT VINAIGRETTE: Cook the port in a saucepan over medium heat until reduced to ¼ cup. Let cool, then whisk in the red wine vinegar and aged balsamic. Slowly whisk in the olive oil and season to taste with salt and pepper. Set aside.

TO SERVE

Toss the Lollo Rossa lettuce with some of the dressing in a bowl and place a mound on each of 4 dinner plates. Drizzle a spoonful of dressing around the perimeter of each plate. Toss the walnuts and parsley in the bowl with the sautéed shallots. Drop the relish in dots and crumble the Roquefort around the salad. Tuck 2 pear quarters into the side of each lettuce pile.

SOUPS

This may be the shortest recipe
we will ever write, but sometimes
simplicity is the height of elegance
and this soup is a testament to both.
Butter, salt, and pepper are all
you need to make this soup divine.
Rarely is such an elegant dish so
easy to prepare.

CAULIFLOWER SOUP WITH MAINE LOBSTER

**MAKES ABOUT
4 (1-CUP) SERVINGS**

CAULIFLOWER SOUP

1 large head cauliflower
(about 2 pounds)
6 cups water
1 tablespoon kosher salt
4 tablespoons unsalted butter,
at room temperature,
plus 1 tablespoon cold
unsalted butter

Meat from a 1¼- to 1½-pound cooked
lobster (about 3½ ounces, see
Basics, page 232), cut into large
bite-size pieces

HERB AND LEMON OIL

2 tablespoons finely sliced fresh
chives
1 tablespoon finely chopped
lemon zest
½ teaspoon freshly ground
black pepper
6 tablespoons extra-virgin olive oil

KITCHEN AND SHOPPING NOTES

It's important not to overcook cauliflower, as it can develop an unpleasant cabbagey odor
if cooked too long. You want it supertender but not mushy or falling apart. The same
principle applies to making the soup in advance. Store the soup covered in the refrigerator
for no more than 4 or 5 hours before serving. When cutting the lobster for the garnish,
don't make the pieces too small; people appreciate identifiable lobster in their soup. Besides,
if you finely chop the lobster, you'll leave most of its flavor on your cutting board.

METHOD

FOR THE SOUP: Remove and discard the outer leaves of the cauliflower, cut out the
core, and then separate into florets. Put the cauliflower florets in a large saucepan with the
water and salt, and bring to a boil over high heat. Maintain a lively simmer and cook for
8 to 12 minutes, or until very tender. Drain into a sieve placed over a bowl. Let cool for a
few minutes, then put the cauliflower and 2½ cups of the reserved cooking liquid into a
blender with the 4 tablespoons butter and puree until smooth. (You may need to do this in
2 batches to avoid a major blender explosion.) Strain through a fine-mesh sieve back into
a saucepan if serving right away or a bowl if serving later. Add more liquid if the soup is
too thick. It should be silky and just coat the back of a spoon. Taste and season with salt if
needed and keep warm, or let cool and refrigerate, covered, for up to 4 hours and reheat
before serving.

FOR THE HERB AND LEMON OIL: Whisk the chives, lemon zest, pepper, and olive oil
together in a small bowl until combined. Set aside for up to 4 hours.

TO SERVE

Heat the lobster meat with the 1 tablespoon cold butter in a skillet until warm. Heat the
soup if necessary, then divide among 4 warm soup bowls. Place a spoonful of the warm
lobster meat garnish in the center of each bowl and drizzle the herb and lemon oil around
the lobster.

WHITE CORN SOUP

. . . .

LITTLE CRAB CAKE "SOUFFLÉS"

. . . .

MAKES ABOUT 8 (1-CUP) SERVINGS

SINGLE CORN STOCK

10 to 12 ears white corn, husks and
    silk removed

2 onions, coarsely chopped

1 leek (white part only), halved
    lengthwise, cleaned, and thinly
    sliced

2 heads garlic, halved crosswise

3 or 4 thyme sprigs

1 bay leaf

10 black peppercorns

4 quarts water

SOUP

3 tablespoons olive oil

2 onions, halved and sliced
    ½ inch thick

2 leeks (white part only), halved
    lengthwise, cleaned, and thinly
    sliced

8 cups corn stock

7 cups reserved corn kernels

4 tablespoons unsalted butter,
    cut into pieces

2 teaspoons kosher salt

Freshly ground black pepper

GARNISH

1 cup reserved corn kernels

1 tablespoon unsalted butter

¼ cup finely sliced fresh chives

LITTLE CRAB CAKE SOUFFLÉS

¾ cup heavy cream or half-and-half

2 large eggs, lightly beaten

2 teaspoons Dijon mustard

1 cup (1-inch) cubes crustless
    sourdough or white bread

2 tablespoons finely diced red onion

2 tablespoons finely diced celery

¼ cup grated Monterey Jack cheese

2 teaspoons chopped fresh
    flat-leaf parsley

½ teaspoon chopped fresh thyme

1 cup cooked crabmeat

Kosher salt and freshly ground
    black pepper

Silky and smooth, this soup is the essence of sweet white summer corn. The secret to its fresh taste is a short cooking time and a double corn stock. Every time we make corn stock, we can't believe how much flavor is locked inside a corncob. It is truly a gift when a pot of boiling water, a few onions, garlic, and herbs, along with the corncobs becomes pure corn flavor.

We make this soup when the sweet local corn arrives and we have an abundance of corncobs in our walk-in refrigerator. We realize you're going to have to buy extra corn to make the stock, but there are always plenty of uses for fresh corn off the cob (see Caramel Corn Ice Cream, page 215, and Fire-Roasted Angus Beef Filet, page 177).

Crab and corn were made for each other, and these delightful little crab cake soufflés are one of our favorite things to eat with this soup. We love them so much, we often serve them on their own with just a little tartar sauce. We used to plop the soufflés right into the soup, but lately our preference is to serve a little stack of them on the side. Prawns, lobster, chanterelles, morels, and summer truffles are all wonderful garnishes, as is heirloom red corn. But the soup is so delicious, that a simple sprinkle of chives is all you need.

continued

KITCHEN AND SHOPPING NOTES

We are committed to the double corn stock, but the soup is almost as delicious made with single corn stock. For a double stock, pour the single corn stock over 10 to 12 more corncobs. Simmer for 30 minutes and reserve the extra corn kernels for another use. Often when people think of soup, they associate it with long, slow cooking, but in this case, the quick cooking of the soup yields the freshest pure corn flavor. Beware of using any of the new supersweet varieties of corn, as they can make this soup taste like a caramelized dessert.

For the crab cakes we use disposable individual 2-ounce aluminum tins, which are available in many grocery stores, but mini-muffin tins or small ramekins will work, too.

METHOD

FOR THE SINGLE CORN STOCK: With a chef's knife, cut the kernels from the corn. You should have about 8 cups. Reserve 7 cups of the corn kernels for the soup and 1 cup for garnish. With the back of the knife, scrape the cobs over a large soup pot to release some of the corn milk. Break the corncobs in half and add them to the pot with the onions, leek, garlic, thyme sprigs, bay leaves, and peppercorns. Add the water and bring to a boil over high heat. Decrease the heat to low and simmer, uncovered, for 45 minutes. Strain the liquid through a sieve into a container or large bowl and set aside, discarding the solids. See Kitchen and Shopping Notes if you want to make a double corn stock.

FOR THE SOUP: Heat the olive oil in a large saucepan over medium heat. Add the onions and leeks. Reduce the heat to low and cook, stirring occasionally, for about 10 minutes, or until translucent and soft. Do not let them color. Add 8 cups corn stock and return to the boil. Add the reserved 7 cups corn kernels and simmer for a final 5 minutes. The corn should be cooked but still have a slightly crunchy texture. Puree the soup with the butter in a blender or food processor in 2 or 3 batches. Add the salt and season to taste with pepper. Strain through a fine-mesh sieve into a container or bowl and refrigerate for up to 3 days.

FOR THE CRAB CAKE SOUFFLÉS: Whisk together the cream, eggs, and mustard in a bowl. Add the bread cubes, onion, celery, cheese, parsley, and thyme. Fold in the crabmeat. Season with salt and pepper. Cover and refrigerate for $1\frac{1}{2}$ hours. Meanwhile, preheat the oven to 375°F. Spray 16 (2-ounce) disposable aluminum muffin tins with nonstick cooking spray. Alternatively, use 2-ounce ramekins or mini-muffin tins. Fill with the soufflé mixture to within $\frac{1}{4}$ inch of the tops. Bake for 20 minutes, or until puffed and golden. Remove and let rest on a counter for 5 minutes before removing from their molds. The crab cake soufflés can be baked up to 2 hours in advance, and reheated in a 375°F oven for 5 minutes.

TO SERVE

Return the soup to a saucepan and reheat. Taste again for salt and pepper. For the garnish, sauté the reserved 1 cup corn in the butter in a small skillet for 1 minute. Reheat the soufflés if necessary, then unmold them, one at a time, by inverting them onto a small plate. Place a soufflé in the center of each soup bowl or serve them alongside piled on a plate. Ladle the soup around the soufflés, sprinkle with the chives, and serve immediately.

ROASTED RATATOUILLE SOUP
WITH WHITE BEANS AND SERRANO HAM

MAKES ABOUT 8 (1-CUP)
SERVINGS

**ROASTED
RATATOUILLE SOUP**

1¾ pounds Roma tomatoes,
    cut into 2-inch pieces

2 large red bell peppers, cut into
    2-inch squares

1 eggplant (about ¾ pound), cut
    into 2-inch cubes

1 red onion, cut into 2-inch pieces

1 fennel bulb, cut into 2-inch pieces

1 zucchini, cut into 2-inch-thick
    rounds

2 tablespoons chopped garlic

½ cup extra-virgin olive oil

¼ cup tomato paste

2 thyme sprigs

2 oregano sprigs

1½ teaspoons kosher salt

½ teaspoon freshly ground
    black pepper

6 to 7 cups Dark Chicken Stock
    (see Basics, page 230)

GARNISH

1 cup drained cooked gigande, Italian
    butter, cannellini, or emergo
    beans (see Basics, page 231)

1 cup Garlic Confit and Gigande Bean
    Fondue (see Basics, page 232)

¼ cup julienned serrano ham

1 teaspoon chopped fresh rosemary
    leaves

Ratatouille is a Provençal word derived from the French *touiller,* meaning "to stir up." Originally from Nice, this hearty stew, made from the rich, ripe vegetables of late summer, has been popularized (for better or worse) around the world. A Niçoise purist would cook the tomatoes, eggplant, and zucchini separately, then combine them with onions, garlic, and herbs and slowly simmer them into a smooth and creamy stew. We take a different approach, however, and encourage this process in the oven. A good long, slow roasting of the vegetables melds the flavors together in a most pleasing way. When the vegetables have caramelized and become soft, we quickly turn them into a satisfying pureed soup, which can be served with just a drizzle of extra-fruity virgin olive oil or, as we serve it at the restaurant, with a spoonful of saucy gigande beans, serrano ham, and chopped fresh rosemary.

KITCHEN AND SHOPPING NOTES

Our current favorite dry bean is the gigande, which we get from Phipps Ranch in Half Moon Bay, California. Phipps Ranch beans are grown, dried, and sold all in one season, ensuring that the beans are plump with a creamy texture inside their tender skins. When fresh shelling beans are available during their short season, we like to feature them in this same preparation, but for most of the year, it's best to look for high-quality new-crop dry white beans. To garnish this dish, we combine whole cooked gigande beans with a puree of the beans that is combined with garlic confit.

continued

METHOD

FOR THE SOUP: Preheat the oven to 350°F. Toss all the vegetables with the garlic, olive oil, tomato paste, thyme sprigs, oregano sprigs, salt, and pepper in a large bowl until well combined.

Spread out in a large roasting pan and roast, turning with a spatula every 20 minutes or so, for 1¼ to 1½ hours, or until the vegetables are golden brown. Meanwhile, heat 6 cups of the dark chicken stock in a large saucepan or small stockpot over a low heat and when the roasted vegetables are done, add them to the stock and cook at a low simmer for 10 minutes. Transfer the soup to a food processor in 2 or 3 batches, and pulse a few times until the vegetables are roughly pureed. Strain through a medium-mesh sieve into a bowl and reheat before serving or refrigerate for up to 2 days.

TO SERVE

Combine the cooked beans and the fondue in a small saucepan and warm slowly. Heat the soup until it's nice and hot, adding more chicken stock if it's too thick, and pour into 8 warm soup bowls. Spoon a generous amount of the saucy beans into the center of the bowls, and scatter the serrano ham and rosemary over the beans.

BRAISED CHESTNUT SOUP

APPLE CREAM AND CRISPY DUCK CONFIT

MAKES ABOUT 8 (1-CUP)
SERVINGS

BRAISED CHESTNUT SOUP

1 cup cognac or brandy

½ cup (1 stick) unsalted butter

2 cups sliced and cleaned leeks,
    white part only

3 cups fresh or frozen peeled
    chestnuts (about 1 pound) (see
    Kitchen and Shopping Notes)

2 thyme sprigs

½ bay leaf

4 cups Dark Chicken Stock (see
    Basics, page 230), heated to
    a low simmer

1 cup heavy cream

Kosher salt and freshly ground
    black pepper

GARNISH

2 duck confit legs (see Basics,
    page 229)

1 cup natural apple juice

¼ cup heavy cream

1 thyme sprig

1 tablespoon unsalted butter

1 cup Fuji apple, peeled and finely
    diced (kept in water to cover
    and 1 tablespoon freshly
    squeezed lemon juice)

Kosher salt and freshly ground
    black pepper

1 tablespoon olive oil

Watercress sprigs (optional)

A lot of menu writing is about seduction. When we put chestnuts on the menu, they conjure romantic visions of holidays out of Charles Dickens, winter walks in Manhattan, and songs about open fires. The reality for the cook, however, is that chestnuts are rich, slightly starchy, and often difficult to peel. But on the positive side, chestnuts are just right for both sweet and savory preparations, and this full-bodied winter soup is a good example. Enhanced by cognac and garnished with sweet apples and slightly salty duck confit, this dish is unimaginably rich and delicious. If you've been very, very good, a nice holiday reward might be this soup topped with a generous shaving of white truffles and a dollop of crème fraîche. But as we all know, being very, very good should be its own reward!

KITCHEN AND SHOPPING NOTES

This soup is cooked in the oven. Roasting intensifies the flavor, controls the rate of evaporation, and prevents the chestnuts from scorching on the bottom of the pot.

We sometimes buy imported Italian chestnuts (see Sources, page 237) that have been peeled and frozen and are an excellent product, but when we're seduced by fresh chestnuts in the fall, this is our method for cleaning them: We give the chestnuts and a sharp paring knife to Cristobal in the Boulevard kitchen and step aside. On his days off when we are forced to take on this task ourselves, we cut an X in the flat side of each chestnut shell with a sharp paring knife, then put them into a saucepan with enough water to cover, and bring to a boil.

continued

We let the chestnuts simmer until they are tender when pierced with a knife. When done, we drain them, and put 1 chestnut at a time into a clean kitchen towel and peel off the outer shell and inner skin. It's necessary to work quickly, however, as they become harder to peel as they cool off. If the chestnuts become too difficult to peel, simply reheat them and proceed with the peeling.

Preparing homemade duck confit sounds like a formidable task, but it is surprisingly easy to do, though it does need to be planned for. Don't make confit just for this soup—make a lot of it when you have the time and can serve it for some impromptu dinners. You can also order confit duck legs by mail (see Sources, page 236) and have them delivered the next day.

METHOD

FOR THE SOUP: Preheat the oven to 375°F. Heat the cognac in a small saucepan over low heat until it's reduced to ¼ cup and set aside. Melt the butter in a sauté pan (that can fit in your oven) or a casserole dish over low heat. Add the leeks and cook, stirring occasionally, until softened but not colored, about 20 minutes. Add the chestnuts, thyme, bay leaf, and hot chicken stock. Transfer the pan to the oven and cook, stirring every 10 minutes or so to make sure all the caramelized liquid is recombined, for 40 minutes. Remove the pan from the oven, stir in the cream, and let cool for 10 minutes. Puree the soup in a blender or food processor in 2 or 3 batches, then strain through a fine-mesh sieve into a bowl. Whisk in the reduced cognac and season to taste with salt and pepper. Reheat before serving or refrigerate for up to 2 days.

FOR THE GARNISH: Remove and discard the skin and bones from the duck and loosely pull the meat apart by hand into not-too-small pieces and set aside. Combine the apple juice, heavy cream, and thyme in a small saucepan over high heat and cook until reduced to ½ cup. Melt the butter in a small sauté pan or skillet over low heat. Drain the apples, add to the pan, and quickly sauté until softened but still slightly crunchy. Discard the thyme sprig from the reduced apple juice–cream mixture and add to the apples, stirring to coat. Season to taste with salt and pepper and set aside. Reheat if necessary just before serving.

TO SERVE

Heat the olive oil in a nonstick skillet over medium-high heat, add the pieces of duck confit, and cook until golden and crispy on the edges. Divide the soup among 8 warm soup bowls. Garnish with the warm apple cream and mound the crispy duck confit on top of the apples. Add something green like a sprig of watercress to each bowl, if you must.

PROVENÇAL FISH SOUP

HERB-ROASTED JUMBO PRAWNS, BOUILLABAISSE RELISH, AND AIOLI

MAKES ABOUT 8 (1-CUP) SERVINGS

FISH SOUP

½ cup fruity extra-virgin olive oil

3 cups (½-inch) diced fennel

1 cup (½-inch) diced onion

10 cloves garlic, minced

2 teaspoons saffron threads

1 cup (½-inch) diced peeled red bell pepper

6 cups (about 4 pounds) peeled, seeded, and diced Roma tomatoes

2 tablespoons fresh thyme leaves

2 cups dry white wine

4 cups Fish Fumet (see Basics, page 229)

2 cups (1½-inch) cubed sea bass, cod, or hake fillet (about 1 pound)

Leaves from 1 bunch basil

½ teaspoon piment d'Espelette (see Sources, page 237) or ¼ teaspoon crushed red pepper flakes

BOUILLABAISSE RELISH

1 tablespoon olive oil

¼ cup (¼-inch) finely diced carrot

¼ cup (¼-inch) finely diced fennel

¼ cup (¼-inch) finely diced celery

2 tablespoons finely diced (¼-inch) onion

⅛ teaspoon saffron threads

3 tablespoons water

CROUTONS

8 (2-by-1½-inch) rectangles *pain levain* or sourdough bread

¼ cup extra-virgin olive oil

¼ cup finely chopped fresh flat-leaf parsley

1 clove garlic, minced

Kosher salt and freshly ground black pepper

HERB-ROASTED PRAWNS

8 jumbo (6 to 8 count) prawns

Kosher salt and freshly ground black pepper

2 tablespoons olive oil

2 cloves garlic, thinly sliced

2 thyme sprigs

¼ teaspoon crushed red pepper flakes

2 tablespoons unsalted butter

AIOLI (see Basics, page 228)

1 tablespoon julienned fresh basil leaves

Best-quality extra-virgin olive oil, for drizzling (optional)

Finely milled fish and vegetables create the luxurious texture of this soup. The rich, warm flavors of ripe tomatoes, olive oil, fennel, and saffron evoke fond memories of the south of France. Our version resembles extracted chowder with a delicate fresh seafood flavor that is somewhere between a bouillabaisse and a classic Provençal fish soup. We use a mild white fish to enhance the flavor of the soup, garnish it with a big, gorgeous roasted prawn, and we're never stingy with the aioli.

KITCHEN AND SHOPPING NOTES

At the restaurant, we fillet and portion hundreds of pounds of fish on a weekly basis, leaving us with lots and lots of little pristine pieces of fish that are perfect for this soup. You'll need to buy a lean white fish, such as cod, bass, rock fish, snapper, or even halibut, for milling into the soup base. Don't feel guilty if you think you're wasting the fish, because all the essence of the fish is actually captured in the finished product. Just don't use an oily fish, such as salmon, tuna, mackerel, or any of their relatives which will impart a strong "fishy" flavor; the fish needs to be lean, white, and delicate.

continued

Remarkable tomatoes are only available in their season; however, sometimes you can find organic, sweet tomatoes, such as Del Cabo, in the off-season, or consider roasting tomatoes (Oven-Roasted Tomatoes, see Basics, page 232) to intensify their flavor. This satisfying soup can easily become lunch or dinner by using more prawns or substituting 3 or 4 ounces of grilled fish fillets.

A food mill is a relatively inexpensive old-fashioned piece of equipment that we've found does certain jobs really well, like this soup, but it's probably worth buying just to make proper mashed potatoes. Without a food mill, the more perilous choice would be to process the hot liquid in a blender (being careful not to inflict yourself or anyone in the vicinity with scalding burns), then push it through a coarse sieve.

METHOD

FOR THE SOUP: Heat the oil in a large saucepan or soup pot over medium-high heat until it shimmers. Add the fennel, onion, and garlic and cook, stirring frequently to prevent sticking, for about 10 minutes, or until very soft. Stir in the saffron and continue cooking and stirring until the saffron starts to color the onions and release its aroma, then add the pepper, tomatoes and thyme. Continue to cook and stir for 8 minutes more. Add the white wine and cook until it has reduced by half, then add the fumet. Increase the heat and bring to a boil. Add the fish and decrease the heat to a simmer. Cook for 5 minutes, add the basil and piment d'Espelette, then turn off the heat and let cool slightly. Set a food mill fitted with a fine strainer plate over another pot and ladle the soup into the food mill; this will strain the liquid and capture all the pieces of vegetable and fish needed to mill into the soup. Process the solids through the food mill. Discard everything that won't go through the food mill and scrape the bits of fish on the bottom of the strainer plate back into the soup. Refrigerate until ready to use. The soup can be made 1 day in advance but it's best served the same day.

FOR THE RELISH: Heat the olive oil in a small skillet over medium heat and sauté the vegetables for about 5 minutes, or until softened but not colored. Add the saffron and water and cook for 2 minutes more. Set aside for up to 4 hours.

FOR THE CROUTONS: Preheat the oven to 400°F. Brush the bread chunks on all sides with some of the olive oil and place on a small baking sheet. Bake for 5 minutes, turn over, and bake for 5 minutes more, or until golden. Meanwhile, combine the remaining olive oil, parsley, and garlic in a small bowl and season with salt and pepper. Remove the croutons from the oven and press both sides of each crouton into the parsley mixture. Return to the baking sheet and bake for 5 minutes. Set aside for up to 2 hours. Reheat for 5 minutes in a 350°F just before serving.

TO SERVE

Peel and devein the prawns, and season with salt and pepper. Heat the olive oil in a skillet over medium-high heat until it shimmers. Add the prawns and cook until golden brown, turning once, about 4 minutes total. Tilt the pan slightly, and add the garlic, thyme sprigs, red pepper flakes, and butter to the part of the pan closest to the heat. When the butter has melted, spoon it several times over the prawns, basting them, for about 2 minutes.

Meanwhile, heat the soup, whisking to reincorporate anything that has settled to the bottom. Keep the soup warm while you cook the prawns. Fill 8 warm soup bowls or plates with the soup and place a warm crouton in the center of each serving. Top each crouton with a dollop of Aioli (if you're going to balance the prawn on top as in the photo), or just prop the prawns against the croutons and spoon over the Aioli. Sprinkle with the basil and spoon some of the relish over the prawns. Drizzle with some exquisite olive oil, if you have it.

ARTICHOKE SOUP

ARTICHOKE HEARTS, MARCONA ALMOND AND MINT PESTO

MAKES ABOUT 8 (1-CUP) SERVINGS

ARTICHOKES

1 onion

2 heads garlic

1 bunch thyme

2 tablespoons black peppercorns

1 bay leaf

1 cup dry white wine

3 tablespoons kosher salt

6 medium to large artichokes

ARTICHOKE SOUP

2 tablespoons olive oil

1 onion, sliced (1 cup)

3 cloves garlic, sliced

1 cup sliced and cleaned leeks,
    white part only

1 cup chopped fennel

5 cups Light Chicken Stock
    (see Basics, page 230)

1 cup heavy cream

Reserved artichoke leaves, chopped
    stems, and bottoms

¼ cup freshly grated
    Parmesan cheese

MARCONA ALMOND AND MINT PESTO

1 clove garlic

¼ cup Marcona or blanched
    regular almonds, toasted

¼ cup extra-virgin olive oil

4 Oven-Roasted Tomatoes (see
    Basics, page 232), diced

2 tablespoons julienned fresh
    mint leaves

Reserved artichoke bottoms

Extra-virgin olive oil

Kosher salt and freshly ground
    black pepper

Many foods grown in California originated somewhere else, thrived here, and then became famous. Such is the case with artichokes, most of which are grown from the original rootstocks that arrived from Italy over a hundred years ago. As you drive south from San Francisco through the central coast area, the sight of artichoke fields unmistakably places you in California. Truly a regional food to be savored and enjoyed at the source, this soup is like eating a whole artichoke with a spoon. Subtle with nutty flavors and a velvety texture, this soup is irresistible.

John Desmond, Boulevard's mad culinary scientist, made the amazing discovery that using the leaves of the artichoke in the soup intensifies the flavor and sets the color. Best of all, most of the meaty artichoke hearts are enjoyed with the pesto instead of being pureed into the soup.

continued

When we order artichokes for Boulevard, they come in a variety of sizes, ranging from very small and loose-packed all the way up to the large and meaty 18-count. The count refers to the number of artichokes per case, so a medium-to-large artichoke would be a 24-count. If you're unsure of the size of artichokes you want to purchase, ask the produce manager what the case count is and adjust the number of artichokes you use in the recipe accordingly. Remember, the larger the artichoke the bigger its heart. When choosing an artichoke, look for ones that feel heavy with tightly closed leaves, which means that the hairy choke will be less developed. Also, look at the stem where the artichoke was cut from the stalk; if it's dry and dark brown or black it means the artichoke is not fresh and will be tough, dry, and flavorless.

Once you've tried the almond and mint pesto, you'll be tempted to put it on everything. It makes an exceptional pasta sauce, it's perfect for a warm green bean salad, and it's wonderful served on warm, crusty French bread. Although you can substitute other almonds, make the effort to find Marcona almonds; they make this pesto exceptional.

It seems like the longer we cook, the fewer gadgets we use, but the immersion blender certainly has a place in our kitchen, particularly for making soups and purees. It is easy to clean, takes up almost no space, and processes hot liquids without having to do them in batches in a blender or food processor.

METHOD

TO COOK THE ARTICHOKES: Place all of the ingredients except the artichokes in a nonreactive pot large enough and deep enough to hold the artichokes with a little headroom. Bend back and snap off the outer 2 rows of green leaves from around the base of each artichoke and cut off the top ½ inch of the artichokes. Using scissors, cut off the tips of the leaves to remove the thorns and lightly press down on the artichokes to open them up. Add them to the pot with enough water to cover. It may be necessary to weight the artichokes down with a plate so they stay submerged. Bring the liquid to a simmer and cook the artichokes for 30 to 40 minutes, or until a leaf can be pulled out easily from the center. Begin testing after 25 minutes and continue testing every 5 minutes until they are done. Take care not to overcook the artichokes, which can turn mushy quickly; you want them just barely tender. Drain the artichokes in a colander and put them on a plate or rimmed baking sheet to cool. Discard other solids.

When the artichokes are cool enough to handle, peel away the outer leaves until you get to the light inner leaves. Set the dark leaves aside and pull off and discard the inner leaves to reveal the choke. Scrape off the hairy choke from the artichoke bottom with a teaspoon. Finally, peel the thick outer layer of the stem with a vegetable peeler or a paring knife and trim base. In the end you will be left with a pile of dark green artichoke leaves for the soup and 6 cleaned artichoke bottoms Cut the stems off of 4 of the artichoke bottoms and add the stems to the pile of leaves reserved for the soup. Set the remaining 4 bottoms aside for garnish, coarsely chop the 2 remaining bottoms, and set aside.

FOR THE SOUP: Heat the olive oil in a nonreactive saucepan over medium-low heat. Add the onion, garlic, leeks, and fennel and cook for about 5 minutes, or until the vegetables begin to soften. Add the chicken stock, heavy cream, artichoke leaves and chopped stems and bottoms. Bring the liquid to a simmer and cook for 25 to 30 minutes. Remove from the heat and pulse on high with an immersion blender for 1 or 2 minutes. This will not work with a blender or food processor, which will mash the leaves into pulp, making the soup bitter and fibrous.

Strain the soup through a medium-coarse sieve into another pot and bring to a simmer; the soup should be thick and velvety. Stir in the Parmesan and keep warm until you are ready to serve or refrigerate for up to 2 days.

FOR THE PESTO: Put the garlic into a food processor and pulse briefly. Add the Marcona almonds and pulse a few more times, then add the olive oil and pulse again. It is important to keep this pesto chunky and full of texture. Put the pesto into a small bowl. Add the tomatoes and mint and give the mixture a little stir. Set aside.

TO SERVE

Slice the reserved artichoke bottoms and heat briefly in a small skillet with a little olive oil and season with salt and pepper. Ladle the artichoke soup into 8 warm bowls, place a generous pile of sliced bottoms in the center, and drizzle a tablespoon of the pesto on top. Serve accompanied by the remaining pesto for your guests to spoon lavishly over the soup.

STARTERS

DUNGENESS CRAB CAKES

ASPARAGUS, LEMON VINAIGRETTE, AND CRAB SALAD

SERVES 4

CRAB CAKES

10 ounces cooked lump
    Dungeness crabmeat
2 tablespoons finely diced celery
1 tablespoon very finely diced
    jalapeño pepper
1 tablespoon chopped fresh
    flat-leaf parsley leaves
2 teaspoons chopped fresh
    thyme leaves
Finely grated zest of 1 lemon
½ cup mayonnaise
2 cups panko (Japanese
    bread crumbs)
2 tablespoons olive oil

ASPARAGUS VINAIGRETTE

12 to 16 medium-thick asparagus
    spears, tough ends
    snapped off and discarded
¼ cup loosely packed fresh
    chervil leaves
¼ teaspoon fine sea salt or
    kosher salt
¾ cup olive oil
¼ cup extra-virgin olive oil

LEMON VINAIGRETTE

1 Meyer lemon, cut into 8 pieces
2 tablespoons light corn syrup
2 tablespoons champagne vinegar
½ teaspoon kosher salt
1 cup grapeseed oil

Kosher salt and freshly ground
    black pepper
Extra-virgin olive oil
8 whole claws and/or "thighs,"
    for plating

TARTAR SAUCE
(see Basics, page 234)

Sometimes it's essential for our mental health to take a break from crab cakes at the restaurant, but it's a decision that is always met with cries of protest from our guests. Removing them and then returning them to the menu is a ritual that predates Boulevard and reaches back over 26 years, but each time the crab cakes return to the menu, they're given new accessories, although the crab cakes themselves never really change.

People may or may not realize that there are, and always have been, two basic crab cake recipes served at the restaurant. The original version has sourdough bread, celery, red onion, thyme, olive oil, egg yolks, and whipped egg whites; the remodeled version has celery, red onion, thyme, and mayonnaise and is patted together with Japanese bread crumbs (panko) on each side. There are no big secrets here; our basic principle is to have lots of crab with just a few ingredients to flavor and hold them together. The key is to use high-quality crab and not to overstir the mixture. Also, crab is very delicate and can be easily overpowered by things like bell peppers, too much onion or strong herbs, and other things that frankly have no business being in crab cakes. That being said, we'll give you both recipes (the other recipe follows this one).

continued

Dungeness crab, considered the quintessential San Francisco seafood, is actually fished up and down the Pacific coast from Southern California to Alaska. Though its main season runs from November to May, the Alaska catch takes place during the summer, making fresh Dungeness available nearly year-round. It's sold live, cooked whole or cracked, or as fresh-picked meat (see Sources, page 236). For this recipe, we use crabmeat for the crab cakes and whole claws or "thighs" for the plate presentation (the thighs coming from the front two meaty legs). Few markets that sell picked meat will also have whole claws or meaty legs available, so if you want to use them you'll most likely need to purchase whole crabs. If you decide to start with whole crabs, a 1¼-pound crab yields about 5 ounces of meat, so for the crab cakes you'll need at least 3 whole crabs, which will give you enough meat for both the crab cakes and the garnish.

It's important the mayonnaise is of good quality, but it doesn't have to be homemade. We like commercial Best Foods (known as Hellmann's east of the Mississippi); just don't use the reduced-fat kind, which is too sweet.

At the restaurant, we form our crab cakes by packing some of the mixture into a 2-inch ring mold (sold in better cookware shops), then we remove the mold and pat on the panko.

METHOD

FOR THE CRAB CAKES: Pick through the crabmeat to remove any bits of shell or cartilage and gently squeeze with your hands to remove any excess liquid. Be careful, you don't want the mixture too dry either. Put the crabmeat into a bowl with the remaining ingredients except the panko and oil and fold the mixture so that it's just combined and the crab is not broken or mashed. Divide the mixture into 4 portions and shape into cakes that are about 2 inches in diameter and 1½ inches high (see Kitchen and Shopping Notes). Refrigerate the crab cakes until ready to serve.

FOR THE ASPARAGUS VINAIGRETTE: Cook the asparagus in a sauté pan or skillet of simmering salted water for 3 to 6 minutes, depending on size, or until the spears are barely crisp but still tender and green. Drain and immerse in a bowl of ice water to stop the cooking. Drain, cut the tips into 3-inch lengths and set aside. Put the asparagus bottoms into a blender and add the chervil and salt. With the machine running, add both olive oils in a slow stream. Blend for 1 minute. Strain through a fine-mesh sieve into a bowl, taste for seasoning, and add water to give the vinaigrette a pourable consistency if necessary. Set aside.

FOR THE LEMON VINAIGRETTE: Put the lemon pieces (peel and all), corn syrup, vinegar, and salt into a blender and puree until smooth. With the machine running, add the grape seed oil in a slow stream. Blend for 1 minute. Strain through a fine-mesh sieve into a bowl, taste for salt, and add water to give the vinaigrette a pourable consistency if necessary. Set aside.

TO COOK THE CRAB CAKES: Preheat the oven to 350°F. Pat the panko onto the tops and bottoms of the crab cakes, then heat the olive oil over medium-high heat in a medium ovenproof skillet. Add the crab cakes and cook for about 2 minutes, or until golden on one side. Flip the cakes over and put the skillet into the oven for 3 minutes to brown the bottom sides.

Sprinkle the asparagus with salt and pepper and drizzle with a little extra-virgin olive oil. Spoon a pool of lemon vinaigrette on one side of each of 4 large dinner plates and top with the asparagus spears. (If you have 4 spears per person you could stack them crosswise 2 over 2. Otherwise line 3 spears side by side.) Toss the crab claws or "thighs" with some of the lemon vinaigrette and place on top of the asparagus. Spoon a pool of asparagus vinaigrette on the other side of the plate and top with a crab cake and a dollop of Tartar Sauce.

BONUS CRAB CAKE RECIPE

MAKES 8 TO 10 LARGE CRAB CAKES OR ABOUT 20 HORS D'OEUVRES

2 cups small (¼-inch) cubes day-old French bread

4 tablespoons olive oil

1 pound fresh Dungeness crabmeat, picked over

⅔ cup finely chopped celery

½ cup finely chopped red onion

1½ teaspoons Worcestershire sauce

½ cup mayonnaise

¼ cup finely chopped fresh flat-leaf parsley leaves

2 tablespoons Dijon mustard

1 teaspoon Tabasco sauce

½ teaspoon crushed red pepper flakes

Kosher salt and freshly ground black pepper

3 large eggs, separated

Preheat the oven to 350°F. Toss the bread cubes with 2 tablespoons of the olive oil in a medium bowl. Stir in everything except the eggs, including salt and pepper to taste, and mix well. Add the egg yolks and stir to combine. Whip the egg whites until they hold a stiff peak and then gently fold into the crab mixture. Form into 3-inch patties. Heat the remaining 2 tablespoons olive oil in a large ovenproof skillet or sauté pan over medium-high heat. Add the crab cakes, cook until golden, and turn over. Finish cooking in the oven, about 8 minutes.

BLACK TRUFFLE PAPPARDELLE

SHAVED BLACK TRUFFLES AND PARMESAN BEURRE FONDUE

SERVES 4

BLACK TRUFFLE PAPPARDELLE

Pasta Dough (see Basics, page 233)
1 fresh black truffle, about 2 ounces
  (1 to 1½ ounces for the pasta
  and the rest for grating over
  the dish)
3 tablespoons semolina or flour

PARMESAN BEURRE FONDUE

¼ cup water
1 cup (2 sticks) unsalted butter,
  cut into ½-inch pieces
½ cup freshly grated Parmigiano-
  Reggiano cheese
Kosher salt and freshly ground
  black pepper

Freshly grated Parmigiano-Reggiano
  cheese

Some things are worth waiting for. Although preserved truffles are available year-round, nothing—absolutely nothing—is comparable to the aroma or flavor of fresh French black or white Italian truffles. A few years ago, Alex Padilla, a brilliant chef who spent many years with us, created this dish, which is not only unbelievably delicious but stunningly beautiful. Gossamer layers of fresh pasta encase shavings of fresh black truffles that, when rolled out, make the dish as beautiful to look at as it is to eat. It's fine to serve the dish with just the truffle pasta and the beurre fondue, but finely grating any "leftover" truffle over the pasta along with some Parmigiano-Reggiano makes the dish truly extraordinary.

KITCHEN AND SHOPPING NOTES

While there are many kinds of truffles (as well as truffle products) available on the market today, for us black truffles from France and white truffles from Italy are always our first choice. In recent years, however, black Himalayan truffles have arrived on the scene, and every year they improve in size as well as in flavor. They are, without a doubt, a great value. There has also been a tremendous improvement in the quality of both black and white truffles from Oregon, the white ones in particular. While we do use them in certain dishes and encourage the producers who are trying to establish the American truffle market, we also regretfully do not consider them equal to their European counterparts.

The use of truffle oil by chefs has come under a lot of fire by truffle purists, perhaps because it has been used to excess and is a laboratory re-creation of the natural flavor and aroma of truffles. We prefer to think of truffle oil as perfume and use it in a diluted ratio of 6 parts olive oil to 1 part truffle oil to "help" those fresh truffles of any given year that seem a little short on flavor or aroma.

When you're using only a few ingredients, they must be absolutely the finest you can get your hands on. While the Parmesan cheese in this dish plays only a small role, it's not an insignificant one, so make sure you use authentic Parmigiano-Reggiano from Italy.

continued

1	4
2	5
3	6

1   Prepare the pasta dough

2   Shave the black truffles

3   Place the shaved truffles in one layer
    on the pasta

4   Place the reserved sheet of pasta on
    top of the truffles. Press together the
    layers and run it through the pasta
    machine again.

5   Cut the pasta into wide pappardelle
    noodles

6   Toss the noodles in semolina

METHOD

making the
pappardelle
<

FOR THE BLACK TRUFFLE PAPPARDELLE: Divide the pasta dough in half. Cover 1 piece with a clean kitchen towel or wrap in plastic to prevent it from drying out. With a pasta machine set on its widest roller setting, run the dough through once. Fold crosswise into thirds and run through once more. Continue feeding the dough through the rollers, decreasing the setting on each pass, until you get to the next to thinnest (number 2) setting. Lay the pasta on a cutting board and cut crosswise into 2 pieces. Thinly shave truffles onto a plate. Brush 1 piece of pasta lightly with water and place shaved truffles (½ to ¾ ounce) evenly over all. Top with the other piece of pasta and press together. Reset the pasta machine roller to a medium-wide setting (number 4), and feed the pasta back through again, making 2 passes per number until you get to the next to thinnest (number 2) setting. Roll up the pasta lengthwise (like a jellyroll) and cut crosswise into 1¼- to 1½-inch-wide-strips. Toss with the semolina or flour, and place on a sheet pan. Repeat the process with the remaining dough and another ½ to ¾ ounce of the truffle. *It's important to note that you'll probably need to shave only 1 to 1½ ounces of the truffle for the pasta. The rest should be reserved for grating over the finished dish.*

FOR THE PARMESAN BEURRE FONDUE: Bring the water to a simmer in a skillet. Whisk in the butter, a few pieces at a time, waiting until they're incorporated before adding more. Whisk in the cheese and strain through a fine-mesh sieve into a bowl, then return to the skillet to keep warm. Season to taste with salt and pepper (though you probably won't need salt).

TO SERVE

Bring an 8- to 10-quart pasta pot or stockpot of salted (2 to 3 tablespoons) water to a boil. Have a large warm bowl near the stove. Add the pasta to the boiling water, stirring to prevent sticking, and cook for 2 to 3 minutes, or until the pasta is tender with a little "tooth" (al dente). Drain and transfer to the warm bowl. Add the beurre fondue and toss to coat the pappardelle well. Divide the pasta among 4 warm dinner plates or shallow soup bowls. Using a Microplane grater (see Kitchen and Shopping Notes, page 60), grate the remaining truffle in generous snowy mounds over all. Finish with another grating of cheese.

PAN-SEARED MONTEREY CALAMARI

FRESH DUNGENESS CRAB LEGS AND OVEN-ROASTED TOMATOES

SERVES 4

BASIL OIL

2 cups loosely packed fresh basil
    leaves

½ cup fresh flat-leaf parsley leaves

1 cup olive oil

SQUID INK VINAIGRETTE

6 tablespoons balsamic vinegar

¼ cup water

1 (2-ounce) package squid ink
    (see Sources, page 237)

¼ cup olive oil

CALAMARI

12 whole cleaned squid, bodies split
    open and tentacles reserved

Kosher salt and freshly ground
    black pepper

1 tablespoon olive oil

TENTACLE SALAD

Reserved tentacles

⅓ cup pine nuts, toasted (see Basics,
    page 234)

¼ cup pitted Niçoise or other good
    small black olives

2 tablespoons julienned fresh
    basil leaves

3 tablespoons unsalted butter

12 Dungeness crab "thighs" from
    large crab legs, or Crab Salad
    (see Basics, page 228)

8 Oven-Roasted Tomatoes (see
    Basics, page 232)

Small, tender, and delicate, our local Monterey squid is all too often relegated to the deep-fryer. (It seems there's no limit to the amount of fried calamari people will order.) Occasionally we prepare calamari in this "flash-in-the-pan" manner to highlight its subtle sea flavor, which is as good as abalone and infinitely more tender. Scoring the insides of the squid bodies causes them to roll up into little purses that beg to be stuffed with our local Dungeness crab. Olives, basil, and roasted tomatoes create layers of taste, and the striking black squid ink vinaigrette has a surprisingly nuanced seafood flavor. Even die-hard fried calamari lovers should give this a try.

KITCHEN AND SHOPPING NOTES

Monterey squid is one of the oldest California fisheries. In a good year, fresh squid is available all twelve months of the year. Its delicate flavor and tenderness make it superior to all other squid and is widely sought after in European and Asian markets. There are only two ways to cook squid with any success, and we adhere to this "3-minute or 3-hour" rule, meaning cook squid either very quickly at high heat or very slowly for a long time over low heat.

continued

Any squid you find already cleaned usually means it's been frozen. Fresh squid is a treat, and it's worth it to learn how to clean it. To clean squid: Holding the squid body in one hand and the head with the other, gently pull the head away from and out of the body, taking the white insides with it. Cut off the tentacles from the head just in front of the eyes. Squeeze out and discard the hard beak (mouth) from the center of the tentacles. While there won't be enough ink contained in the squid for this recipe, you can remove the ink sac (it's in the intestines), cut it open, and freeze the ink for later. (It freezes well and can be accumulated over time.) Many Japanese and Spanish markets sell 2- to 4-ounce packages of squid ink, or it can be purchased online (see Sources, page 237).

The West Coast crab fishery has excellent sustainability and is one of the best-managed fisheries in the world. The sweet, succulent meat is easy to "pick" or remove from the shell in large pieces, making it one of our favorites. When we call for "crab thighs," we mean the meat from the large front crab legs. Monterey Fish Market in Berkeley, California, has an excellent website that contains a wealth of information on Dungeness crab and many other varieties of West Coast fish, and they sell and ship retail (see Sources, page 236). The proprietor, Paul Johnson, has supplied fish of the highest quality to restaurants and consumers for years, as well as having authored several cookbooks.

METHOD

FOR THE BASIL OIL: Blanch the basil and parsley leaves in a large saucepan of boiling water for 20 seconds. Drain, rinse with cold water, and drain again. Squeeze out the excess liquid. Put the blanched basil, parsley, and olive oil into a blender and puree until smooth. Let the puree sit for 2 hours at room temperature so the basil and parsley have time to infuse the oil. Strain the oil through a very fine-mesh sieve or a medium sieve lined with a coffee filter into a bowl, then discard the solids. The infused oil can be refrigerated for up to 1 week.

FOR THE SQUID INK VINAIGRETTE: Put the balsamic vinegar, water, and squid ink into a blender. With the machine running, gradually add the olive oil until well combined.

FOR THE CALAMARI: Lay the squid bodies on a cutting board and lightly score them in a ½-inch crosshatch, making sure not to cut too deeply into the flesh. Season with salt and pepper. Heat the oil in a large skillet or sauté pan over medium heat and place 3 or 4 of the squid bodies in the pan, unscored side down. Using tongs, quickly turn the squid over onto the scored side. The calamari should immediately curl up. Transfer to a plate and cook the remaining squid bodies. Add the tentacles and cook for about 1 minute, or until they're opaque. Set aside on the plate with the bodies.

FOR THE TENTACLE SALAD: Toss the cooked tentacles with the pine nuts, olives, basil, and 1 teaspoon of the basil oil in a small bowl. Set aside.

TO SERVE

Melt the butter in a small skillet, add the crab thighs, and heat them just enough to warm them through. Stuff them into the curled squid bodies. Place 2 roasted tomatoes on each of 4 dinner plates and top with 3 of the crab-stuffed calamari. Top with the tentacle salad and drizzle the squid ink vinaigrette and basil oil around the plate.

FRIED GREEN TOMATO
AND CRISPY HAMA HAMA OYSTER "BLT"

TARTAR SAUCE AND GREEN TOMATO VINAIGRETTE

SERVES 4

GREEN TOMATO VINAIGRETTE

1 green garden tomato or ripe green
    variety, such as Green Zebra
3 tablespoons chopped fresh
    tarragon leaves
2 tablespoons chopped fresh chives
3 tablespoons white verjus
¾ cup extra-virgin olive oil
Kosher salt and freshly ground
    black pepper

OYSTERS

12 small to medium Hama-Hama
    oysters, shucked (see Kitchen
    and Shopping Notes)
¼ cup buttermilk
¼ cup all-purpose flour
¼ cup rice flour
¼ cup cornstarch
¼ teaspoon cayenne pepper
Kosher salt and freshly ground
    black pepper

TOMATOES

½ cup all-purpose flour
¼ teaspoon cayenne pepper
2 large *unripe* red (still green)
    tomatoes, cut crosswise into
    4 (¾-inch-thick) slices
3 large egg whites, lightly beaten
½ cup yellow or white cornmeal
Kosher salt and freshly ground
    black pepper

1 to 1½ cups canola oil, for frying
4 slices good-quality thick-sliced
    bacon, cooked until crisp
¼ cup Tartar Sauce (see Basics,
    page 234)
1 cup julienned romaine, Tango, or
    other green leaf lettuce
½ cup green grape tomatoes, halved,
    or red currant or blue tomatoes
    (see Sources, page 237)

TARTAR SAUCE

(see Basics, page 234)

Trying to choose favorite dishes to include in this book led us to examine what it is that we love about a recipe. This Fried Green Tomato and Oyster "BLT" has come to represent for us American food at its finest. Tart fried green tomatoes, briny, plump oysters, creamy tartar sauce, and smoky, salty bacon are what compelled us to choose this "knife-and-fork BLT." Warm and crisp with enough tartar sauce to make anyone feel better, this is the food we often crave: excellent seasonal ingredients with irresistible textures, simply prepared. Try this dish when the weather is still cold enough for good oysters, but in your heart you're already impatient for the foods of summer.

KITCHEN AND SHOPPING NOTES

The flavor of oysters depends on their freshness, variety, and where they're cultivated. We happen to prefer the crisp, briny-sweet oysters from cold Pacific waters, such as Hama Hama, Quilcene, and Pearl Points, but it's a matter of personal taste. Many oysters are suitable for frying, though for this recipe you will be happiest with a medium-size oyster. Avoid small oysters, like Kumamotos, which are difficult to dredge and fry, or large oysters, which some people find unpalatable.

continued

Try this dish when the weather is still cold enough for good oysters, but in your heart you're already impatient for the foods of summer.

Shucking oysters can be tricky for the novice, but once you have learned the technique it's an impressive skill. It's important to invest in a sturdy oyster knife with a pointed tip. To shuck an oyster, thoroughly wash the oysters. Opening an oyster depends a lot on leverage, so put an oyster on a flat countertop. Using a heavy kitchen towel, place the oyster, cup side down, in a corner of the towel and fold the towel over the top of the oyster, leaving the hinged side exposed. Wiggle the tip of the oyster knife into the hinge and, with a twist of your wrist, pop open (hopefully) the shell (this takes practice). After the shell has been opened, slide your knife along the upper shell and cut through the connective muscle that holds the shells together. Remove the top shell and slide your knife under the oyster to loosen it from the bottom shell. Put the oyster in a bowl along with its liquid. Repeat with the remaining oysters. Oysters can be opened 2 to 3 hours in advance and stored in their liquid in the refrigerator.

When frying, it's important to get your oil hot (about 350°F) but not smoking (see Our Frying Manifesto, page 126). In this case, however, when you're shallow frying and not deep-frying, the oil is not deep enough to insert a thermometer. We can tell if the oil is hot enough if it starts to show a little wave or shimmer on the surface. You can also drop in a tiny piece of bread and see if it bubbles and turns golden within 20 seconds.

METHOD

FOR THE GREEN TOMATO VINAIGRETTE: Put the tomato into a blender with the tarragon, chives, and verjus and puree on high speed until smooth. With the machine running, slowly add the oil until blended. Taste for seasoning, strain through a fine-mesh sieve into a bowl, and refrigerate if not using within a few hours.

FOR THE OYSTERS: Soak the oysters in the buttermilk for 10 minutes. Combine the all-purpose flour, rice flour, cornstarch, and cayenne in a bowl and season with salt and pepper. Set aside.

FOR THE TOMATOES: Combine the all-purpose flour with the cayenne in a bowl and season with salt and pepper. Coat the tomatoes, one at a time, with the flour mixture, dip into the egg whites, and then coat, a few at a time, with the cornmeal. Set aside on a baking sheet.

TO FRY THE TOMATOES AND OYSTERS: Preheat the oven to 350°F. Have a baking sheet lined with paper towels near the stove. Heat the canola oil in a medium skillet over medium-high heat until the oil is hot but not smoking or the surface shimmers (see Kitchen and Shopping Notes). Carefully slide the coated tomatoes into the oil and cook for about 2 minutes, or until golden brown. Gently turn over and fry until the other side is golden. Remove with a slotted spatula to the prepared baking sheet and keep warm in the oven while you fry the oysters. Line a large plate with paper towels and place near your stove, and add the remaining oil to the skillet if needed. Fry the oysters, turning once, for about 1 minute, until crisp all over. With a slotted spoon, transfer to the paper towels to drain.

TO SERVE

Place a fried tomato in the center of each of 4 dinner plates. Place the bacon strips on top of the tomatoes and then arrange 3 oysters on the bacon. Finish with a dollop of Tartar Sauce and some of the julienned lettuce. Drizzle the green tomato vinaigrette around and garnish with the small tomatoes.

GOAT CHEESE AND TRUFFLE RAVIOLI

PINE NUT PESTO, BASIL AND TINY FAVA PESTO, ROASTED TOMATOES,
WHITE ASPARAGUS AND TRUFFLES

SERVES 4

RAVIOLI

Pasta Dough (see Basics, page 233)
½ pound fresh goat cheese, softened
2 ounces mascarpone cheese,
    softened
1 tablespoon julienned fresh black
    or Himalayan truffle
½ teaspoon truffle oil
Kosher salt and freshly ground
    black pepper
Semolina flour

PINE NUT PESTO

½ cup pine nuts, toasted (see Basics,
    page 234)
3 tablespoons finely grated
    Parmigiano-Reggiano or
    domestic Parmesan cheese
1 small clove garlic
3 tablespoons extra-virgin olive oil

BASIL AND TINY FAVA PESTO

1 cup packed fresh basil leaves
1 cup fresh flat-leaf parsley leaves
2 tablespoons cold water
⅓ cup olive oil
½ cup shelled very small fava beans,
    peeled (see Basics, page 229)
Kosher salt and freshly ground
    black pepper

WHITE ASPARAGUS

4 white asparagus spears
Kosher salt and freshly ground
    black pepper

ROASTED TOMATOES

1 tablespoon extra-virgin olive oil
1 small clove garlic, chopped
Oven-Roasted Tomatoes (see Basics,
    page 232), diced
¼ teaspoon fresh thyme leaves
Kosher salt and freshly ground
    black pepper

Beurre Fondue (see Basics,
    page 228)
Piece of Parmigiano-Reggiano
    cheese for grating
1 ounce black truffle, for grating
Freshly ground black pepper

A simple plate of food, deliciously prepared, is certainly pleasing, but we often are left wondering what the dish would taste like with, say, white asparagus, or truffles, or maybe it would be better with tomatoes. We often use contrasting flavors to prevent palette fatigue, as with this very simple goat cheese ravioli, served with various accompaniments. Try all three on the same plate with the ravioli, or choose the one that appeals most and enjoy it all by itself.

KITCHEN AND SHOPPING NOTES

Himalayan truffles are available from November through mid-March, depending on the weather of that year. They are also known as Chinese black truffles *(Tuber indiccum)* and have the same striking black color, but are less pungent than their European cousins *(T. aestivum)*. They're also much less costly. We like to enhance their flavor with the addition of a little "truffle helper," aka truffle oil. In the end, the Himalayan truffles are similar to their cousins though not equal, but we look forward to their seasonal arrival nonetheless.

Tiny, tender fava beans are one of the joys of spring. For this recipe we prefer to use only the smallest favas, found early in the season. In Italy you'll often see tiny favas served skin and all, but we prefer to remove the slightly bitter skin and just serve the sweet, tender beans. As the season progresses and the weather warms, favas grow larger, less tender, and lose some of their sweetness, but they're still appropriate in this recipe.

An inexpensive tool we find essential for this recipe (and many other recipes as well) is a Microplane grater. With a few zips across its razor-sharp teeth, you can create what we like to call Parmesan or truffle snow. It's also wonderful for finely grating citrus zest or nutmeg.

METHOD

FOR THE RAVIOLI: Stir together the goat cheese, mascarpone, truffle, truffle oil, and a little salt in a bowl.

Divide the Pasta Dough in half. Wrap one of the pieces in plastic and save it for another meal. With a pasta machine set on its widest roller setting, run the dough through once. Fold the dough crosswise into thirds and run through once more. Continue feeding the dough through the rollers, decreasing the setting on each pass, until you get to the next to thinnest (number 2) setting. Cut the dough into 12 (3½-inch) squares. Sprinkle each square with a little flour, then stack them and cover with a damp towel to keep them from drying out while you fill the ravioli.

Place 1 heaping tablespoon of the goat cheese mixture in the center of a pasta square. Bring the 4 corners up and over the filling to form a pyramid. Tightly press all the edges together to form a tight seal. To make a decorative edge, trim the edges with pinking shears or a scalloped pasta cutter (see page 174). Place the ravioli on a baking sheet dusted with semolina flour. Make the rest of the ravioli with the remaining pasta squares and filling. The ravioli can be refrigerated uncovered for up to 8 hours.

FOR THE PINE NUT PESTO: Put the pine nuts in a blender with the Parmesan and garlic. Pulse until the mixture is coarsely chopped. With the blender running, add the olive oil, and process until the mixture is smooth. Transfer the pesto to a bowl and set aside.

FOR THE BASIL AND FAVA PESTO: Bring a large saucepan of salted water to the boil and have a bowl of ice water nearby. Blanch the basil and parsley leaves for a few seconds, then quickly scoop out with a sieve and plunge into the ice water. Drain and squeeze dry. Coarsely chop the herbs, put in a blender with the olive oil, and process until smooth. Push the herbs through a fine-mesh sieve, stir in the fava beans, season with salt and pepper, and set aside.

FOR THE WHITE ASPARAGUS: Trim off the tough bottom ends and then peel the asparagus stalks. Cook in a large sauté pan of boiling water for 6 to 8 minutes, or until just tender. Transfer to a bowl of ice water to stop the cooking, then drain and place on a clean kitchen towel to dry. Cut each stalk in half lengthwise and then in half crosswise, season with a little salt and pepper and set aside.

TO SERVE

Have the Beurre Fondue warming in a skillet over low heat. Bring a large pot of salted water to the boil and reduce the heat to a simmer. With a slotted spoon, gently lower half of the ravioli into the simmering water and cook for 5 to 7 minutes, or until tender with a little "tooth." Using the slotted spoon, carefully transfer the ravioli to the skillet with the warm Beurre Fondue. Repeat with the remaining ravioli and keep warm while you plate the dishes.

Put the Basil and Fava Bean Pesto in a small skillet and warm over low heat. Put the asparagus in a small skillet with a little water and warm over low heat. To prepare the Roasted Tomatoes, heat the olive oil in a small sauté pan over medium heat. Add the garlic, cook for a few seconds, and then add the tomatoes and thyme leaves. Season with salt and pepper, and remove from the heat. Place a tablespoon or so of the Basil and Fava Bean Pesto on each of 4 dinner plates alongside a small mound of asparagus and a spoonful of the tomatoes. Place 1 ravioli on each pile. Using a Microplane grater, grate a flurry of Parmesan and then truffle snow over the ravioli on top of the asparagus. Spoon the Pine Nut Pesto over the ravioli on the tomatoes, and finish with a grinding of black pepper over the ravioli on the basil and fava pesto.

TRIO OF TUNA TARTARES

JALAPEÑO AND GINGER, SPICY RED CHILE, SHIITAKE, AND WHITE SOY

SERVES 4

JALAPEÑO AND GINGER TARTARE

3 ounces sushi-quality ahi tuna, cut into small (¼-inch) dice, (see Kitchen and Shopping Notes)

3 tablespoons seeded, deribbed, and (⅛-inch) diced jalapeño pepper

1 tablespoon finely diced ginger

3 tablespoons grape seed oil

1 tablespoon Thai sweet chile sauce

1 tablespoon white soy sauce

1 tablespoon rice vinegar

1 ripe avocado

1 lime, halved

Kosher salt and freshly ground black pepper

SPICY RED CHILE TARTARE

3 ounces sushi-quality ahi tuna, cut into small (¼-inch) dice (see Kitchen and Shopping Notes)

¼ cup mayonnaise

1 teaspoon Chinese chile garlic paste or *sambal oelek*

SHIITAKE AND WHITE SOY TARTARE

3 ounces sushi-quality ahi tuna, cut into small (¼-inch) dice (see Kitchen and Shopping Notes)

6 ounces fresh shiitake mushrooms

2 tablespoons white soy sauce

1 tablespoon grape seed oil

2 teaspoons Asian sesame oil

3 tablespoons thinly sliced scallions

1 tablespoon mixed black and white sesame seeds, toasted

Kosher salt and freshly ground black pepper

MISO VINAIGRETTE

1 tablespoon yellow miso

1 tablespoon rice vinegar

1 tablespoon mirin

2 tablespoons canola oil

2 teaspoons regular soy sauce

2 cups canola or grape seed oil, for frying

24 wonton wrappers, cut into 1½-inch rounds

GARNISH

1 ounce *tobiko* or trout roe

1 tablespoon finely sliced fresh chives

We're not sure if the true culinary origins of tuna tartare can be traced, but its popularity can be compared to the "shot heard round the world." Most certainly overexposed, tuna tartare has been keelhauled through every ethnic identity possible, yet somehow its bright, shiny appeal remains untarnished. At least fifteen years into the raw tuna craze, the popularity of tuna tartare is dwarfed at Boulevard only by crab cakes and lobster bisque. In spite of its cliché, when we actually sit down to a meal in the restaurant dining room, chances are good that we'll start with tuna tartare. Just one bite of sushi-grade ahi tuna, pristinely cleaned, cut into jewel-like cubes, and dressed with herbs, oil, spices, and just a touch of lemon or lime says it all.

KITCHEN AND SHOPPING NOTES

We like to serve these three favorite tuna tartares all on one plate so we can compare the different flavors; each is distinct and delicious on its own. It's also a great way to get a party started. Put out bowls of the three tartares with some wonton crisps or cucumber rounds for dippers, and let guests help themselves.

Dense, meaty, and full-flavored fresh yellowfin tuna, more familiarly known these days as *ahi,* is available in most markets around the country. Because the meat deteriorates rapidly when exposed to air, often you'll find slices from the whole loin wrapped in plastic, although many fishmongers will cut slices to order. Superfresh tuna has a subtle translucent sheen, with no rainbow opalescence or brown color and is sometimes labeled as sushi-grade or sashimi-grade. To prepare the tuna, trim off as much sinew as possible and discard the dark blood line before cutting it into small dice. Make sure you cut the tuna instead of chopping it, which breaks down the fibers and gives the tartare a mushy texture.

White soy sauce, which we like because it has soy flavor without the dark color, is available in specialty markets and online. All of the other Asian ingredients we used here (Thai sweet chile sauce, Chinese chile garlic sauce, *sambal oelek, tobiko,* miso, and mirin) are fairly common and can often be found not just in Asian markets, but in the international-food sections of many supermarkets, as well as by mail order.

METHOD

FOR THE JALAPEÑO AND GINGER TARTARE: Just before you want to serve the tartare, combine the tuna, jalapeño, ginger, oil, chile sauce, soy, and vinegar in a small bowl. Cut the avocado into ¼-inch dice and squeeze the lime juice over. Season with salt and pepper, then gently stir the avocado mixture into the tuna mixture.

FOR THE SPICY RED CHILE TARTARE: Just before you want to serve the tartare, combine the tuna, mayonnaise, and chile paste in a small bowl.

FOR THE SHIITAKE AND SOY TARTARE: Preheat the oven to 350°F. Remove the stems from the shiitakes and cut the caps into small (¼-inch) dice. Toss the shiitakes with the white soy sauce, grape seed oil, and sesame oil in a small baking dish. Roast for about 5 minutes, or until tender, then set aside to cool. Just before serving, stir in the tuna, scallions, and sesame seeds. Season to taste with salt and pepper.

FOR THE MISO VINAIGRETTE: Whisk the miso, rice vinegar, and mirin together in a small bowl until smooth, then whisk in the oil and soy sauce.

TO FRY THE WONTONS: Heat the oil in a wok or sauté pan until it reaches 325°F on a deep-fry thermometer. Add the wontons, a few at a time, turning them with tongs after a minute or so, for about 2 minutes total, or until they're brown and crisp. Transfer to paper towels to drain. Set aside for up to 2 hours.

TO SERVE

Using a small ice-cream scoop or spoon, scoop a mound of tuna tartare from each bowl onto 4 plates, spacing the mounds evenly apart. To garnish, place a small spoonful of *tobiko* on the spicy red tuna, sprinkle the chives on the tuna with avocado, and drizzle the miso vinaigrette around the shiitake-flavored tuna. Serve the wontons alongside.

SEARED SEA SCALLOPS

FRESH SHELLING BEANS, LOMO EMBUCHADO, SMOKED SPANISH PAPRIKA

SERVES 4

SHELLING BEANS

1 carrot, halved lengthwise and
    cut crosswise into thirds
1 celery rib, cut crosswise into thirds
1 small onion, quartered
1 bay leaf
2 thyme sprigs
2 quarts cold water
2 cups mixed shelled fresh borlotti,
    cannellini, cranberry, garbanzo,
    and/or flageolet beans
    (about 2 pounds unshelled)
Kosher salt

2 ounces thinly sliced *lomo
    embuchado* (about 20 slices)

SCALLOPS

8 large dry-packed sea scallops
    (1½ ounces each)
Kosher salt and freshly ground
    black pepper
2 tablespoons olive oil

SHELLING BEAN SALAD

Unfiltered Arbequina olive oil (see
    Sources, page 237) or any
    artisanal extra-virgin olive oil
¼ cup finely diced shallots
½ teaspoon minced garlic
Cooked shelling beans
1 tablespoon chopped fresh
    flat-leaf parsley leaves
Kosher salt and freshly ground
    black pepper

½ cup finely diced Manchego cheese
Spanish smoked paprika
Aged Spanish sherry vinegar

Fresh, sweet sea scallops, salt-cured pork, and fresh shelling beans have a special affinity for one another. During the short season when fresh flageolets, cannellini, borlotti, and cranberry beans are available, they are a special treat not to be missed. Here a mixture of beans, including fresh garbanzos, are prepared in a warm "salad" with shallots, herbs, excellent Spanish olive oil, and spiked with tiny cubes of aged Manchego cheese. With a sprinkling of smoked *pimentón* (Spanish paprika) and a drizzle of very lovely aged sherry vinegar, you'll add two small but exceptional details that will take this dish from simple to extraordinary.

KITCHEN AND SHOPPING NOTES

The quality of the scallops you use can turn this dish from triumph to tragedy. When purchasing scallops, the current vocabulary can be confusing, but whether they're labeled "day-boat" or "diver," the most important thing to know is if they're "dry-packed" or "chemical free," which means that they haven't been treated with preservatives (sodium tripolyphosphates, or STP) to prevent moisture loss. Treated scallops are not sweet tasting and release their excess water as they cook, preventing them from developing a nice brown crust. When shopping, look for scallops that are translucent, ivory to light tan—never white—and with little or no milky liquid in the tray. To be sure, ask your fishmonger if they've been treated; by law their shipping cases must be labeled.

continued

Spanish *lomo embuchado* is dry-cured and spiced pork loin that is often served in tapas bars alongside serrano ham. See Sources (page 236) for purveyors that sell fresh mail-order scallops, *lomo embuchado,* smoked Spanish paprika, and aged sherry vinegar.

A combination of shelling beans, as shown in the photo (page 66), is not only delicious but pretty as well. The beans must all be cooked separately since certain beans can stain the cooking water. If you combine them after cooking, you'll need fresh water to store them in. The beans must be cooled and refrigerated in their cooking liquid, but nothing goes badder than a bean that's turned sour and fizzy, so keep your fingers out of the container while they're being stored.

METHOD

TO COOK THE SHELLING BEANS: Put the carrot, celery, onion, bay leaf, thyme sprigs, and water into a large saucepan and bring to a boil. Decrease the heat to maintain a simmer and cook for 30 minutes. Strain and discard the solids. Return the vegetable water to the saucepan. Add the beans, bring to a boil, and skim off and discard the foam. Decrease the heat to maintain a simmer and cook for 10 to 20 minutes, or until the beans are tender to the bite and no hard or chalky core remains. Scoop out with a slotted spoon and plunge into a bowl of ice water. If you're cooking more than one kind of bean, add them to the liquid, cook, scoop them out, and add to the ice water. When all the beans have been cooked, stir in salt until the water is well seasoned and return the beans to the pot of liquid (they will absorb flavor from the liquid). Refrigerate the beans in their cooking liquid for up to 4 days.

TO PREPARE THE PLATES: Arrange the sliced *lomo* in a ring in the center of each of 4 dinner plates (leaving a space in the center). Set the plates aside.

TO COOK THE SCALLOPS: Season the scallops with salt and pepper. Heat a large skillet over high heat, add the oil, and heat for a few seconds more until it shimmers. Add the scallops and cook, turning once, for about 5 minutes total, or until golden brown on both sides. (The scallops should be 90 percent opaque on the inside.) Remove the pan from the heat.

TO PREPARE THE BEAN SALAD: While the scallops are cooking, warm the beans. Heat 2 tablespoons of the olive oil in a small skillet or sauté pan over medium heat. Add the shallots and garlic and cook for 1 minute. Add the beans and 2 tablespoons of their cooking liquid and warm though, stirring occasionally, for 2 to 3 minutes. Remove from the heat, add the parsley, and season to taste with salt and pepper. Toss the Manchego cheese with the warm beans.

TO SERVE

Mound the beans in the center of the arranged *lomo*. Place the scallops on top of the beans. Dust the perimeter of the plates with paprika and drizzle with some oil and sherry vinegar.

Mild, sweet little sand dabs are a San Francisco delicacy that is still abundant, probably because most people don't like to eat fish with tiny bones and there are just two guys who fish for them (and then only if it isn't crab season). Panfried on the bone and served that way, it was once a San Francisco dining rite of passage to learn how to deftly lift the entire skeleton out of a sand dab. Although not often seen on restaurant menus or even in fish markets, don't hesitate—if the opportunity presents itself—just order them because these tasty little guys are a local treasure.

SAND DABS STUFFED WITH LOBSTER

. . . .

ARTICHOKE CONFIT, PARSLEY BEURRE FONDUE

. . . .

SERVES 4

SAND DABS

8 sand dab fillets (from 4 whole fish)
(see Kitchen and Shopping
Notes)

Kosher salt and freshly ground
black pepper

¼ pound (½-inch) diced, cooked
lobster meat (see Basics,
page 232)

4 teaspoons mayonnaise

½ teaspoon finely chopped fresh
flat-leaf parsley leaves

2 tablespoons grape seed oil

BABY ARTICHOKES

16 to 18 baby artichokes

Juice of 1 lemon

4 cloves garlic

3 thyme sprigs

2 teaspoons kosher salt

ARTICHOKE CONFIT

1 clove garlic, lightly crushed

1 shallot, halved

1 thyme sprig

1 bay leaf

16 to 18 cooked baby artichokes

2 cups olive oil

½ teaspoon kosher salt

PARSLEY BEURRE FONDUE

2 cups fresh flat-leaf parsley leaves
(from 1 large bunch)

2 tablespoons water

½ cup (1 stick) cold butter, cut into
½-inch pieces

Kosher salt and freshly ground
black pepper

½ cup fresh flat-leaf parsley leaves

1 lemon, peeled and cut into
segments (see Kitchen and
Shopping Notes)

2 tablespoons unsalted butter

4 lobster claws

Chive blossoms, for garnish
(optional)

Filleting sand dabs before cooking is a bit like kitchen microsurgery and should be classified as an act of love. Which is in fact how we feel about this dish: a succulent, boneless sand dab filled with lobster and sitting on generous spoonfuls of tender Artichoke Confit, scented with thyme and garlic.

KITCHEN AND SHOPPING NOTES

Sand dabs are plentiful and available all year, as long as you can find someone to fish for them. Short of that, you can order them from Monterey Fish Market (see Sources, page 236) and have them shipped to your door. Typically they're sold "dressed," or "pan-ready," which means that the head, fins, and viscera have been removed. Because the scales are so small, there's no need to scale them.

Lobster is extravagant, so crab and shrimp can be used in its place. Whichever shellfish you choose, dice it in medium (½-inch) pieces to better appreciate its flavor and texture. If you do opt for lobster, save the claws to go on top of the sand dabs for a more glamorous presentation.

The parsley salad calls for lemon segments. The technique for sectioning citrus fruit is the same no matter whether you're segmenting a grapefruit, an orange, or a lemon. Begin by taking a small slice off each end. Put the fruit on a work surface, one of the cut sides down, and slice away the peel and pith without cutting into the flesh. Once it's free of its peel, put the fruit in one hand and carefully cut along both sides of each segment, freeing it from the membrane.

METHOD

TO COOK THE ARTICHOKES: To prepare the artichokes, cut ¼ to ½ inch off the top of each artichoke. Peel away the tough outer green leaves until you get to the pale inner leaves, then drop the artichokes into a bowl of water to which you've added the lemon juice.

Remove the artichokes from the water and transfer to a medium saucepan along with the garlic, thyme sprigs, and salt and cover with fresh water. Bring to a simmer over medium heat and cook for 15 to 20 minutes, or until the artichokes are tender but not mushy. Drain, discard the garlic and thyme, and set aside in a bowl or on a plate to cool. When cooled, cut the artichokes lengthwise into ¼-inch-thick slices and use for the confit.

FOR THE ARTICHOKE CONFIT: Wrap the garlic, shallot, thyme sprig, and bay leaf in a piece of cheesecloth and tie with kitchen string. Put it in a medium saucepan with the cooked and sliced artichokes. Add the oil and salt and bring to a low simmer. Cook for 10 minutes, remove from the heat, cover, and set aside until cool. Pull out and discard the cheesecloth bag, then strain the olive oil through a fine-mesh sieve into a glass measuring cup and reserve for drizzling over the finished dish; save the rest for another use (it's great in salad dressings). The artichokes can be refrigerated for up to 2 days.

FOR THE PARSLEY BEURRE FONDUE: First make a parsley puree by blanching the parsley leaves for 1½ minutes in a small saucepan of boiling salted water. Drain and reserve ½ cup of the cooking water. Put the parsley into a blender and puree until smooth, adding just enough of the reserved water to get the blender blade whirring. Strain through a fine-mesh sieve into a bowl and set aside. Bring the 2 tablespoons water to a simmer in a small skillet or saucepan. Working quickly, whisk in the butter, piece by piece, until it's fully incorporated and creamy. Whisk in the parsley puree and season to taste with salt and pepper. Keep it warm while you cook the fish. The parsley puree can be made up to 4 hours in advance, but don't add it to the beurre fondue until you are ready to serve the dish; you'll lose the brilliant color of the parsley sauce if it is kept warm for too long.

FOR THE FISH: Lay the 8 fillets on a cutting board and season with salt and pepper. Combine the lobster meat with the mayonnaise and parsley in a small bowl and season with salt and pepper. Place equal spoonfuls of the lobster mixture on 4 of the fish fillets, then top with another fillet, pressing down lightly. Heat the oil in a large nonstick skillet over medium-high heat until it shimmers. Place the stuffed fillets in the pan and cook for about 3 minutes on the first side, or until golden. Using a spatula, carefully turn the fillets over and cook on the second side for 2 to 3 minutes more, or until golden.

TO SERVE

Toss the parsley leaves and lemon segments together in a small bowl. Melt the butter in a small saucepan and warm the lobster claws. If the artichokes have been refrigerated, warm them with a little of their cooking oil in a small skillet. Place the warm artichokes in the center of 4 warm dinner plates. Drizzle the beurre fondue around, top with a fish, and place a lobster claw on top. Place a mound of parsley salad to the side of each lobster claw. Drizzle some of the reserved artichoke oil over all and garnish with chive blossoms if you have them.

MAINE LOBSTER TAIL
WITH JOHN DESMOND'S BLACK PUDDING

POTATO MOUSSELINE, FENNEL AND LEEK RELISH, BLOOD ORANGE JUS

SERVES 4

(with lots of leftover black pudding)

BLACK PUDDING

1 tablespoon olive oil

1 onion coarsely chopped (1 cup)

3 cloves garlic

2 tablespoons port, sherry, or
    Madeira

1 teaspoon yellow mustard seeds

½ teaspoon cumin seeds

½ teaspoon coriander seeds

½ teaspoon crushed red
    pepper flakes

¼ teaspoon fennel seeds

1 bay leaf, crumbled

¾ pound Boston butt, cut into
    1-inch cubes

¼ pound fatback, cut into
    1-inch cubes

1½ cups pork blood (see Kitchen
    and Shopping Notes)

½ cup cooked long-grain white rice

½ cup cooked pearl barley

¼ cup cooked steel-cut rolled oats

¼ cup chopped fresh flat-leaf
    parsley leaves

½ teaspoon chopped fresh
    sage leaves

½ teaspoon chopped fresh
    thyme leaves

½ teaspoon chopped fresh
    oregano leaves

1 tablespoon kosher salt

1 teaspoon smoked Spanish paprika
    (*pimentón*) (see Sources,
    page 237)

1 teaspoon freshly ground
    black pepper

¼ teaspoon ground allspice

1 large egg, lightly beaten

2 tablespoons unsalted butter

POTATO MOUSSELINE

½ pound russet potatoes

½ cup (1 stick) unsalted butter,
    at room temperature

BLOOD ORANGE JUS

3 cups freshly squeezed blood
    orange juice, (from about
    8 oranges)

¾ cup white port

1 teaspoon brown sugar

1 cup Dark Chicken Stock (see
    Basics, page xxx)

Kosher salt and freshly ground
    black pepper

1 tarragon sprig

FENNEL AND LEEK RELISH

¼ cup finely diced fennel

¼ cup finely diced leek,
    white part only

¼ cup extra-virgin olive oil

¼ cup water

2 teaspoons finely chopped fresh
    tarragon leaves

Kosher salt and freshly ground
    black pepper

2 tablespoons unsalted butter

2 cooked Maine lobster tails (see
    Basics, page 232)

¼ cup Beurre Fondue (see Basics,
    page 228)

John Desmond hails from County Cork, a region in Ireland renowned for black puddings. Far from just a traditional Irish blood pudding, John has drawn on all of his culinary experience to create what turns out to be a magnificent full flavored terrine. The black pudding terrine can then be cut and pan-fried, acquiring a crispy, dark crust and creamy, rich interior, making it, in short, irresistible.

We are always surprised and thrilled by the response to this dish. We suspect it is the lobster that entices people to order it, aided by the fact that we've glossed over the blood issue by calling it black pudding. In the end, it turns out to be the black pudding that receives the accolades.

continued

KITCHEN AND SHOPPING NOTES

The black pudding recipe will leave you with quite a bit more pudding than is called for in this dish. However, it freezes very well. After it has been steamed and cooled, slice it, then wrap the pudding in plastic and it will keep for up to 3 months in the freezer. A more traditional way to serve black pudding is with chunky applesauce and mashed potatoes. It can also be crisped and browned and served alongside poached eggs. In Spain we've been served blood sausage in the more traditional casing along with various types of shellfish. Though the ingredient list is lengthy and the method makes it a project, one bite of this rich and aromatic pudding will make all the time and effort seem well spent.

We've looked all over the internet to find mail-order sources for pork blood, to no avail. Your best bet is to go to a Latin or Asian butcher or call local butchers or slaughterhouses. Farmers or ranchers in your area might also be helpful, and restaurants can sometimes get blood from their wholesale suppliers, so ask a chef you're friendly with.

METHOD

FOR THE BLACK PUDDING: Have a meat grinder and an electric mixer set up. Heat the olive oil in a skillet over medium heat. Add the onions and garlic and cook, covered, stirring occasionally, for 5 minutes. Stir in the port and cook, covered, for about 20 minutes, or until the onions are quite soft. Transfer to a bowl, along with any liquid, and cool in the refrigerator while you prepare the rest of the ingredients.

Heat a small skillet over medium heat and add the mustard seeds, cumin seeds, coriander seeds, red pepper flakes, fennel seeds, and bay leaf. Toast the spices, shaking the pan continuously, for 2 to 3 minutes, or until aromatic. Let cool for a few minutes, then finely grind in a spice grinder or coffee grinder. Set aside.

Combine the pork butt, pork fat, and reserved onion mixture in a bowl. Using a meat grinder fitted with the ¼-inch plate, grind the mixture into the large bowl of an electric mixer. Add the blood, reserved spice mixture, rice, barley, oats, parsley, sage, thyme, oregano, salt, paprika, pepper, allspice, and egg. Mix on medium speed for 2 to 3 minutes, or until the mixture is well combined. Alternatively, stir the mixture by hand with a wooden spoon for about 5 minutes. Transfer the mixture to a 7-cup (9-by-5-inch) loaf pan. Seal the pan tightly with foil.

Meanwhile, place a rack in the middle of the oven and preheat to 325°F. Put on some water in a kettle to boil. Set the loaf pan in a large roasting pan or baking dish and put the roasting pan in the oven on the middle rack. Add boiling water to reach two-thirds up the sides of the loaf pan. Bake the pudding for 1½ hours, or until an instant-read thermometer inserted into the center reads 160°F. Remove from the oven. Take the loaf pan out of the water and let cool on a wire rack for 2 hours. Remove the foil, then wrap with plastic wrap and refrigerate overnight.

FOR THE MOUSSELINE: Peel the potatoes, cut into quarters, and place in a large saucepan with generously salted water to cover. Bring to a boil over medium high heat. Cook until the potatoes are soft but not falling apart. Drain and reserve ½ cup of the potato liquid. Put the potatoes and softened butter into a blender with ¼ cup of the reserved cooking liquid. Pulse just until smooth, adding more liquid if necessary. Be careful not to overmix the potatoes, as they will become gluey very easily. Transfer to a bowl and keep warm by setting over a saucepan of warm water until serving.

FOR THE BLOOD ORANGE JUS: Reduce the blood orange juice with the port and sugar in a saucepan over medium-high heat until thick and syrupy. Reduce the chicken stock by half in another saucepan over high heat, and then whisk the 2 liquids together. Season to taste with salt and pepper. Add the tarragon sprig, cover the pan, and let the tarragon steep for 20 minutes. Strain through a fine-mesh sieve into a small bowl. Set aside and keep warm.

FOR THE RELISH: Put the fennel, leek, 2 tablespoons of the olive oil, and the water into a small saucepan and cook over medium heat and until the vegetables are tender and the water has almost completely evaporated. Let cool. Stir in the remaining 2 tablespoons olive oil and the tarragon. Season to taste with salt and pepper and set aside.

TO SERVE

Unmold the pudding onto a cutting board. Cut off a 1-inch-thick slice and cut the slice into quarters. Melt 2 tablespoons of the butter in a nonstick skillet over medium heat and add the pieces of black pudding. Cook for 3 to 5 minutes, or until the pudding is brown and crisped. Turn over and cook on the other side for another 3 or 4 minutes. The pudding can be kept warm in a 250°F oven while you heat the lobster and set up the plates.

Cut the lobster tails in half, remove all but the last segment of tail, and warm the Beurre Fondue. Spoon some of the potato mousseline in the center of each of 4 dinner plates and spread it around with the back of the spoon to make a 3-inch circle. Place a piece of black pudding in the center of each potato circle and place a lobster tail half on each piece of pudding. Spoon a small amount of the sauce on the lobster and around the potato mousseline. Dot the fennel relish around the plate in the sauce.

PAN-SEARED FOIE GRAS

BOSC PEAR CONFIT, ALMOND PAIN PERDU, SHERRY VINEGAR REDUCTION,
AND ASSORTED SALTS AND PEPPERS

SERVES 4

BOSC PEAR CONFIT

2 cups poire William

1 cup natural apple juice

½ cup granulated sugar

4 Bosc pears, peeled and cut into
    ½-inch dice

SHERRY VINEGAR
REDUCTION

1 cup Spanish sherry (see Kitchen
    and Shopping Notes)

1 cup Spanish sherry vinegar (see
    Kitchen and Shopping Notes)

2 tablespoons brown sugar

ALMOND PAIN PERDU

1 cup whole blanched almonds

4 tablespoons unsalted butter,
    at room temperature

Kosher salt

1 large egg white

2 (1-inch-thick) slices *pain d'mie*
    or other high-quality dense
    white bread (see Kitchen
    and Shopping Notes)

½ cup sliced almonds

2 tablespoons granulated sugar

FOIE GRAS

10 to 12 ounces fresh grade A foie
    gras, cut into 4 equal portions
    (1 to 1¼ inches thick) (see
    Sources, page 236)

Kosher salt and freshly ground
    black pepper

ASSORTED SALTS
AND PEPPERS

(one or any combination you like)

Fleur de sel

Maldon sea salt

Hawaiian red salt

Mediterranean sea salt

Himalayan pink salt

Cracked black pepper

Grains of paradise (see Sources,
    page 237)

Pink peppercorns

Fat liver (*foie gras* in French), is the creamiest and richest ingredient in a cook's arsenal. It really needs nothing more than salt, pepper, and toast. Anything more is just window dressing, although that doesn't stop us from experimenting with the tastes, textures, and aromas of foods that could accompany foie gras. In this preparation, some interesting salts and peppers, a concentrated confit of Bosc pears, and a thick reduction of fine dark sherry and aged sherry vinegar are offered alongside the quickly seared foie gras. Crisp almond-coated *pain perdu,* which means "lost bread" is included, probably more to enjoy with the pears than anything else. Each element on the plate affects the flavor of the foie gras in a slightly different way and is meant to be enjoyed either separately or together.

continued

An impeccable liver is off-white to yellow in color. It's supple, almost stretchy, and smooth to the touch. Avoid foie gras that's dull gray or has any red marbling or hints of green bile. When you get the liver home, soak it in salted ice water overnight. To prepare your foie gras for cooking: Lay the foie gras, smooth side down, on top of an inverted bowl, allowing the liver to curve and "spread" open. With a small sharp knife, expose the main vein and with a dry paper towel, pick up the vein and gently pull it out. If the vein tears, leave it as is. With your hands, gently pull apart the lobes to separate them.

The quality of the sherry and sherry vinegar used for the reduction is important because all the flavors (both good and bad) are intensified when they are reduced. Many Americans know only two kinds of sherry: dry and cream, but the world of true Spanish sherry is quite complex and varies in flavor, color, and sweetness. Authentic sherry is only produced in the Jerez region of Spain, primarily from Palomino Fino grapes and using a method of aging called the *solera* system, where older sherries are topped off with newer ones. The four main types of sherry are pale and dry fino, dry and subtly salty Manzanilla, semidry, amber-colored amontillado, and sweet, dark oloroso. Sherry vinegar can be made from any of the four types of sherries, but the best are aged to develop a rich, nutty, mellow flavor. Some of the premium aged sherry vinegars are more than 50 years old, rival *aceto balsamico tradizionale di Modena,* and can be quite costly. For this recipe, we suggest using good amontillado sherry and sherry vinegar that has aged for 10 years or so.

Using salt as a condiment is a fairly recent phenomenon, coinciding with the production of artisanal salts and their purveyors. Given how foie gras always seemed incomplete without a sprinkling of *fleur de sel,* we thought it would be fun to try some of these less familiar salts (and peppers) with it. Many upscale grocers carry the salts and peppers, and they're also available by mail order (see Sources, page 237). A salt and pepper tasting is interesting but not necessary.

Our recipe for *pain perdu* uses *pain d'mie,* a fine-textured white bread that is baked in a closed bread pan, giving it four even sides with a dense crumb and homemade flavor. Any good-quality, firm-textured white bread could be substituted. Instead of serving pain perdu, toasted artisanal French or whole-grain bread is also excellent with foie gras.

METHOD

FOR THE PEAR CONFIT: Heat the poire William, apple juice, and granulated sugar in a saucepan over medium-high heat until almost boiling. Add the pears and decrease the heat to maintain a low simmer. Cook for 20 to 30 minutes, or until the pears have softened. Strain through a fine-mesh sieve into a bowl, reserving the liquid. Put the pears into a bowl, mash with a fork, and set aside. Return the pear liquid to the saucepan and reduce over high heat until it's syrupy. Set aside.

FOR THE SHERRY VINEGAR REDUCTION: Simmer the sherry, sherry vinegar, and brown sugar in a saucepan until it's reduced to ¼ cup. Set aside or cover and refrigerate for up to 1 week.

FOR THE ALMOND PAIN PERDU: Preheat the oven to 350°F. Spread the almonds out in a shallow pan and toast for 8 to 12 minutes, or until golden. Transfer the still-warm almonds to a food processor and puree along with 2 tablespoons of the butter. Season with salt and set aside or refrigerate for up to 2 months. Raise the oven temperature to 400°F. Whisk the egg white in a small bowl until it's frothy, then stir in the sliced almonds and granulated sugar. Spread 1 tablespoon of the softened butter on one side of each slice of bread and spread the other side with the almond butter. Place on a cookie sheet, almond butter side up, and toast for 10 to 12 minutes, or until golden. Set aside.

TO SERVE

Heat a sauté pan or skillet over medium-high heat. Season the foie gras on both sides with salt and pepper and slip into the skillet. Cook for 2 to 3 minutes, or until it begins to turn brown along the edges, and flip over. Cook for about 2 minutes more, or until the meat is still pink. Transfer the foie gras to a clean kitchen towel or paper towels to blot excess fat, and then place a portion on each of 4 warm dinner plates. Cut the pain perdu into small triangles or rectangles. Place a spoonful of pear confit on one side of the plate with a piece of the pain perdu. Drizzle the plates with the vinegar reduction and serve with small piles of the various salts and peppers.

QUAIL STUFFED WITH FOIE GRAS
AND ROASTED PORCINI MUSHROOMS

KABOCHA SQUASH PUREE AND ASIAN PEAR, THYME AND SPANISH SHERRY RELISH

SERVES 8

SAUTÉED SPINACH

2 tablespoons olive oil

½ teaspoon finely diced shallot

1 small clove garlic, chopped

½ pound spinach, cleaned and
     tough stems removed

QUAIL

4 boned quail

8 to 10 ounces fresh Grade A fresh
     foie gras, cut into 4 equal
     pieces

Kosher salt and freshly ground
     black pepper

1 tablespoon olive oil

8 to 10 ounces fresh porcini
     mushrooms, brushed clean

1 shallot, peeled

1 clove garlic, peeled

2 thyme sprigs

1 tablespoon unsalted butter

SPANISH SHERRY SAUCE

2 tablespoons olive oil

Reserved wings and legs from
     the quail

1 small onion, coarsely chopped

2 cloves garlic

½ cup fine-quality dry (fino) sherry

1½ cups Dark Chicken Stock (see
     Basics, page 230)

3 thyme sprigs

Kosher salt and freshly ground
     black pepper

KABOCHA SQUASH PUREE

1 (2- to 3-pound) kabocha squash

Olive oil

4 tablespoons unsalted butter,
     cut into pieces

Kosher salt and freshly ground
     black pepper

ASIAN PEAR RELISH

2 tablespoons finely diced shallots

¼ cup extra-virgin olive oil

¼ cup fine-quality dry (fino) sherry

1 tablespoon fresh thyme leaves

1 small Asian pear, peeled and finely
     diced (⅛ inch)

Kosher salt and freshly ground
     black pepper

2 tablespoons grape seed or olive oil

2 tablespoons unsalted, butter,
     at room temperature

Choose a nice fall day—preferably a rainy one—when you have absolutely no other plans. Invite your most appreciative friends to dinner and treat them to this special-occasion quail. We usually reserve this dish for wine dinners, culinary events, tasting menus, and New Year's Eve.

KITCHEN AND SHOPPING NOTES

Boneless quail, which are really only partially boned with just the rib cages removed and the tiny legs and wing bones left in, are as readily available as bone-in quail—though many butchers need to special order them. For this recipe, you need to remove the leg and wing bones as follows: For the leg, cut off the tip of the drumstick (sharp scissors work) and gently pull the bones away from the meat. For the wing, cut off the first joint, scrape the meat from the bone, and pull through and out the body. Reserve all the bones for the sauce. Keep in mind that it's important to keep as much skin on the birds as possible in order to enclose the stuffing.

continued

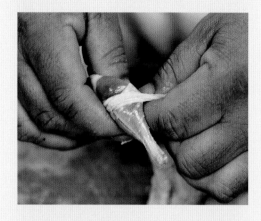

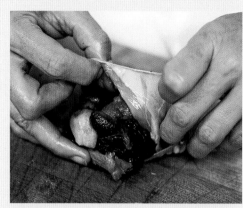

1 4
2 5
3 6

1   French the wings and remove the bone

2   Cut off the tip of the drumstick and pull
    the meat and bone from the skin

3   The parted quail breast, legs, and wings

4   The foie gras, spinach, and porcini
    package; the quail breast ready to
    be stuffed

5   Stuff the quail breast

6   The stuffed quail breast, ready to
    be seared

Kabocha squash has dark green skin, fine-grained orange flesh, and deep flavor. They weigh anywhere from 2 to 3 pounds. Be aware that hard winter squashes, such as kabocha, can be difficult to cut, so use a sharp knife or cleaver carefully when you cut them in half. You end up with more squash than you need for this recipe; use the extra for soup or risotto. It can also be frozen.

Porcini means "little pigs" in Italian, a silly name for such stately mushrooms. The buttery flavor and firm, meaty texture of porcini make them one of the most sought-after fresh wild mushrooms in the world. Available for only a short time in the spring and fall, they're quite perishable and should be used the day purchased. Out of season, porcini are available frozen and dried, but only fresh will do for this dish.

METHOD

FOR THE SPINACH: Heat the olive oil in a large sauté pan over medium heat. Add the shallot and garlic and cook for 1 minute, then add the spinach, turning with tongs, for about 2 minutes, or until wilted. Drain in a colander. When cool enough to handle, squeeze to remove as much moisture as possible and set aside.

FOR THE QUAIL: Bone out the legs and wings of the quail (see Kitchen and Shopping Notes). Heat a skillet over high heat for 1 minute. Season the foie gras with salt and pepper and sauté, turning once, for 2 minutes on each side, or until golden brown and still slightly pink in the center. Transfer to a plate and chill in the refrigerator for at least 30 minutes. Separate the caps and stems of the porcini and slice both ½ thick. Heat the same skillet over medium-high heat. Add the olive oil, porcini, shallot, garlic clove, and thyme sprigs. Cook for about 5 minutes, or until the porcini begin to brown. Lower the heat to medium-low and continue to cook for about 5 minutes, or until the porcini are tender. Season with salt and pepper and add the butter, tossing to combine well. Transfer the porcini mixture to a plate (discard the shallot, garlic, and thyme) and chill in the refrigerator for at least 30 minutes or up to several hours ahead.

To stuff the quails, put them on a work surface, breast side down. Assemble the sautéed spinach, seared foie gras, and cooked porcini, and season everything with salt and pepper. Place the 4 pieces of foie on your work surface, and top each with a small pile of the spinach and 1 or 2 slices of porcini. Lightly press down on the layers to form compact packages. Insert a package into the cavity of each quail, foie gras side closest to the breast. Pull the skin taut and put the stuffed quail on a plate, cover with plastic wrap, and refrigerate for at least 1 hour or up to overnight.

continued

FOR THE SHERRY SAUCE: Heat the olive oil in a saucepan over medium heat. Add the reserved quail pieces, onion, and garlic. Increase the heat to high and cook, stirring occasionally, for 5 to 8 minutes, or until browned. Add the sherry and cook until the pan is almost dry. Add the chicken stock and thyme sprigs and cook over medium heat until reduced by half, skimming occasionally. Strain through a fine-mesh sieve into a small saucepan, season with salt and pepper, and set aside or refrigerate for up to 1 day.

FOR THE SQUASH PUREE: Preheat the oven to 350°F. Cut the squash in half, scoop out and discard the seeds, and rub the cut sides with a little olive oil. Place the squash, cut side down, on a baking sheet or in a roasting pan and roast for 30 to 45 minutes, or until tender when pierced with a knife. Set aside to cool slightly. Scoop out the flesh into a blender or food processor. Add the butter and puree until smooth. Strain through a fine-mesh sieve into a bowl and season to taste with salt and pepper. The puree can be made up to 1 day ahead and refrigerated. Reheat before serving.

FOR THE PEAR RELISH: Cook the shallots in 1 teaspoon of the olive oil in a small skillet until softened. Add the sherry and reduce to 2 tablespoons. Stir the shallots and sherry reduction in a small bowl with the thyme and Asian pear and season to taste with salt and pepper. The relish can be made up to 6 hours ahead but the pear should be added no more than 1 hour before serving. Season to taste with salt and pepper.

TO COOK THE QUAIL: Preheat the oven to 425°F. Heat the grape seed oil in a large ovenproof skillet over medium-high heat. Add the quail, breast side down, and cook for about 3 minutes, or until golden brown. Carefully turn the birds onto their backs, cook for 1 minute, and put the skillet in the oven. Roast the quail for 12 minutes, or until an instant-read thermometer inserted into a thigh reaches 110° to 115°F. Remove from the oven and let rest for 5 minutes.

TO SERVE

Rewarm the squash puree and the sauce separately. Whisk the butter into the sherry sauce until melted and smooth. Cut the quail crosswise in half. Place a spoonful of the kabocha puree in the center of 8 warm dinner plates and place a quail half in the center of the puree. Spoon the sauce around the puree and break up the sauce with dots of the relish.

GLAZED SWEETBREADS IN POTATO CRUST

CHANTERELLE MUSHROOMS AND RED WINE REDUCTION

SERVES 4

RED WINE SAUCE

2 cups dry red wine, such as Pinot
    Noir, Sangiovese, or Merlot

1 tablespoon olive oil

1 carrot, chopped

1 celery rib, chopped

4 large shallots, chopped

1 small clove garlic

2 teaspoons tomato paste

2 cups Dark Chicken Stock (see
    Basics, page 230)

2 thyme sprigs

½ bay leaf

½ teaspoon black peppercorns

1 tablespoon unsalted butter

Kosher salt and freshly ground
    black pepper

SWEETBREADS

½ pound veal sweetbread "hearts"
    (see Kitchen and Shopping
    Notes)

Kosher salt and freshly ground
    black pepper

2 cloves garlic

4 thyme sprigs

1 bay leaf

About 2 cups olive oil

4 large green Swiss chard leaves,
    stemmed and halved if large

1 tablespoon unsalted butter

1 tablespoon extra-virgin olive oil

2 large Yukon Gold potatoes,
    unpeeled (about ½ pound each)

CHANTERELLES

6 ounces small chanterelle
    mushrooms, brushed clean

1 tablespoon unsalted butter

1 tablespoon olive oil

1 teaspoon chopped fresh
    thyme leaves

Kosher salt and freshly ground
    black pepper

GARNISH

2 cups loosely packed cleaned
    mâche

1 tablespoon extra-virgin olive oil

¼ teaspoon Banyuls vinegar

Sweetbreads can sometimes cause confusion in the dining room at Boulevard. On more than one occasion, an order was promptly returned to the kitchen because it wasn't the basket of yummy little dinner rolls someone expected. Experience has taught us that sweetbreads aren't for everyone, but for the true connoisseur who adores their smooth texture and delicate veal flavor, we love having them on the menu. In this recipe, we've wrapped the sweetbreads in a crisp potato crust, which contrasts and accentuates their sublime texture. A small, slightly acidic salad is the perfect complement to the crisp, creamy sweetbreads and earthy flavors of the mushrooms.

continued

KITCHEN AND SHOPPING NOTES

We use only the top, rounded, heart-shaped lobe of the sweetbreads, what we call "sweethearts," which have very little connective tissue and membrane. (The bottom portion is irregularly shaped and has more sinew. You might have to ask your butcher if he'll sell you just the heart-shaped lobe.) The cook-friendly characteristics of the heart make it possible to confit the sweetbreads, a novel technique that our friend Franco Dunn brought back from Italy. This dish takes a little planning, not because it's complicated but because the sweetbreads take a day or two to prepare.

We recommend purchasing a spiral vegetable slicer (see Sources, page 237). It makes beautiful continuous strands and ribbons of vegetables, perfect for salads and for wrapping around things like sweetbreads. While it's essential for this recipe, we also think it will become a much-used and valuable piece of equipment in your kitchen.

METHOD

FOR THE RED WINE SAUCE: Cook the red wine in a saucepan over high heat until reduced to a thick syrup. Heat the oil in a small saucepan over medium-high heat. Add the carrot, celery, shallots, and garlic and cook for about 5 minutes, or until the vegetables begin to turn golden. Add the tomato paste and cook for 1 minute more. Add the chicken stock, thyme sprigs, bay leaf, and peppercorns. Increase the heat to high and reduce the liquid by half. Whisk in the red wine reduction, then strain through a fine-mesh sieve into a bowl. The strained liquid can be refrigerated for up to 2 days before adding the butter. Return to the pan, whisk in the butter until it melts, and season to taste with salt and pepper. Set aside or refrigerate for up to 2 days.

FOR THE SWEETBREADS: Soak the sweetbreads in cold water to cover for at least 6 hours, changing the water 2 or 3 times. Preheat the oven to 300°F. Drain the sweetbreads and pat dry with paper towels. Season with salt and pepper and put into a small casserole dish along with the garlic, thyme sprigs, and bay leaf. Add the 2 cups olive oil or as needed to cover the sweetbreads, and bake for 1½ hours. Using a slotted spoon, transfer the sweetbreads to a plate or small rimmed baking sheet. Let the liquid from the sweetbreads settle to the bottom of the casserole, then strain the oil, leaving as much of the sweetbread liquid behind as possible. Reserve the confit oil for frying the potato-crusted sweetbreads. (The oil can be strained and stored in the refrigerator for up to 2 weeks.) The sweetbreads can be refrigerated for up to 2 days.

Blanch the Swiss chard leaves in a large pot of boiling water for about 30 seconds, or until wilted. Drain, rinse well with cold water to stop the cooking, and lay the leaves out flat on clean kitchen towels to dry.

Cut the sweetbreads into 4 equal portions. Heat the butter and 1 tablespoon olive oil in a skillet or sauté pan over medium-high heat. Season the sweetbreads with salt and pepper and cook, turning as needed, for about 4 minutes, or until golden on all sides. Remove from the skillet and set aside to cool. Season once more with salt and pepper. Wrap each sweetbread piece in a chard leaf so it forms a neat package. Set aside briefly or refrigerate for up to 6 hours until you're ready to cut and wrap in the potatoes. Once the sweetbreads are wrapped in potato they must be cooked or the potatoes will darken.

To make the potato strands, use a spiral slicer set with the $\frac{1}{8}$-inch julienne blade. Set the thickness blade so it cuts the potato strands into linguine-like strips that are thinner than they are wide. Cut $\frac{1}{3}$ inch off each short end of the potatoes to create a flat surface, then put 1 of the potatoes onto the spiral slicer and cut into thin strands. Lay the strands on a cutting board to form 8 sets that are 5 strands wide and about 12 inches long. Put one sweetbread package lengthwise on 1 group of the strands (parallel to the ribbons) and roll up. Wrap it up by winding another set of strands crosswise around the potato. Set the potato-wrapped sweetbread package aside on a plate. Repeat with the remaining sweetbread portions, spiral cutting the remaining potato.

Meanwhile, heat 2 cups of the reserved sweetbread-cooking oil in a large sauté pan until it reaches 300°F on a deep-fry thermometer. Cook the sweetbreads without crowding them and turning with a slotted spoon until golden on all sides, about 8 minutes. Transfer to paper towels to drain.

FOR THE CHANTERELLES: Cut the chanterelles lengthwise into $\frac{1}{4}$-inch-thick slices. Heat the butter and oil in a skillet over high heat. Add the mushrooms and sauté for 1 minute, then add the thyme. Continue to sauté for 1 to 2 minutes, or until the mushrooms are golden. Season to taste with salt and pepper.

TO SERVE

Place an equal pile of the chanterelles in the center of each of 4 dinner plates. Cut the sweetbreads crosswise in half and nestle into the middle of the chanterelles, with one cut surface facing up so it can be seen. Spoon the sauce around the plate. Toss the mâche with the oil and vinegar in a bowl and put a little mound on top or off to the side of each plate.

PAN-ROASTED MEDITERRANEAN ROUGET BARBET

MELTED EGGPLANT, SHRIMP AND BASIL BEIGNETS, HEIRLOOM TOMATO CARPACCIO

SERVES 4

CREAMY ROASTED EGGPLANT

1 Rosa Bianca, globe eggplant
    or your favorite variety
    (¾ to 1 pound)
1 teaspoon balsamic vinegar
1 tablespoon capers, rinsed
1 tablespoon extra virgin olive oil
2 tablespoons Melted Garlic
    (see Basics, page 232)

ROCK SHRIMP BEIGNETS

¼ pound fresh rock shrimp
1 teaspoon extra virgin olive oil
Pinch of Aleppo pepper
Kosher salt and freshly ground
    black pepper
8 large fresh basil leaves, about
    3½ to 4 inches long

BEIGNET BATTER

¼ cup plus 2 tablespoons cake flour
¾ cup soda water
1 cup olive oil

TOMATO CARPACCIO

2 large (3-inch-diameter) vine-
    ripened or heirloom tomatoes
1 teaspoon fresh thyme leaves
Coarse sea salt
½ teaspoon Aleppo pepper
Special extra-virgin olive oil,
    for drizzling

ROUGET BARBET (RED MULLET)

2 tablespoons olive oil
8 *rouget barbet* fillets, skin on
    and pin bones removed
    (see Sources, page 236)
Kosher salt and freshly ground
    black pepper

Vine-ripened tomatoes, heirloom eggplants, and fresh tender basil leaves are all signals that summer is in full force. Midsummer, when tomato season is well underway, is absolutely the perfect time to enjoy all of the summer "icons" in this recipe.

Even with these summer ingredients at the peak of their flavor, we suspect that the shrimp and basil beignets are the primary reason our guests order this dish. The kitchen receives a huge number of "emergency" second orders of these beignets. We understand; the beignets deserve all of the attention they receive, and while it would be a prodigious amount of work to make a big, wonderful plateful of these treats, it would also be worth every bit of the effort.

Rouget barbet, the beloved little Mediterranean red mullet, has a beautiful red skin and rich flavor that is the perfect complement to the creamy eggplant and thin slices of ripe tomatoes dressed with the best olive oil you can find. Just remember to have a few extra shrimp and basil beignets ready to fry for those emergency extras your guests are sure to request.

continued

KITCHEN AND SHOPPING NOTES

The tomato carpaccio should only be prepared during the height of tomato season because there is no recipe that will make bland tomatoes delicious. If you are intrigued by the *rouget*, eggplant, and beignets, they make a superb dish on their own. If you're lucky you have a farmers' market in your area, a friend who's an avid gardener, or, best of all, your own tomato plants! If not, refer to Sources (page 237) for a list of mail-order companies that can ship heirloom tomatoes directly to you. There is a dizzying array of varieties with crazy colors, wild names like Green Zebra, Brandywine, and Marvel Stripe (to name a few of our favorites), and different shapes and sizes each with its own distinct flavor and texture.

Eggplants are at their best in summer when their flesh is sweetest with none of the bitterness, but be adventurous and try an heirloom variety like Rosa Bianca or an all white Italian. In choosing any eggplant, pick one that is unwrinkled, unblemished, firm, and feels heavy for its size (it will have fewer seeds). Aleppo pepper from Syria has a complex spicy flavor and adds more than just heat to a dish. It's usually sold beautifully cleaned and devoid of pesky seeds and can be substituted for red pepper flakes in any recipe.

Rouget barbet is not widely available, although it can often be found in Asian markets on the coasts. It has a rich, mild ocean flavor that has endeared it to chefs, but really any small fish with skin that crisps up nicely when cooked will do. You can also serve the dish with just a few beignets on top of the creamy eggplant and tomato carpaccio.

METHOD

FOR THE EGGPLANT: Preheat the oven to 375°F. Prick the eggplant all over with a fork and roast the eggplant for 30 to 40 minutes, or until it is soft and melting, then set aside to cool. Peel and remove any large seed sacks. Coarsely chop the eggplant with the Melted Garlic. Add the balsamic vinegar, olive oil, and capers and season to taste with salt and pepper. The eggplant can be refrigerated for several hours or overnight, but bring to room temperature or heat slightly before serving.

FOR THE ROCK SHRIMP BEIGNETS: Coarsely chop the rock shrimp and combine in a small bowl with the olive oil and Aleppo pepper and season with salt and pepper. Stir vigorously for a minute so the stuffing binds.

Place $\frac{1}{2}$ to $\frac{3}{4}$ teaspoon of the mixture into each basil leaf and fold in half lengthwise. Make sure the stuffing doesn't pop out of the sides. They'll remind you of pea pods when they are stuffed. Since people really do love these beignets, use all the shrimp stuffing to make a few extra because you will certainly have enough batter. We guarantee that not a crunchy morsel will be left. Refrigerate before frying for up to 4 hours.

FOR THE BEIGNET BATTER: In a medium bowl, gently stir together the cake flour and soda water with a whisk. It's okay if a few lumps remain in the batter. Refrigerate for up to 1 hour.

FOR THE TOMATO CARPACCIO: About 15 or 20 minutes before you plan on serving the dish, place the tomatoes on a cutting board and, with a very sharp knife or serrated knife, slice the tomatoes $\frac{1}{8}$ inch thick. Season to taste with salt and pepper. Arrange 5 or 6 tomato slices on each of 4 plates, alternating colors if you have them. Sprinkle Aleppo pepper and thyme leaves over the tomatoes, then drizzle a generous amount of olive oil over all.

TO SERVE

Just before you are going to cook the fish and fry the beignets, place a nice oval spoonful of room-temperature eggplant in the center of the tomatoes. Put the 1 cup olive oil into an 8-inch sauté pan, (any larger and the oil will not be deep enough to fry the beignets) and heat the oil to 350°F on a deep-fry thermometer. Put several of the stuffed basil leaves in the batter and turn them gently so they're completely coated. Fish one out with tongs and place it in the hot oil. Repeat this process with 3 more of the stuffed leaves. When they are golden brown, turn over and continue frying until they are puffed and golden. Transfer the beignets to paper towels to drain and sprinkle immediately with salt. Repeat with the remaining stuffed basil leaves. (The beignets stay crisp long enough for you to cook the fish, so don't worry about having to do 2 things at once.) Just don't cover them in any way; they'll go from magnificently crisp to soggy in an instant.

Heat a large, heavy skillet or sauté pan over medium heat and add the olive oil. Generously season both sides of the fish with salt and grind a little fresh pepper on the flesh side. Place skin side down in the pan; the fish will start to curl up, so just press the fillets with a spatula for a minute. Continue to cook on the skin side for about 2 minutes; you'll notice the flesh on the sides cooking. Small, skinned fish fillets cook mostly from the bottom up, so don't be tempted to turn them until the skin is crisp; turn the fillets so they just kiss the sauté pan for a few seconds on the other side, remove from the pan, and blot gently with paper towels.

Drizzle the special extra-virgin olive oil on and around the tomatoes and plate. Place 2 fish fillets on each plate and top with 2 beignets, or serve the beignets separately on a plate in the center of the table and take your chances on getting your share.

FISH

CALIFORNIA WHITE SEA BASS ROASTED WITH OLIVES AND BASIL

POTATOES CRUSHED WITH GARLIC, CHILES, AND ARUGULA, TOMATO VINAIGRETTE

SERVES 4

OLIVE FILLING

2 tablespoons chopped pitted
    Kalamata or other brine-cured
    black olives (see Kitchen and
    Shopping Notes)
1 teaspoon finely diced preserved
    lemon (see Basics, page 234)
¼ teaspoon fresh thyme leaves

SEA BASS

4 (6-ounce) California white sea bass
    fillet, at least 1 inch thick
3 tablespoons Pesto (see Basics,
    page 233)
Kosher salt and freshly ground
    black pepper

CRUSHED POTATOES

1½ pounds medium to large Yukon
    Gold potatoes, peeled and
    quartered
8 cloves garlic, peeled
3 tablespoons unsalted butter,
    cut into pieces
3 tablespoons mascarpone cheese
2 tablespoons extra-virgin olive oil
3 cups chopped cleaned arugula
1 teaspoon crushed red pepper
    flakes
Kosher salt and freshly ground
    black pepper

TOMATO VINAIGRETTE

3 large vine-ripened red tomatoes
    (about 1¼ pounds)
1 tablespoon balsamic vinegar
½ cup extra-virgin olive oil
Kosher salt and freshly ground
    black pepper

2 tablespoons olive oil

Sometimes a great side dish becomes the driving force behind the entire plate; this is just that side dish. Yukon Gold potatoes, gently crushed with olive oil, carry the flavors of chile, garlic, and peppery arugula in a way that a simple pureed potato never could. We have an ever-expanding list of variations for crushed potatoes, but we always seem to return to this simple and rustic version that exemplifies California and Mediterranean cuisine in one bite. A thick fillet of white sea bass, slashed and seasoned with olives and basil pesto and complemented by the remarkable potatoes, needs only a fresh tomato, coarsely grated and whisked with extra-virgin olive oil to make it complete. This dish is truly greater than the sum of its parts.

KITCHEN AND SHOPPING NOTES

California white sea bass is an elusive fish that shows up year-round in California. We're particularly fond of large California white sea bass because they have a delicate flavor and firm white flesh. The thick fillets can be cooked by most methods. Other thick white fish, such as striped bass, halibut, and grouper (grouper is in the bass family), are appropriate substitutes.

We recommend a yellow-fleshed potato like the Yukon Gold or Yellow Finn for this recipe. Their golden-colored buttery flesh can be crushed and still maintain its texture. These potatoes have both visual appeal and flavor, which makes them a superior choice for this dish.

Choose well-made black olives that really taste good. The assertive flavor of olives stands out in this recipe. Some olives we like are Niçoise, Ligurian, and Spanish Arbequina. Large, briny artisanal Kalamatas can be excellent, but it depends on the brand and few good varieties of olives are sold pitted, as it compromises their quality. Kalamatas are the exception, but again check the brand. We recommend that you rinse the olives before proceeding with the recipe.

METHOD

FOR THE OLIVE FILLING: Gently stir the olives with the preserved lemon and thyme until combined and set aside.

FOR THE SEA BASS: Make 4 diagonal evenly spaced cuts, about ½ inch deep, on the flesh side of each piece of fish. Stuff about ½ teaspoon of the olive-lemon mixture into every other cut. Stuff the pesto into the remaining 2 cuts. Season with salt and pepper, cover, and refrigerate the fish for up to 2 hours before cooking.

FOR THE POTATOES: Put the potatoes into a large saucepan with generously salted water to cover by 1 inch and bring to a boil over high heat. Add the garlic and lower the heat to a simmer. Cook for about 15 minutes, or until the potatoes are just tender when pierced with a knife but not falling apart. Drain the potatoes and garlic, transfer to a bowl, and add the butter and mascarpone cheese. Using a large spoon or fork, mix the potatoes with the butter and cheese, making sure to leave some of the potatoes in large chunks, mashing the garlic on the side of the bowl. Heat the oil in a small skillet and sauté the arugula with the red pepper flakes for about 3 minutes, or until the arugula has wilted. Add the arugula mixture to the potatoes, gently folding it in so it looks like green marble streaks. Season to taste with salt and pepper. The potatoes can be cooked and mashed up to 4 hours ahead, but do not add the cooked arugula mixture until you are ready to serve.

FOR THE TOMATO VINAIGRETTE: Cut the tomatoes crosswise in half. Gently squeeze out the seeds and set tomatoes, cut side down, on a paper towel to drain for 5 minutes. Using the largest holes of a box grater set over a bowl, grate the tomatoes until only the skins of the tomatoes remains. Discard the skins. Add the balsamic vinegar and then slowly whisk in the olive oil until well combined. Season to taste with salt and pepper and set aside. The vinaigrette is best made just before cooking the fish and should be served at room temperature.

TO SERVE

Preheat oven to 450°F. Heat a large ovenproof nonstick sauté pan over medium-high heat until hot, then add the olive oil. Place the fish, stuffed side down, into the pan and decrease heat to medium-low. Cook for about 2 minutes, or until golden brown, then carefully turn the fish over. Transfer the pan to the oven and roast for about 4 minutes, or until just cooked through (note that the slashes in the fish cause it to cook more quickly). Remove from the oven and set aside. Place a scoop of the potatoes on each of 4 warm dinner plates, top with a fish fillet, and spoon the tomato vinaigrette around.

PAN-ROASTED HALIBUT FILLETS AND CHEEKS

FRESH MOREL MUSHROOMS, SPRING VEGETABLES, GREEN GARLIC PESTO, AND MOREL MUSHROOM JUS

SERVES 4

MOREL MUSHROOM JUS

½ ounce dried morel mushrooms

1 cup hot water

1 tablespoon olive oil

1 onion, coarsely chopped
(1 cup)

1 shallot, thinly sliced

½ cup dry white wine

6 black peppercorns

3 thyme sprigs

2 cups Dark Chicken Stock (see
Basics, page 230)

GREEN GARLIC PESTO

2 cups chopped green garlic, white
and green parts

2 cups loosely packed fresh flat-
leaf parsley leaves

1 cup olive oil

Kosher salt and freshly ground
black pepper

SPRING VEGETABLES

½ pound English peas, shelled
(½ cup shelled)

20 sugar snap peas, stems and
strings removed

½ cup shelled fava beans (see
Basics, page 229)

¼ pound pea shoots or tendrils

HALIBUT

1 tablespoon olive oil

4 (4-ounce) pieces halibut fillet,
skin on

½ pound halibut cheeks or sea
scallops

Kosher salt and freshly ground
black pepper

24 fresh morel mushrooms (each
about 2 inches long), cleaned
(see Kitchen and Shopping
Notes) or dried morels

4 tablespoons olive oil

1 tablespoon unsalted butter

¼ cup water

Kosher salt and freshly ground
black pepper

"Are they here yet?" That's the call that mycologist and mushroom purveyor Connie Green hears from the Boulevard kitchen at least a month before fresh morels are actually available. By the time March arrives, we don't want to see another parsnip, rutabaga, or turnip. By April, we definitely anticipate the arrival of fresh morels and all of the delights of spring, so when English peas, green garlic, fava beans, and fresh morels arrive in the kitchen at the same time, carpe diem—seize the day! It's certainly a full-blown restaurant production to prepare two "cuts" of halibut, but with all of these spring vegetables along with the fresh morels, it's a splendid way to celebrate the arrival of spring.

KITCHEN AND SHOPPING NOTES

At the restaurant, we use two types of halibut: California, which is a bit smaller and leaner, and Alaskan, which is larger, fattier, and thicker. Halibut cheeks are relatively unknown outside coastal fishing ports, but many people consider them the best part of the fish. They're denser than the fillets and have a more concentrated sweetness, much like scallops, which can be substituted in this recipe. Alaskan halibut cheeks can be ordered by mail (see Sources, page 236). Because halibut is such a lean fish, it can quickly overcook, so err on the side of being underdone, and let it finish cooking outside the oven.

continued

Fresh morels make their appearance in spring and can be purchased throughout the summer. Look for those that are firm and dry with no damp soft spots or off odor. Morels can be as short as ½ inch or up to 4 inches long. For this recipe, choose small- to medium-size specimens about 2 inches in length. To clean fresh morel mushrooms, we use the "soak and float" method: Put them into a large bowl of cold water, swish them around, then let them sit for a few seconds until they float to the surface. The dirt will settle to the bottom of the bowl. Scoop out the morels, drain the water, and repeat the procedure 2 or 3 times. Spread the morels out on a sheet pan or plate lined with paper towels and pat dry. You can do this a few hours ahead of time, then set them aside at room temperature or in the refrigerator.

Pea shoots and pea tendrils (the smaller, more delicate, curly ends of the shoots) were once only seen in Chinese markets. Today you can find them at many upscale urban grocers and farmers' markets. The cut ends of the shoots can often be dry and tough, so we prefer the tendrils, which are sweet and delicately flavored.

The freshest fava beans have smooth, firm, moist-looking pods. For this recipe, their size doesn't matter, however, smaller favas beans are sweeter.

Immature bulbs of garlic, called green garlic, arrive—usually in farmers' markets—in the spring. They look like giant green onions with bulbous white ends and have a very sweet, delicate flavor.

METHOD

FOR THE MOREL JUS: Soak the dried mushrooms in the hot water in a small bowl for 15 minutes. Drain and discard the water. Heat the oil in a saucepan over medium-high heat. Add the onion and shallot and cook, stirring occasionally to prevent burning, for 8 to 10 minutes, or until the onions begin to caramelize. Add the wine, then add the morels. Add the peppercorns, thyme sprigs, and chicken stock. Increase the heat to high and cook until the liquid has reduced by half. Put the morels and their liquid into a blender or food processor and pulse until the mushrooms are coarsely chopped (be careful not to puree them). Strain through a fine-mesh sieve into a bowl and discard the solids. You should have about ¾ cup jus. Set aside or refrigerate for up to 2 days.

FOR THE GREEN GARLIC PESTO: Trim off the tough green ends from the garlic. Bring a large pot of water to a boil and cook the garlic for about 5 minutes, or until it's tender and softened but still green. Using tongs, remove the garlic and plunge into a bowl of ice water to stop the cooking. Scoop out with a sieve or slotted spoon and set aside on a plate. Blanch the parsley leaves in the same boiling water for 30 seconds, then scoop out and plunge into the bowl of ice water. Drain and transfer to the plate with the garlic. Put the garlic and parsley into a blender and puree with ¼ cup of the olive oil. With the machine running slowly, slowly add the remaining ¾ cup olive oil until the mixture has formed an emulsion. It may be necessary to stop and scrape down the sides of the blender several times with a rubber spatula. Season to taste with salt and pepper. Using the spatula, press the pesto through a medium or fine-mesh sieve into a small bowl. The pesto will be quite thick but you should have about ¾ cup. Set aside or refrigerate for up to 24 hours.

FOR THE VEGETABLES: Bring the same pot of water back to a boil (unless you made the pesto ahead of time). Blanch the English peas and sugar snap peas together for 1 minute and drop into another bowl of cold water. Drain and set aside.

FOR THE HALIBUT: Preheat the oven to 400°F. Heat the olive oil in a large ovenproof nonstick sauté pan over medium-high heat. Season the skin side of the halibut fillets and both sides of the halibut cheeks with salt and pepper. Put the halibut fillets in the pan, skin side down. Sauté for 1 minute, then add the cheeks to the pan. Sauté both for about 2 minutes more, or until golden brown. Turn all the fish over and sprinkle just the fillets with a little salt. Put the pan into the oven and roast for 4 to 6 minutes, or until the fillets are springy to the touch and the center is translucent (make a discreet cut with a knife to check). Remove the pan from oven before the fish seems done; the residual heat will finish the cooking.

TO SERVE

If using dried morels, rehydrate as directed for morel jus. Heat 2 tablespoons of the olive oil in a skillet over high heat. Add the morels and cook, stirring, for about 1 minute, or until lightly browned. Add the mushroom jus and reduce until the liquid is thick and syrupy. Swirl in the butter. Heat the remaining 2 tablespoons of olive oil in a large skillet over medium-high heat. Add the favas, English peas, and sugar snap peas and cook for 1 minute. Add the pea shoots and water and cook for about 30 seconds, or until the pea shoots have softened. Stir in the pesto. The vegetables should move freely in the sauce; add a little water if the mixture is too thick. Taste for salt and pepper and season if necessary.

Place some of the vegetables into the center of 4 warm dinner plates. Place a halibut fillet on top of the vegetables and top with the halibut cheeks. Spoon the morel jus over, making sure each plate is topped with some of the morels.

PAN-ROASTED WILD KING OR IVORY SALMON

POTATO, BACON, AND WATERCRESS CAKE, SHAVED APPLE AND FENNEL SALAD, CIDER SAUCE,
AND MUSTARD VINAIGRETTE

SERVES 4

POTATO CAKES

1 to 1¼ pounds Yukon Gold potatoes
(about 5 ounces each)

1 large onion, cut into ½-inch dice

5 tablespoons olive oil

2 cloves garlic, minced

¼ pound watercress (stemmed),
arugula, or stinging nettles (see
Kitchen and Shopping Notes)

1 tablespoon Dijon mustard

Kosher salt and freshly ground
black pepper

16 very thin slices good-quality
bacon

CIDER SAUCE

1 tablespoon olive oil

¼ cup minced shallots

1 cup hard cider

¼ cup cider vinegar

2 tablespoons heavy cream

½ cup (1 stick) cold butter,
cut into tablespoons

MUSTARD VINAIGRETTE

2 teaspoons mixed yellow and black
mustard seeds or all yellow

½ teaspoon dry mustard

3 tablespoons cider vinegar

1 tablespoon Dijon mustard

½ cup olive oil

Kosher salt and freshly ground
black pepper

SALMON

2 tablespoons olive oil

4 (5- to 6-ounce) skinless wild king or
ivory salmon fillets

Coarse sea salt and freshly ground
black pepper

APPLE AND FENNEL SALAD

1 bunch watercress, thick stems
removed

1 Gravenstein apple (or your favorite
eating apple), unpeeled and
thinly sliced

1 fennel bulb, thinly sliced lengthwise
on a mandoline

It's good to be a patient cook and wait for each season to unfold. Although we're not particularly known for our patience, we do try to wait until late summer to put this dish on the menu. This stellar season, when wild king salmon is running, fresh Gravenstein apples have come to market, fennel is small and tender, and watercress is abundant, is the time for us to reap the rewards of living in California.

The slightly sweet and vinegary cider sauce, spiked with spicy mustard vinaigrette, enhances the rich flavor of the salmon and unifies all of the components of this dish. Fresh and crunchy, the fennel-apple salad is nice alongside the salmon, but consider enjoying it on its own or with just the addition of some good blue cheese. We cannot say enough about this potato cake. It's the proverbial little black dress of the food world; with or without the bacon, it goes with everything. When in Ireland, we were allowed to gleefully forage wild nettles and watercress, and we devised these potato cakes to keep up with our energetic harvesting. If you happen to have some pesky stinging nettles in your yard or in a nearby field, your best revenge is to eat them. Harvest the tender, young sprigs with gloves and scissors, and plunge them into boiling water with tongs, and substitute the nettles for the watercress in this recipe. Try the bacon-wrapped potato cakes with poached eggs, it's one of our favorite breakfasts.

continued

KITCHEN AND SHOPPING NOTES

The committed and patient cook waits for Pacific wild salmon, wild Alaskan king salmon, and the splendid fish from the Colombia and Copper rivers. We especially look forward to the rare ivory salmon with its delicate flavor and pale flesh. Although we pan-roast the salmon for this dish, you could grill it if you're so inclined.

We feel strongly about the harsh environmental impact of most commercial fish farms and, in truth, we find the flavor of farmed salmon to be strong and oily with fishy overtones but, of course, there are always exceptions (see Sources, page 236).

Gravenstein apples are the first fresh apples to come into season in California. They have a short season and a short shelf life. Green and tart, they're magnificent for baking or eating out of hand. See the Endive and Heirloom Apple Salad (page 9) for more on apples.

Bacon quality varies wildly, so we urge you to find a product that is lean, not too salty or heavily smoked, and with a hint of sweetness (see Sources, page 236). For this recipe, it's important that the bacon is thinly sliced. Thick-cut slices that are good for breakfast just won't work when you need to wrap them around the potato cakes.

METHOD

FOR THE POTATO CAKES: Preheat the oven to 375°F. Scrub the potatoes and pat dry with paper towels. Bake for 30 to 40 minutes, or until soft. Remove from oven and peel when they're cool enough to handle. Put the potatoes into a bowl and break them into large chunks with a fork. While the potatoes are cooking, heat 2 tablespoons of the olive oil in a skillet over medium heat and sauté the onion for about 5 minutes, or until softened. Add the garlic and watercress and cook, stirring, just until the watercress has wilted. Put into the bowl with the potatoes and add the Dijon mustard. Stir to combine and season to taste with salt and pepper.

Divide the potato mixture into 4 equal portions and shape into patties about 3 inches in diameter and 1½ inches thick. Cut the bacon strips crosswise in half. On a work surface, crisscross 2 bacon strips, put a potato cake on top, and bring the ends of the bacon up and over to wrap around the potato cake. Heat the remaining 3 tablespoons olive oil in a large ovenproof skillet or sauté pan over medium heat and cook the potato cakes for about 5 minutes, or until the bacon is crisp and the potatoes are golden. Turn the cakes over and put the pan into the oven. Cook for 8 to 10 minutes, or until the bacon is crisp on the bottom and the cakes are heated through. You can form the potato cakes early in the day, then sauté them and finish the cooking in the oven just before serving.

FOR THE CIDER SAUCE: Heat the olive oil in a small saucepan over medium heat. Add the shallots and cook for about 2 minutes, or until softened but not colored. Add the cider and cider vinegar, increase the heat to high, and reduce the liquid until thick and syrupy. Decrease the heat to medium, add the cream, and bring to a boil. Whisk in the butter, a few tablespoons at a time, whisking well until the butter has melted before adding more. Strain and keep warm in a small heatproof container set into a larger pan of barely simmering hot water. The sauce will hold for up to 2 hours. You can also keep it warm in a small thermos.

FOR THE MUSTARD VINAIGRETTE: Soak the mustard seeds in hot water in a cup until plumped and softened, about 10 minutes. Drain and transfer to a small bowl. Dissolve the dry mustard in the vinegar and whisk in the Dijon mustard. Gradually whisk in the olive oil until emulsified, then add the mustard seeds. Season to taste with salt and pepper and set aside.

FOR THE FISH: Preheat the oven to 400°F. Heat the olive oil in a large ovenproof nonstick skillet or sauté pan over high heat. Season the fish fillets on the skin side with salt and pepper. Put the fish in the pan, flesh side down, and sauté for about 2 minutes, or until golden brown. Turn the fish over and put the pan into the oven. Roast the fish for about 5 minutes, or until it is medium or still translucent in the center (make a discreet cut with a knife to check). Transfer to a plate and set aside.

FOR THE SALAD: Toss the watercress, apple, and fennel together in a bowl with the mustard vinaigrette.

TO SERVE

Place a potato cake on each of 4 warm dinner plates and nestle a piece of salmon next to each potato cake. Drizzle the cider sauce and a little mustard vinaigrette around the plate and top with the fennel salad.

ROASTED TRUE COD

. . . .

TOMATO GRATIN, PANCETTA AND BABY SPINACH SALAD, PINE NUT RELISH

. . . .

SERVES 4

TOMATO GRATIN

1 clove garlic, sliced into shavings
   on a mandoline
1 cup heavy cream
16 Oven-Roasted Tomatoes
   (see Basics, page 232)
1 cup bread crumbs (see Basics,
   page 228)
2 tablespoons freshly grated
   Parmesan cheese
1 tablespoon olive oil
1 teaspoon fresh thyme leaves

PINE NUT RELISH

⅓ cup pine nuts, toasted (see Basics,
   page 234)
2 tablespoons finely chopped celery
2 teaspoons finely chopped shallots
1 teaspoon finely minced fresh
   flat-leaf parsley leaves
2 tablespoons best-quality extra-
   virgin olive oil

BABY SPINACH SALAD

3 thin slices pancetta
1 tablespoon extra-virgin olive oil
2 teaspoons red wine vinegar
2 cups loosely packed, cleaned, and
   stemmed baby spinach leaves
Kosher salt and freshly ground
   black pepper

TRUE COD

3 tablespoons olive oil
4 (6-ounce) pieces skinless
   cod fillet
Kosher salt and freshly ground
   black pepper
2 cloves garlic, lightly crushed
4 thyme sprigs

ACETO BALSAMICO

(see Sources, page 237)

It's naughty for us to be amused, but you're always requesting a thick, mild, moist, flaky, and boneless fish, and then when we put it on the menu, you don't even order it. We're talking about cod. When Alain Senderens first put fresh-roasted cod on his menu in 1976, no one ordered it until he started calling it fresh salt cod or *morue fraîche,* at which point it became one of his signature dishes. In his words, "Cod is so beautiful the way the flesh unfolds in white leaves." How eloquent. And it's only taken a worldwide shortage for people to begin to appreciate one of the best fish in the sea. Because of its aforementioned qualities, cod goes extraordinarily well with the cream-enriched tomato gratin, warm spinach salad, and crunchy pine nut relish. Cod has certainly been one of the most important fish in the history of mankind. The hunger for this fish, which was once so abundant and takes so well to salt preservation, has sent men out in search of new fishing grounds, expanding the world's maps. If you read Mark Kurlansky's excellent book *Cod,* you'll come away with an understanding of how the trade in cod led to the exploration of the New World and the founding of our country.

KITCHEN AND SHOPPING NOTES

In spite of everything we just said about cod, we must admit that it's not so easily found, particularly away from the eastern seaboard. Other thick white fish, such as halibut, hake, haddock, lingcod, or sea bass, will also work in this recipe.

continued

Oven-drying the tomatoes with herbs and garlic intensifies their flavor and is particularly essential when tomatoes are out of season. When vine-ripened tomatoes are available, they only need to be peeled—not roasted—to be used here. For a more casual or family-style presentation, the tomato gratin can be made in a large casserole and served on the side along with a big bowl of the spinach salad, the pine nut relish, and the *aceto balsamico* (use the eye dropper it comes with to control the amount used of this luscious substance).

Pine nuts from Italy and the Mediterranean, while more expensive, are larger and have a superior flavor to the broader and more triangular Chinese pine nuts. Always toast the nuts to an even golden brown to develop their flavor. The pine nut relish is delicious tossed with caramelized cauliflower florets and served with roasted prawns or scallops or as a sauce for fresh hot pasta.

METHOD

FOR THE TOMATO GRATIN: Preheat the oven to 375°F. Put the garlic and cream into a small saucepan and cook over medium heat until reduced to ¾ cup. Put 3 tablespoons of the reduced cream in each of 4 (10-ounce) greased soufflé dishes or baking dishes. Arrange 4 tomatoes in each of the dishes. Mix the bread crumbs, Parmesan, olive oil, and thyme leaves together in a small bowl and sprinkle 2 tablespoons of the mixture on top of each gratin. Bake for 30 minutes, or until browned and bubbly. The gratins can be made earlier in the day and reheated before serving.

FOR THE PINE NUT RELISH: Stir all the ingredients together in a small bowl and set aside. The relish can be made several hours ahead, but leave out the pine nuts until you are ready to serve.

FOR THE SPINACH SALAD: Put the pancetta into a skillet and cook over medium heat until crisped and golden. Cut the pancetta into thin crosswise pieces and set aside. Whisk the olive oil and vinegar into the pancetta fat in the pan and set aside for up to 2 hours. Just before serving, add the pancetta to the vinaigrette.

FOR THE COD: Heat the olive oil in a large skillet or sauté pan over high heat. Season both sides of the cod fillets with salt and pepper. When the oil is hot, add the fish to the pan, skin side up, immediately shaking the pan as you put the fish in to prevent the fillets from sticking. Decrease the heat to medium and cook for 4 to 5 minutes. Using a spatula, turn the fish over and add the garlic and thyme sprigs. Cook for 2 to 3 minutes longer, or until the fish begins to flake and the interior is still moist.

TO SERVE

While you're cooking the fish, if necessary reheat the tomato gratins in a 350°F oven for 10 minutes, or until warmed through. Heat the pan with the pancetta over medium-low heat until the vinegar and oil begin to bubble. Remove from the heat and add the spinach leaves and stir until the leaves are just coated with the warm oil and vinegar. Season to taste with salt and pepper and set aside. Invert a gratin onto each of 4 warm dinner plates. Place a cod fillet on top of each tomato gratin and spoon a little of the pine nut relish on the fish and around the plate. Neatly mound the spinach leaves on top of the fish and drizzle around the *aceto balsamico*.

To say that all cooks love black bass is a sweeping generalization, but there is truly something wonderful about this fish, with its firm white meat and stylish black-and-white skin that can be cooked to crispy perfection. In this recipe, the East Coast bass and sweet West Coast spot prawns combine in perfect partnership with lush cauliflower "risotto." Tiny cauliflower florets masquerading as risotto substitute for the rice, and a puree of cauliflower stands in for the "crema."

PAN-ROASTED BLACK BASS

SANTA BARBARA SPOT PRAWNS, CAULIFLOWER "RISOTTO"

SERVES 4

CAULIFLOWER "RISOTTO"

2 large heads cauliflower (about
    4 pounds)
6 tablespoons unsalted butter,
    at room temperature

SPOT PRAWNS

¾ pound medium heads-off spot
    prawns or other fresh shrimp
    or prawns, or 1 pound with
    heads on
2 tablespoons grape seed oil
1 cup Fish Fumet (see Basics,
    page 229)
1 tablespoon unsalted butter
2 tablespoons chopped shallots
¼ cup dry white wine
1 thyme sprig
½ cup (1 stick) cold unsalted butter
    cut into ½-inch pieces
Kosher salt and freshly ground
    black pepper

BLACK BASS

1 tablespoon grape seed oil
5 (4-ounce) pieces black bass
    fillet, skin on
Kosher salt and freshly ground
    black pepper

2 tablespoons olive oil
Chopped fresh flat-leaf parsley
    leaves, for garnish

KITCHEN AND SHOPPING NOTES

Black bass is a small (2 pounds or so) Atlantic fish and is common in fish markets on the East Coast. As other seafood markets are getting requests from chefs and consumers for this delectable fish, it's becoming more widely available across the country. If your fishmonger doesn't carry black bass yet, raise your voice to request it.

In our opinion, sweet, luscious Pacific spot prawns vie with Dungeness crab for the title of "Best Shellfish" in West Coast waters, and they certainly rank as one of our local treasures. Spot prawns are sold with or without heads, or alive in tanks (though the tanks are primarily in Asian markets). Live shrimp go bad quickly and should be cooked as soon as possible. Pass on any head-on prawns with blackening on the head area, which is a sure sign of deterioration. The prawn heads and shells are used here for the sauce. We also love Maine shrimp, whose short season is January and February. Like spot prawns, they have a sweet, buttery flavor and are also sold head-on but are much smaller. Any prawns or shrimp, as long as they're fresh, may stand in for the spot prawns.

METHOD

FOR THE CAULIFLOWER "RISOTTO": Remove and discard the outside leaves of the cauliflowers, cut out the cores, and separate the heads into florets. Using your hands, break apart half of the large florets into tiny florets (what we like to call microflorets) and set aside. Put the remaining large florets (about 4 cups) into a large saucepan with generously salted water to cover and bring to a boil over high heat. Lower the heat to maintain a lively simmer and cook for 8 to 12 minutes, or until tender. Drain and reserve the liquid. Let the cauliflower cool for a few minutes, then put 2 cups of the large florets and ½ cup of the reserved cooking liquid into a blender with the butter and puree until smooth. Transfer to a bowl and set aside. Bring a large pot of water to a boil and cook the tiny florets for about 1 minute, or until slighltly tender but not mushy.

FOR THE SPOT PRAWNS: Peel the prawns and reserve the shells and heads. Heat 1 tablespoon of the grape seed oil in a skillet over medium-high heat. Add the shells and cook for about 2 minutes, or until they turn pink, then add the fumet. Simmer until the liquid has reduced by half. Strain through a fine-mesh sieve into a bowl, discarding the shells and reserving the liquid. Melt the butter over medium heat in the same skillet, add the shallots, and cook for 1 minute. Add the wine, thyme sprig, and reduced fumet and cook until reduced by half. Decrease the heat to low, and whisk in the cut-up butter, one piece at a time, adding each piece after the previous one has melted. Strain through a fine-mesh sieve into a small bowl and season with salt and pepper. Set the bowl into a small saucepan of hot water to keep warm.

Clean the skillet and heat the remaining 1 tablespoon grape seed oil over medium-high heat. Add the prawns and cook, stirring frequently, for about 2 minutes, or until just pink. Set aside.

FOR THE BLACK BASS: Heat the oil in large skillet or sauté pan over high heat. Season the flesh side of the fish with salt and pepper. Put into the pan, skin side down, and cook for about 3 minutes, or until the skin has crisped. Using a spatula, turn the fish over and cook for 2 to 3 minutes more.

TO SERVE

Reheat the cauliflower "crema" in a small saucepan, add the microflorets, and warm over low heat. Put a spoonful of warm risotto in the center of 4 warm dinner plates and top with the fish. Spoon a ring of warm sauce around the fish and arrange the spot prawns in the sauce, then drizzle a little more sauce over them. Sprinkle the parsley over all.

CRISPY-SKINNED ONAGA

BRAISED SHELLFISH MUSHROOMS AND FRESH HEARTS OF PALM

SERVES 4

BRAISED SHELLFISH MUSHROOMS

1 abalone mushroom (about
    4 ounces), sliced ¼ inch thick
3 ounces clamshell mushrooms,
    trimmed and broken into
    large pieces
3 ounces oyster mushrooms
1 cup Dark Chicken Stock (see
    Basics, page 230)
¼ cup dry white wine
½ cup (1 stick) plus 1 tablespoon
    unsalted butter, cut into pieces
2 cloves garlic, thinly sliced
2 thyme sprigs
Kosher salt

BRAISED LOBSTER MUSHROOMS AND SAUCE

3 ounces fresh lobster mushrooms,
    sliced ¼ inch thick
Reserved mushroom braising liquid
    (about 1 cup)
4 tablespoons cold unsalted butter,
    cut into ½-inch pieces

HEARTS OF PALM

2 tablespoons olive oil
¼ pound fresh hearts of palm, sliced
    ¼ inch thick (see Kitchen and
    Shopping Notes, page 21)
1 tablespoon unsalted butter
Kosher salt and freshly ground
    black pepper

ONAGA

1 tablespoon grape seed oil
4 (5-ounce) pieces onaga fillet,
    skin on
Kosher salt and freshly ground
    black pepper

2 tablespoons chopped fresh
    flat-leaf parsley leaves

Dramatic in appearance yet simple and delicious, the highlight of this recipe is the variety of what we like to call "shellfish mushrooms," which are slowly braised rather than quickly sautéed. Gentle braising is the best way to coax the subtle flavors of abalone, lobster, oyster, and clam out of the eponymous mushrooms. Enchanted by nature's ability to reflect itself in unexpected forms, we've taken advantage of this coincidence by pairing the thick, moist, deep-water fish fillets with these sneaky forest imposters. We also love the nutty, lemonlike quality that the sautéed fresh hearts of palm bring to this dish.

continued

Fish from the snapper family are valued for their lean, moderately firm flesh, and mild flavor, as well as the beautiful appearance of their skin. There are many varieties of snapper found in tropical waters, but most of the "true" red snapper sold in the United States is found in the Caribbean, the Gulf, and along the southern Atlantic seaboard. Onaga, considered the "king" of snappers, is a Pacific variety that has the same characteristics as "true" red snapper. We like it because the fillets are thicker and take better to pan-roasting. Other fish we know and love are opakapaka, red alphonse, and red reef fish, such as Pacific rockfish (often sold as snapper).

Not only is perfectly crisped fish skin an important element of this recipe, but for cooks it's a culinary achievement to be mastered as well. Excess moisture in the fish skin prevents it from crisping quickly and makes it necessary to leave the fish in the pan for so long that the flesh becomes overcooked. The simplest way to remove excess moisture from fish skin is to place the fillets, skin side down, on superabsorbent paper towels for 20 to 30 minutes. A little messier but quicker method is to scrape a knife blade over the skin, pressing down to force out the excess water. You then need to clean the blade and repeat the procedure several times until most of the visible water is gone.

Many varieties of lean fish that are soft to moderately firm will pair nicely with the braised mushrooms. The crisp skin is included because we think it's delicious, but it's not essential. We chose red-skinned fish because we were inspired by the red and gold hues of the mushrooms and sauce.

Lobster mushrooms are so named because of their red "shell," white interior, and flavor that is slightly reminiscent of lobster. The lobster mushroom's firm texture makes it the perfect candidate for braising, and it imparts a lovely yellow hue to the braising liquid, which turns into a striking sauce. Lobster mushrooms can be purchased fresh in the summer and fall and are found dried year-round, but we prefer to make this dish when lobster mushrooms are fresh.

Oyster mushrooms are prized for their smooth texture and subtle oysterlike flavor. Abalone mushrooms are a species of oyster mushrooms that are giants by comparison. They're so large they can be sliced into thick, meaty pieces for braising. Both oyster and abalone mushrooms are grown commercially and are available year-round; abalones are most commonly found in Asian markets. Clamshell mushrooms are another cultivated species; they have a creamy gray color, firm texture, and mild flavor similar to oyster mushrooms. To prepare them, cut off the bottom ½ inch and break their clusters apart into pieces.

METHOD

FOR THE BRAISED SHELLFISH MUSHROOMS: Preheat the oven to 350°F. Place all the mushrooms in a roasting pan large enough to hold them in one layer. Add the chicken stock, wine, $\frac{1}{2}$ cup butter, garlic, and thyme sprigs and roast, stirring once or twice, for 20 minutes, or until the mushrooms have softened. Drain the mushrooms into a sieve over a bowl. Remove the garlic and thyme sprigs. Set aside.

FOR THE LOBSTER MUSHROOMS AND SAUCE: Preheat the oven to 350°F. Put the lobster mushrooms into a small casserole dish or ovenproof saucepan with the reserved mushroom liquid. Cook, stirring once or twice, for 15 to 20 minutes, or until tender. Drain the mushrooms into a sieve over a bowl. Reserve the mushrooms. Pour the liquid into a skillet. Heat to a simmer, then whisk in the butter, piece by piece, until smooth and the sauce has thickened. Set aside.

FOR THE HEARTS OF PALM: Heat the olive oil in a skillet or sauté pan over medium-high heat. Add the hearts of palm and cook for 3 to 4 minutes, stirring a few times. Add the butter, and cook until the hearts of palm are lightly browned. Season with salt and pepper, set aside, and keep warm.

FOR THE ONAGA: Heat the oil in a large skillet or sauté pan over high heat. Sprinkle the flesh side of the fish with salt and pepper. Put the fish in the pan, skin side down, pressing down with a spatula. Cook for about 4 minutes, or until the skin is crisp. Using a spatula, turn the fish over and cook for 3 to 4 minutes more. If your fish is particularly thick (more than $1\frac{1}{2}$ inches), it may need 5 minutes in a 375°F oven, so plan ahead and preheat your oven if needed.

TO SERVE

Meanwhile, heat the shellfish mushrooms in a saucepan with 1 tablespoon butter and 2 tablespoons water. Add the parsley, and keep warm. Mound a generous spoonful of mushrooms in the center of 4 warm plates. Spoon the sauce over and around the mushrooms, create a bridge of hearts of palm over the mushrooms, and set the fish on top.

BACON-WRAPPED MAINE MONKFISH STUFFED WITH LOBSTER AND AVOCADO

FRESH CORIANDER RISOTTO AND GREEN ALMONDS

SERVES 4

MONKFISH

2 (6-ounce) monkfish fillets,
　　membrane removed (see
　　Kitchen and Shopping Notes)
Kosher salt and freshly ground
　　black pepper
½ cup Crab Salad (see Basics,
　　page 228)
4 Oven-Roasted Tomatoes (see
　　Basics, page 232)
2 ripe, but firm avocados, each
　　halved, pitted, peeled, and
　　halved lengthwise
10 thin slices good-quality bacon
2 tablespoons olive oil

CORIANDER RISOTTO

1 cup fresh flat-leaf parsley leaves
3 tablespoons finely sliced fresh
　　chives (about 1 bunch)
2 cups fresh coriander leaves
4 cups Light Chicken Stock (see
　　Basics, page 230)
2 tablespoons olive oil
1 cup finely diced onion
1 cup arborio or carnaroli rice
1 cup dry white wine
2 tablespoons unsalted butter
Kosher salt and freshly ground
　　black pepper

GREEN ALMONDS AND FRIED FRESH CORIANDER LEAVES

½ cup olive oil
½ cup large, unblemished fresh
　　coriander leaves
18 to 24 peeled fresh green
　　almonds (see Kitchen and
　　Shopping Notes)
Kosher salt

Every time we make this dish, or some version of it, we're haunted by Calvin Trillin's humorous but disdainful description of restaurant menus that have "stuff stuffed with stuff." In defense of stuffing and wrapping, the combination of flavors—meaty monkfish, tart tomatoes, creamy avocado, and salty bacon—plus the eye-popping appearance of this dish, is enough to make us ignore the cautions of one of our favorite food writers.

People have a love-hate relationship with fresh coriander, more commonly known as cilantro. We find its distinctive flavor captivating. Once the fresh coriander leaves are blended with the parsley and chives, the herb's unique pungent citrus flavor is released into the risotto and turns it an intense emerald green. Tart, fresh green almonds with their liquid centers are a surprising complement to all the flavors in this dish.

KITCHEN AND SHOPPING NOTES

Monkfish is usually found in fish markets skinned and filleted but covered with a thin grayish membrane that needs to be removed before cooking. Pull off the membrane, using a sharp knife to get it started if necessary, before proceeding with the recipe.

Our friends at Lucedio, outside of Turin, who grow some of the finest rice in Italy, would insist that a proper risotto requires 30 minutes of a cook's undivided attention. It's not that we disagree, but this two-part method allows you to cook the rice partially earlier in the day and reduces the final cooking time to 10 minutes. For this method, follow the instructions in the recipe through the first addition of stock, cook the rice until almost dry but before it begins to color, then immediately spread it out on a rimmed baking sheet to cool. Put it into the refrigerator until ready to use. Just before serving, resume the process by putting the rice into a saucepan with $\frac{1}{2}$ cup stock and complete the cooking. This method will help you to handle the challenge of cooking the monkfish and risotto simultaneously.

In California, with 600,000 acres planted with almond trees, it's pretty easy for us to get green almonds. Though well-known in the Mediterranean, they're still a bit of a novelty here. Every year our produce purveyors announce the arrival of fuzzy green almonds as if they are diamonds. We especially like the almonds very early in the season when their second skin has not developed and they have a jellylike consistency and delicate nutty flavor. Using a sharp paring knife, follow the seam of the almond, split open the soft shell, and gently pop the tender green almond out intact.

METHOD

TO STUFF AND WRAP THE MONKFISH: Place the cleaned monkfish on a cutting board and, working with 1 fillet at a time, cut it lengthwise three-quarters of the way through and open it up like a book. With your knife parallel to the board, butterfly the 2 halves and spread them out to form 2 flaps. Season with salt and pepper. Stuff 2 tablespoon of Crab Salad into each of 2 of the tomatoes and place the stuffed tomatoes in the center of the fish fillet. Lay 4 avocado quarters on top of the tomatoes and fold the 2 flaps over the stuffing so it's completely enclosed and forms a neat open-ended roll. Repeat with the second monkfish fillet.

Place 4 slices of bacon on the work surface, overlapping them slightly, then place 1 slice on top, perpendicular to the 4 slices, to form a cross. Put 1 of the stuffed monkfish fillets on top, parallel to the single bacon slice, and bring the ends of the bacon up over the open ends of the fish. Tightly roll the fish up in the 4 bacon strips to form a neat package. Repeat with the other fillet. Refrigerate the stuffed and wrapped monkfish for at least 1 hour, but not more than 6 hours because the bacon will begin to cure the fish.

FOR THE CORIANDER RISOTTO: Make a coriander puree by blanching the parsley leaves and chives for 1 minute in a saucepan of boiling salted water. After 1 minute, add the coriander leaves and cook for 30 seconds longer. Drain, reserving ½ cup of the cooking water. Put the herbs into a blender and puree until smooth, adding just enough of the cooking water to get the blender blade whirring. (You can push the puree through a *tamis* or *chinois* if you're going for absolute perfection.)

To make the risotto, heat the chicken stock in a saucepan and keep hot. Heat the olive oil in a heavy saucepan over medium heat. Add the onion and sauté until very soft, translucent, and just before it begins to turn color, about 5 minutes. Stir in the rice and cook until the rice grains become opaque, about 2 minutes. Add the wine and cook until the wine has evaporated, stirring often. Continue to cook, adding the warm stock ½ cup at a time, stirring occasionally to prevent sticking and making sure the liquid is almost completely absorbed before adding more. After 15 minutes, begin checking the rice to see if it's tender. Test by biting into a couple of grains—it's done when you meet some resistance. We also like to cut into a few individual grains and look at the center; if there's a white dot, it's done. Remove from the heat and let sit while you finish the dish. The rice will continue to cook and absorb liquid even after it's removed from the heat, so err on the side of undercooked. When the rice is done, stir in the coriander puree and butter, and season to taste with salt and pepper.

TO COOK THE MONKFISH: Preheat the oven to 375°F. Heat the 2 tablespoons oil in a large ovenproof skillet or sauté pan over medium-high heat. Put the monkfish fillets in the pan, seam side down, and cook for 2 minutes. Continue to cook, using tongs to turn the fish to brown the bacon on all sides, for about 5 minutes more. Put the pan in the oven and cook the fish for 4 to 5 minutes. Remove from the oven and let rest for 5 minutes before serving.

FOR THE GREEN ALMONDS AND FRIED CORIANDER: Heat the oil in a small saucepan until a drop of water spatters as it hits the oil. Have a plate lined with paper towels and a slotted spoon near the stove. Drop in the coriander leaves; when the oil stops bubbling and foaming, use the slotted spoon to transfer the coriander to the paper towels to drain. Season with salt. Drain off the oil, leaving 2 tablespoons in the pan. Add the green almonds to the oil to warm slightly, for about 1 minute. Scoop out with the slotted spoon and put on the lined plate to drain next to the coriander.

TO SERVE

Cut each monkfish roll crosswise into 4 equal pieces. Put some risotto into the center of 4 warm dinner plates and top each with 2 pieces of the monkfish. Spoon the green almonds around the fish with a little bit of the oil and sprinkle the fried coriander around the plate.

At Boulevard we have complicated this simple, rustic dish by applying our own restaurant logic.

SPINY LOBSTER PAELLA

WITH A POT OF STEAMED CLAMS AND CHORIZO

SERVES 4

PAELLA STOCK

Shells from the bodies and legs
of 2 spiny lobsters (or Maine
lobsters)

8 large prawns, shelled and
deveined, with tails left on
(bodies and shells reserved
separately)

¼ cup olive oil

1 cup coarsely chopped fennel

1 small leek, halved lengthwise,
cleaned, and white and green
parts thinly sliced

1 onion, coarsely chopped

4 cloves garlic, lightly crushed

4 ripe tomatoes, coarsely chopped

4 tablespoons unsalted butter

Pinch of saffron threads

2 cups dry white wine

3 cups Light Chicken Stock (see
Basics, page 230)

5 thyme sprigs

5 flat-leaf parsley sprigs

¼ teaspoon smoked Spanish paprika
(*pimentón*)

Kosher salt and freshly
ground pepper

PAELLA RICE

½ cup olive oil

1 onion, finely diced (¼ inch)

1 clove garlic, minced

¼ teaspoon saffron threads

1 cup Spanish paella rice (see
Kitchen and Shopping Notes) or
Italian Arborio or Carnaroli rice

2 cups Paella Stock

1 tablespoon salt

POT OF CLAMS AND CHORIZO

2 tablespoons olive oil

¼ pound chorizo

2 cloves garlic, thinly sliced

2 tablespoons seeded and thinly
sliced piquillo peppers (see
Kitchen and Shopping Notes)

3 to 4 dozen (depending on their
size) hard-shell clams, such as
Manila or small cherrystones,
scrubbed

½ cup dry white wine

¼ cup water

¼ cup Paella Stock

2 tablespoons chopped fresh
flat-leaf parsley leaves

2 tablespoons chopped fresh
coriander leaves

2 tablespoons olive oil

1 tablespoon tomato paste

2 cups Paella Stock

Reserved 8 prawns from Paella Stock

1 large ripe tomato, peeled, seeded,
and diced

½ pound English peas, shelled and
blanched

2 tablespoons unsalted butter,
cut into small pieces

Cooked meat from 2 lobsters (see
Basics, page 232)

A simple paella of rice and sausage cooked over an open fire in an orange orchard, with a few added finds like rabbit, frogs, and snails, completed the field workers' lunch. Such were the inauspicious beginnings of a dish that has become the national culinary symbol of Spain. Paella has survived many transformations as cooks around the world tasted the soulful flavors of rice and saffron and were inspired to contribute their own regional ingredients.

At Boulevard we have complicated this simple, rustic dish by applying our own restaurant logic. Our biggest issue with paella is that each of the variously sized and shaped ingredients has a different cooking time, so nothing ends up properly cooked, including the rice. This is particularly true of seafood paellas, where we've actually become so neurotic about the cooking time that we've relegated the clams to their own little pot. To compensate for this separation, we make an enriched stock flavored by the clams, shrimp, and lobster. The rice absorbs the heady perfumes of saffron and *pimentón* from the paella stock, and each lovely piece of seafood gets the individual attention that it deserves.

continued

Paella is made with Spanish medium-grain rice that has Valencia or Calasparra as its designation of origin. This rice has the ability to absorb the flavor from the stock and saffron and hold its shape when cooked (see Sources, page 237). Italian rice such as Carnaroli or Arborio has similar qualities and can be substituted. Spanish piquillo peppers are flavorful, sweet, thick-walled red peppers that come peeled and canned. Look for them in the specialty section of some markets and delis, or purchase them online (see Sources, page 237). If you can't find piquillos, substitute whole pimientos or fire-roasted red bell peppers. Spiny lobster, also called rock lobster, is native to the warm Pacific waters, and when it's in season (from fall to spring) we prefer to use it in our paella. It's very similar to Maine lobster, and we think it's just as sweet. Either one works in this recipe.

METHOD

FOR THE PAELLA STOCK: With a chef's knife, cut the lobster bodies into 3 pieces each. Remove the lungs and sand sack from behind the eyes. Heat a large saucepan over medium heat and add the olive oil. Add the fennel, leek, onion, and garlic and cook, stirring occasionally, for about 10 minutes, or until the vegetables are soft and translucent. Increase the heat to high; add the lobster bodies and reserved prawn shells and cook, stirring frequently, for 3 to 5 minutes. Lower the heat to medium and add the tomatoes, butter, and saffron. Cook for 5 minutes. Increase heat to high, add the wine and cook for about 5 minutes, or until reduced by half. Add the chicken stock, and water if needed, to cover. Bring to a simmer, add the thyme, parsley, and paprika, and simmer, uncovered, for 45 minutes, skimming occasionally. Strain through a fine-mesh sieve into a large bowl, pressing on the solids with the back of a spoon or ladle to extract as much flavorful liquid as possible. Cool the stock and refrigerate for up to 2 days.

FOR THE RICE: Heat the oil in a saucepan over medium-high heat. Add the onion and cook, stirring occasionally, for about 5 minutes, or until golden. Stir in the garlic and saffron. Add the rice and stir for about 2 minutes, or until the grains begin to turn translucent. Add the stock and salt and decrease the heat to low. Cover the pan and cook for about 20 minutes, or until all the liquid is absorbed. Remove from the heat and let stand for 10 minutes. You can make the paella rice early in the day you plan to serve it, but remove it from the heat about 5 minutes before you think it's done. Let sit at room temperature, then reheat and finish the cooking before serving.

FOR THE CLAMS AND CHORIZO: While the rice is cooking, prepare the clams and chorizo. Heat the oil in a large skillet over medium heat. Crumble the chorizo into the pan and cook for about 5 minutes, or until it shows almost no pink. Drain off all but 2 tablespoons of the oil. Add the garlic and piquillo peppers and toss well to combine with the chorizo. Add the clams, wine, and water. Cover, increase the heat to high, and cook for about 4 to 5 minutes, or until the clams pop open. Discard any that do not open. Stir in the stock and some of the parsley and coriander.

TO SERVE

Warm 4 small iron pots or ramekins and 4 dinner plates. Cut the lobster tails in half lengthwise and loosen the shell, leaving the meat attached at the tail end only. Heat the olive oil in a large skillet over high heat. Add the tomato paste and sauté for 1 minute. Whisk in the stock and cook until reduced by half. Add the reserved prawns and decrease the heat to medium. Cook for 1 minute, then add the diced tomato, peas, and butter. Stir and cook for 1 minute more. Stir in the lobster meat and turn off the heat. Divide the clam-chorizo mixture among the small pots and mound equal amounts of the paella onto the plates.

POULTRY and GAME

Our Frying Manifesto

There is nothing better for frying than a deep cast-iron skillet. Seventy-five percent of perfect frying is keeping the oil at a constant 350°F, the magic temperature at which the oil will not be absorbed into the food. Hotter than that and the coating will burn before the meat is cooked through—particularly the larger pieces. The other 25 percent is in dredging the pieces of food correctly and allowing them to rest on a rack, uncovered, in the refrigerator, for 1 to 6 hours.

BUTTERMILK-BRINED FRIED LITTLE CHICKENS

MASHED POTATOES, GRAVY, AND CREAM BISCUITS

SERVES 4

BUTTERMILK-BRINED GAME HENS

2 Cornish game hens

1 quart buttermilk

¼ cup kosher salt

3 tablespoons freshly squeezed lemon juice

2 tablespoons chopped fresh thyme leaves, or 1 tablespoon dried

2 tablespoons Dijon mustard

1 tablespoon freshly ground black pepper

Canola, safflower, or peanut oil, for frying

FLOUR COATING

4 cups self-rising flour

2 tablespoons dry mustard (we like Colman's)

2 teaspoons kosher salt

2 teaspoons Hungarian sweet paprika

GRAVY

1 pound chicken wings

Reserved backbones from the game hens

2 tablespoons olive oil

1 onion, coarsely chopped

1 carrot, coarsely chopped

4 cups Dark Chicken Stock (see Basics, page 230)

4 thyme sprigs

4 tablespoons unsalted butter

¼ cup all-purpose flour

Kosher salt and freshly ground black pepper

MASHED POTATOES

2 pounds Yukon Gold potatoes, peeled and quartered

1 cup whole milk

⅓ cup heavy cream

4 tablespoons unsalted butter

Kosher salt and freshly ground black pepper

CREAM BISCUITS

1½ cups self-rising flour

1 tablespoon sugar

½ teaspoon kosher salt

1 cup heavy cream (plus a few more tablespoons if necessary)

⅓ cup unsalted butter, melted

Unsalted butter and honey, for serving

Fried chicken calls out to everyone, "Abandon your dietary commitments!" We celebrate with fried chicken and we console with fried chicken. There's always an animated discussion about authentic fried chicken, as well as many schools of thought on the subject: crispy coating, lightly floured, deep fried, pan fried with a cover, or no cover at all. To put it simply, this rendition is ours. We all agree on it, and it's what we cook for ourselves.

KITCHEN AND SHOPPING NOTES

There's a lot of talk these days about good and bad fats, so we use canola and rice bran oils exclusively for frying now. Hydrogenated vegetable oil is out because of its trans fats. Whatever you use, just make sure it's clean and fresh.

Self-rising flour has baking powder and salt already added. In addition to saving a little measuring time, we find it makes an especially light coating on fried foods, as well as guaranteeing a consistent "lift" to our biscuits and shortcakes. Check the expiration date on the package, though, to make sure the baking powder hasn't lost its oomph.

continued

We like to fry Cornish game hens because in a single serving you get a taste of all the different parts. The petite stature of this bird also makes the presentation, well . . . adorable.

Cornish game hens are little chickens. Originally they were a cross between Cornish and White Rock chickens, but now they're their own little breed and widely available. Game hens average 1½ to 2 pounds. A half bird per person is plenty, but keep in mind that most people like to eat fried chicken cold, so fry some extras.

With our buttermilk brine, flour coating, and cooking method, you can fry almost anything to absolute perfection. We include buttermilk in the brine for tender moistness; add mustard and lemon for tang, the self-rising flour for lightness, and drying after dredging for crunch.

These are James Beard's absolutely brilliant cream biscuits. It's a recipe we've used for years, and the only thing we've changed is that we use self-rising flour, making them unbelievably quick and easy to put together. They can even be made ahead, dipped in butter, and refrigerated for up to 6 hours. (Just be aware that the longer they sit, the less they'll rise in the oven.) Another time-saver is to measure out the dry and liquid ingredients separately in advance, then combine and bake at the last minute. Be mindful that biscuits are like people: they don't like to be overworked; it just makes them tired and tough.

METHOD

TO BRINE THE GAME HENS: Remove the backbones and reserve for the gravy. Cut the hens into 8 pieces: drumsticks, thighs, breasts, and wings. Stir the buttermilk, salt, lemon juice, thyme, mustard, and pepper together in a large bowl, and then immerse the hens. (You can also put the hens into a large zippered bag and pour the brine over them.) Refrigerate the hens in the brine for a minimum of 4 hours or up to 12 hours.

TO DREDGE THE HENS: Whisk the flour coating ingredients together in a bowl. Place 1 or 2 wire racks on a rimmed baking sheet, making sure there's enough room to accommodate all the hen pieces without touching. Working with 1 piece at time, remove the hens from the brine, leaving a fair amount of brine on each piece as it goes into the flour mixture. As you work little clumps will form. Let a few clumps stay in the coating, as these will become little extracrunchy bits when you fry the hens, but don't get too carried away because too many bits will turn the coating gummy. Place the coated hen pieces on the rack so they don't touch. Refrigerate for at least 1 hour or up to 6 hours.

FOR THE GRAVY: Preheat the oven to 375°F and put the chicken wings and reserved backbones on a rimmed baking sheet. Roast, turning once, for 30 to 40 minutes, or until golden brown. Heat the olive oil in a large saucepan or small stockpot over medium-high heat. Add the onion and carrot and cook, stirring occasionally, for about 7 minutes, or until softened and beginning to brown. Using tongs, transfer the chicken wings and hen backs to the saucepan with the vegetables, discarding any fat left on the baking sheet. Add the chicken stock and thyme sprigs and bring to a simmer, skimming a few times. Cook until reduced by one-third. While the stock is cooking, melt the butter in a small saucepan over medium heat and whisk in the flour until smooth. Decrease the heat and cook, stirring occasionally, for about 10 minutes, or until the raw taste is gone from the flour. Strain through a fine-mesh sieve into a saucepan. Add the butter-flour mixture to the stock, whisking continuously to prevent lumps. Simmer for 10 minutes, strain one more time into another saucepan, and season to taste with salt and pepper. Keep warm.

FOR THE MASHED POTATOES: Put the potatoes into a large saucepan and cover with generously salted water by 1 inch. Bring to a boil, decrease the heat to a simmer, and cook for about 20 minutes, or until tender when pierced with a fork. Meanwhile, combine the milk, cream, and butter in a small saucepan and heat almost to a boil. Drain the potatoes, and mash with a potato masher (or put through a food mill fitted with a medium-hole disk), whisk in the heated milk mixture, and season to taste with salt and pepper. Keep warm.

FOR THE CREAM BISCUITS: If you're planning to serve the biscuits soon after they're baked, preheat the oven to 425°F. (If making them ahead, see Kitchen and Shopping Notes.) Combine the self-rising flour, sugar, and salt in a bowl. Using a fork, slowly stir in the cream until the mixture just begins to come together to form a dough. If it feels dry and there are too many pieces falling away, add a little more cream, 1 tablespoon at a time. Turn the dough out on a lightly floured cutting board and pat and shape with your hands into a ½-inch-thick square. Cut into 9 squares (2 per serving and 1 for the cook) and dip each square into the melted butter. Place the biscuits on a baking sheet and bake for 15 minutes, or until lightly golden. Serve hot from the oven, or they can be baked up to 2 hours ahead and reheated.

TO FRY THE GAME HENS: Lower the oven temperature to 250°F and have a baking sheet lined with paper towels or brown paper bags ready nearby. Put enough oil into a large, deep skillet to come halfway up the side and heat to 350°F on a deep-fry thermometer. Carefully add enough hen pieces to fit comfortably without crowding. Increase the heat to bring it back up to 350°F as quickly as possible, then regulate the heat to maintain a constant temperature. Fry for 4 to 5 minutes per side, using tongs to turn the pieces and to remove them when they are golden brown. Put them on the lined baking sheet to drain and keep warm in the oven while you fry the remaining pieces.

TO SERVE

To serve individual portions, place a mound of mashed potatoes in the center of each of 4 warm dinner plates and lean a serving of fried game hen pieces against the potatoes. Ladle some gravy around the plate and pass the biscuits, butter, and honey. Alternatively, serve everything family style on big platters.

ROASTED POUSSIN WITH SPICY CORN BREAD STUFFING

ANDOUILLE GUMBO SAUCE

SERVES 4

CORN BREAD

1 cup all-purpose flour

¾ cup yellow cornmeal

1 teaspoon baking powder

1 teaspoon kosher salt

1 cup buttermilk

2 large eggs

⅓ cup honey

4 tablespoons unsalted
    butter, melted

SPICY CORN BREAD STUFFING

½ recipe corn bread

¼ cup olive oil or vegetable oil

1 onion, diced (½-inch)

1 cup (¼-inch) diced andouille
    sausage

½ cup (¼-inch) diced tasso

1 teaspoon minced garlic

1 cup white corn kernels (cut from
    2 ears corn)

½ cup sliced green onions, green
    and white parts

2 teaspoons chopped fresh
    sage leaves

1 teaspoon chopped fresh
    thyme leaves

Kosher salt and freshly ground
    black pepper

½ cup grated jack cheese

¼ cup chopped fresh flat-leaf
    parsley leaves

¾ cup Light Chicken Stock (see
    Basics, page 230), warm

DARK ROUX

½ cup canola or safflower oil

½ cup all-purpose flour

¼ cup minced celery

¼ cup minced carrot

¼ cup minced onion

½ teaspoon dried thyme

GUMBO SAUCE

2 slices apple wood–smoked
    bacon, cut crosswise into
    ½-inch pieces

½ cup (½-inch) diced tasso

½ cup (½-inch) diced andouille
    sausage

½ cup chopped celery

½ cup chopped onion

½ cup chopped green bell pepper

½ cup chopped red bell pepper

1 tablespoon sliced garlic

2 jalapeño peppers, seeded and
    thinly sliced crosswise

3 thyme sprigs

1 bay leaf

2 teaspoons smoked Spanish
    paprika (*pimentón*) or
    sweet paprika

1 cup dry white wine

4 cups Dark Chicken Stock (see
    Basics, page 230)

½ cup Dark Roux

Kosher salt and freshly ground
    black pepper

POUSSINS

4 poussins, left whole and boned
    through the neck, thigh bones
    removed, and drumsticks
    frenched

Kosher salt and freshly ground
    black pepper

4 tablespoons olive oil

Sautéed spinach, braised collards,
    or mustard greens, for serving

At Boulevard we don't have a claim on authentic New Orleans cuisine, but every year when Fat Tuesday rolls around we get out the gumbo. There are two clear reasons for this: Chef Gaines Dobbins, a transplanted southerner who helped open Boulevard and gave us a true appreciation for all things southern (especially his charming vernacular, which we regrettably can't print here), and Bruce Aidells, Nancy's husband, who founded Aidells Sausage Company, which specializes in smoky andouille sausage and tasso ham. Both people have left us with an everlasting appreciation of the spicy flavors of Louisiana.

Poussin is our choice for this recipe. There's something very deluxe about having your own little boneless bird, plumped up and roasted with spicy corn bread stuffing. It's easy eating with a knife and fork until you pick up the tiny drumsticks with your fingers to finish them off.

continued

KITCHEN AND SHOPPING NOTES

A poussin (also known as "spring chicken") is a young chicken that weighs between 10 and 12 ounces. Unfortunately, they enjoy only limited popularity in the United States, though their meat is tender and delicately flavored. We've chosen poussin for this recipe because it's one of the few small birds you can purchase already boned through the neck, which creates a perfect pouch for stuffing. Other whole small birds that are boned through the neck, such as quail and squab, are suitable substitutes in this dish. A whole Cornish game hen could be roasted until crisp and brown and then served with the gumbo sauce and stuffing alongside, if you like. For some things, however, there are no substitutes: smoked andouille sausage and tasso, which is spicy cured pork shoulder, are the essence of Louisiana cooking and without them this dish just won't taste right.

One poussin per person make a generous main course. If you're having a first course (see Fried Green Tomato and Crispy Hama Hama Oysters "BLT," page 57, or Dungeness Crab Cakes, page 46), consider serving half a bird per person.

METHOD

FOR THE CORN BREAD: Preheat the oven to 425°F. Butter an 8-inch square baking pan or cast-iron skillet. Stir the flour, cornmeal, baking powder, and salt together in a bowl. Whisk the buttermilk, eggs, honey, and melted butter together in another bowl, then pour over the dry ingredients. With a wooden spoon or rubber spatula, stir just until combined (don't overmix!) and pour the batter into the prepared pan. Bake for 20 minutes, or until golden or a skewer inserted near the center comes out clean. Cool the corn bread for 10 minutes in the pan, then turn out onto a wire rack to finish cooling. The corn bread can be wrapped in plastic and stored at room temperature up to 2 days ahead.

FOR THE STUFFING: Break the corn bread into 1-inch chunks onto a rimmed baking sheet. Set it out to dry overnight or toast it in a low (200°F) oven for about 1 hour. Heat the oil in a large skillet over medium heat. Add the onion and cook, stirring occasionally, for about 10 minutes, or until soft and translucent. Increase the heat to high, add the andouille and tasso, and cook for 4 minutes. Add the garlic, cook for another minute or so, then add the corn, green onions, sage, and thyme. Cook for 4 minutes more, and then transfer to a large bowl. Season with salt and pepper, let cool for 5 minutes, and stir in the cheese, parsley, and warm chicken stock. Mix well, then set aside to cool completely. The stuffing can be made 1 day ahead and stored in a covered container in the refrigerator.

FOR THE DARK ROUX: Heat the oil in a heavy saucepan over medium heat until it shimmers. Whisk in the flour until thoroughly combined and smooth. Decrease the heat to very low and cook the roux, stirring constantly for about 20 minutes, or until it is dark golden brown and smells nutty. Be careful not to let the roux scorch—it can go from brown to black quickly. Stir in the celery, carrot, onion, and thyme. The mixture will start to bubble and spurt, but keep stirring and cook for another 10 minutes. Remove the pan from the heat and set aside to cool. The cooled roux can be stored in the refrigerator for up to 1 week. You only need ½ cup for this recipe; the remainder can be frozen for up to 2 months.

FOR THE GUMBO SAUCE: Heat a large saucepan over medium heat and add the bacon, tasso, and andouille. Cook, stirring, until the bacon becomes translucent and begins to release its fat, then add the celery, onion, bell pepper, garlic, and jalapeños and cook until the vegetables have softened but not browned. Add the thyme sprigs, bay leaf, and paprika. Cook, stirring often to keep the mixture from burning, for 5 minutes more, then add the wine. Increase the heat to medium-high and cook, stirring, until the pan is almost dry. Add the chicken stock and decrease the heat to low. Cook for 20 minutes, then whisk in the roux and cook, stirring occasionally, for 10 minutes longer. Strain the sauce through a medium-mesh sieve into a bowl, pressing on the solids with a spoon to extract all the liquid. Season with salt and pepper. Store, covered, in the refrigerator for up to 2 days.

FOR THE POUSSINS: Rinse the birds and pat thoroughly dry with paper towels. Season them inside and out with salt and pepper and place ¾ cup stuffing in the cavity of each bird. Skewer the neck flaps closed with toothpicks, then plump up and smooth the birds with your hands to reshape them nicely. Truss the legs by making a small incision in one leg near the ankle and then inserting the other leg through the incision. The poussins can be stuffed up to 8 hours ahead (but no more than that!) and kept loosely covered in the refrigerator.

Preheat the oven to 400°F. Heat 2 tablespoons of the oil in a large, heavy ovenproof skillet or sauté pan over medium-high heat. Carefully add the 2 of the poussins to the pan and cook, turning them with tongs, for 6 to 8 minutes, or until golden on all sides. Transfer the birds to a plate and set aside while you cook the other birds. Discard the cooking oil and add the remaining 2 tablespoons oil. Cook the other 2 poussins. Again discard the cooking oil, then return all the poussins to the pan. Place the pan in the oven and roast for 20 to 25 minutes, or until an instant-read thermometer inserted in the thickest part of the leg (not touching bone) reaches 155° to 160°F. Remove from the oven and let rest for 5 minutes before serving.

TO SERVE

Place a bed of greens on each of 4 warm dinner plates. Top each with a poussin and ring the plate with the gumbo sauce.

POT-ROASTED GUINEA HENS

TWICE-COOKED POTATOES WITH GARLIC MOUSSELINE, WARM ARUGULA AND OLIVE SALAD
WITH GLAZED WALNUTS

SERVES 4

TWICE-COOKED POTATOES WITH GARLIC MOUSSELINE

4 (5- to 6-ounce) Yukon Gold
   potatoes
3 tablespoons unsalted butter,
   cut into ½-inch pieces
¼ cup water
8 large cloves garlic
1 cup heavy cream
Kosher salt and freshly ground
   black pepper

GLAZED WALNUTS

1 cup walnut halves
2 tablespoons light corn syrup
1½ teaspoons sugar
¼ teaspoon kosher salt
¼ teaspoon freshly ground
   black pepper

ROSEMARY VINAIGRETTE

1 cup pitted Niçoise olives
3 rosemary sprigs
½ cup extra-virgin olive oil
1 tablespoon finely diced shallots
1 tablespoon freshly squeezed
   lemon juice
¼ teaspoon kosher salt

GUINEA HENS

2 (2½- to 3-pound) guinea hens
⅓ cup olive oil
1 large onion, coarsely chopped
2 celery ribs, coarsely chopped
4 cloves garlic, peeled
2 to 3 thyme sprigs
3 cups dry white wine
2 cups Dark Chicken Stock (see
   Basics, page 230)
Kosher salt and freshly ground
   black pepper
1 tablespoon unsalted butter

1 tablespoon olive oil

WARM ARUGULA SALAD

1 bunch arugula, cleaned and dried
Reserved olives from the vinaigrette
Rosemary vinaigrette
Glazed walnuts

Guinea fowl or "yard birds," as Gaines Dobbins, a former chef in our kitchen, affectionately called them, were originally brought to this country from Africa. In France the guinea hen is called a *pintade,* in Italy it is a *faraona,* and it also goes by the name African pheasant. Though this bird may not be very well known in the United States, it's steadily gaining in popularity because of its deep flavor, which is reminiscent of free-range farm chickens.

Pot-roasting the whole bird creates a comforting yet elegant dish that develops a rich and soulful sauce, while the hens cook to moist perfection. The twice-cooked potatoes with garlic mousseline combine two recipes that are easily made ahead and are a perfect accompaniment to all kinds of roasted meats and braised dishes. Warm olives and glazed walnuts with lemons, rosemary, and arugula add a welcome flavor balance.

continued

Fresh guinea fowl can be found at many butchers and specialty meat markets and by mail order (see Sources, page 236). They vary in size from 2 to 4 pounds; for this recipe you'll need 2½- to 3-pound hens (not toms, which are tough).

We recommend the short extra step of trussing the guinea hens because trussed hens form neat packages that cook more evenly and are easier to turn during browning. To truss the guinea hens, cut 2 pieces of kitchen twine, each about 2½ feet long. Place a hen on a cutting board with the legs facing you, place the middle of one piece of string at the legs and loop one end over each leg and pull tight. Next, bring the ends of the string back along the sides of the hens, running the strings between the legs, and pull the string over the thighs, breast, and wings. Turn the bird on its side and wind the ends of the string over the neck. Knot the string and trim it off close to the knot. Repeat with the second hen.

The trick to keeping the hens from sticking to the casserole is to let the pan get very hot, add the oil, let it heat for a few seconds, and then put in one bird. Lower the heat and don't move it for at least a minute—once it gets a nice crust, you can use your tongs to turn it. Repeat the process, turning the bird until it's golden brown all over.

We suggest that you double or triple the recipe for the glazed walnuts. They're great to toss into a salad, to serve with cheese or, our favorite option, to snack on. If you store them in an airtight container in a dry place, they should stay fresh and crisp for up to 2 weeks. One more tip, always taste the nuts before you commit them to a dish since they're full of oil and can turn rancid easily.

METHOD

FOR THE POTATOES WITH GARLIC MOUSSELINE: To make the potatoes, preheat the oven to 400°F. Cut off a ¼-inch-thick slice from the two opposite long sides. Place the potatoes, cut side down, in an ovenproof skillet or baking dish with water and butter pieces scattered around. Bake, turning once, for about 1 hour, or until the potatoes have softened.

Meanwhile, make the garlic mousseline. Put the garlic cloves in a microwave-safe container with water to cover and cook on HIGH for 3 minutes. Drain, add more water to cover, and cook for 6 minutes, or until soft. Drain again and set aside. When the potatoes are done, remove from the oven and scoop out some of the middle of the potatoes, leaving about ¼ inch of potato on the sides and bottom so that you have what looks like a little boat. Heat the cream until just below boiling and put into a blender with the scooped out potato and soft garlic. Puree until blended and smooth, then season to taste with salt and pepper. Set the potatoes and garlic mousseline aside.

FOR THE GLAZED WALNUTS: Lower the oven temperature to 300°F. Blanch the walnuts in boiling water for 3 minutes. Drain and spread out in a sheet pan. Dry in the oven for 10 minutes. Remove the walnuts from the oven and set aside to cool. Stir the corn syrup, sugar, salt, and pepper together in a bowl. Add the walnuts and stir to coat well.

Line a baking sheet with parchment or a nonstick baking liner (see Sources, page 237) and spread the coated walnuts out in a single layer. Increase the oven temperature to 325°F and bake the walnuts, stirring them once or twice, for 15 to 20 minutes, or until golden brown and crispy. Remove from the oven, season the nuts with a little more salt and pepper if necessary, and let them cool. Gently break apart any nuts that are stuck together.

FOR THE VINAIGRETTE: Combine the olives, rosemary sprigs, and olive oil in a small saucepan. Heat over medium-high until just sizzling, then remove from the heat and let sit for 5 minutes. Strain the mixture through a sieve into a small bowl. Reserve the oil and olives in separate bowls and discard the rosemary. Whisk the shallots, lemon juice, and salt together in a small bowl. Slowly whisk in the reserved rosemary oil until well combined. Set aside.

FOR THE GUINEA HENS: Increase the oven temperature to 400°F. Cut off the first 2 joints of the wings and reserve. Truss the hens (see Kitchen and Shopping Notes). Heat the olive oil in a lidded casserole dish that is large enough to hold both hens with a little room between them over high heat. Lower the heat to medium-high and brown the hens on all sides, turning them with tongs but being careful to not tear the skin, about 8 minutes total. (It may be easier for you to brown them one at a time). When the hens are browned, discard the fat in the casserole dish and add the onion, celery, garlic, thyme sprigs, and reserved wing tips. Lower the heat to medium-low and sauté the vegetables and wing tips for about 6 minutes, or until the vegetables have softened and are beginning to color. Add the wine, increase the heat to high, and reduce the liquid to 1½ cups. Add the chicken stock and hens and cover the casserole. Roast for 30 minutes. Uncover the casserole dish and increase the oven temperature to 500°F. Roast for 15 minutes more, then check the internal temperature of the hens in the thickest part of the leg with an instant-read thermometer; it should be 155° to 160°F. Transfer the hens to a cutting board or platter and let rest for 10 minutes. Strain the liquid in the casserole dish through a fine-mesh sieve into a saucepan. Skim off the fat and reduce over high heat until syrupy and about 1 cup of liquid remains. Season the sauce with salt and pepper and whisk in the butter to give it a silky texture and rich flavor.

TO SERVE

While the hens are resting, heat the 1 tablespoon olive oil in a skillet over medium-high heat. Add the potatoes and cook until golden brown on both sides. Meanwhile, heat the garlic mousseline until warm, either in a microwave or in a small saucepan on top of the stove. Warm the olives and walnuts in a small skillet, add the vinaigrette, and remove from the heat.

Carve the hens into 4 breast-wing and 4 leg-thigh pieces. Toss the arugula with the vinaigrette mixture. Place a potato on each of 4 warm dinner plates, pour some garlic mousseline into the "bowl" in each potato, and lean the guinea hen pieces up against the potatoes. Spoon the sauce over the hens and in the front of the plate. Top with a generous handful of the warm arugula salad.

PAN-ROASTED CALIFORNIA PHEASANT BREAST

SPRING ONIONS, PRUNES IN ARMAGNAC, BRAISED BACON, AND SAVOY SPINACH
LISA'S POTATO PANCAKES

SERVES 4

PHEASANT

2 whole pheasants (about
    3 pounds each)
½ cup heavy cream
2 tablespoons kosher salt
½ teaspoon freshly ground
    black pepper
3 thyme sprigs

PHEASANT SAUCE

12 pitted prunes
1 cup Armagnac
¼ cup olive oil
Reserved legs, thighs, necks,
    wing tips, and carcasses
    from the pheasants
1 small onion, coarsely chopped
3 shallots, sliced
3 cloves garlic, lightly crushed
2 cups Dark Chicken Stock (see
    Basics, page 230)
5 thyme sprigs
5 flat-leaf parsley sprigs
1 teaspoon black peppercorns

LISA'S POTATO PANCAKES

1 pound Yukon Gold potatoes, peeled
Juice of ½ lemon
½ teaspoon kosher salt
⅓ cup chopped onion
1 to 2 tablespoons all-purpose flour
1 large egg, lightly beaten
Olive oil, for frying

3 tablespoons olive oil
2 tablespoons unsalted butter, cut
    into pieces
4 spring onions, trimmed of roots
    and all but 3 inches of green
Braised Bacon and Bacon Braising
    Stock (see Basics, page 228)
⅓ cup crème fraîche
4 cups loosely packed cleaned
    Savoy spinach leaves, or
    regular spinach leaves, tough
    stems removed
Kosher salt and freshly ground
    black pepper

Pheasant has a certain cachet. The name stirs up "pheasant-under-glass" fantasies, but in the wrong hands, cachet turns into catastrophe when a tough, dry bird hits the table. With proper care in the kitchen, pheasant has much in its favor—its meat has a very pure, delicate flavor that is worth uncovering with some time and effort in the kitchen. If you are lucky enough to have friends or loved ones who offer you some of their hunting bounty, or you're just in the mood for a romantic endeavor, this recipe contains *the* essential ingredient for success—cream. An overnight soak in cream ensures that your pheasant will be tender and moist but, unfortunately, nothing can save it if overcooked.

To complement the lean meat of the pheasant breasts, we serve wonderfully rich bacon, braised until it's crisp on the outside and gooey on the inside. When the pheasant braising juices combine with the prunes and Armagnac, the three elements form a luscious sauce that has both perfect texture and a perfect balance of flavor. This recipe also features our favorite potato pancake recipe from Lisa Weiss, our coauthor. Easy to prepare, it yields a crispy potato cake that's creamy on the inside—the perfect latke.

continued

KITCHEN AND SHOPPING NOTES

The availability of commercially raised fresh pheasant varies throughout the country. We recommend you search for a fresh farm-raised bird (see Sources, page 236) because the leanness of the meat is affected by freezing, rendering it less tender. Pheasant ranges in size from 2 to 5 pounds, but we prefer 3-pound females; they have much juicier flesh than the males. Bone the pheasant just as you would a chicken, and proceed with the recipe by making the sauce first. Of course, a good butcher will be able to do the boning for you, but make sure you get the bones to take home for the sauce. Keep in mind that the pheasant must be boned ahead, allowing enough time for the breasts to marinate.

Spring onions are sweet young onions, pulled out of the ground with their green shoots attached and the bulbs about golf-ball size. In some areas of the country they're also called "short-day" onions or green onions. Look for spring onions in the spring, of course. If they're not available, pearl onions can be substituted.

We like to use Savoy spinach, a variety that has a thicker, crinkly leaf that we find holds up better for sautéing, but any kind of spinach will do. A favorite Savoy type is Bloomsdale, which you can eat stems and all. If you use flat-leaf spinach, trim and remove any tough stems.

METHOD

FOR THE PHEASANT BREAST: Bone the pheasants leaving the wings attached to the breasts. Remove the first two joints of the wings. French the wing joints that are still attached to the breasts by scraping the meat away from the wing bones Remove the legs and thighs and set aside for the sauce with the carcass, wing tips, and necks.

To marinate the pheasant breasts, combine the cream, salt, pepper, and thyme sprigs in a shallow baking dish. Add the pheasant breasts, turn to coat, and cover with plastic wrap. Refrigerate overnight. (You can also put the breasts in a large zippered bag and pour the marinade over them.)

FOR THE PHEASANT STOCK: Soak the prunes in the Armagnac in a small bowl for about 30 minutes, or until plumped. Strain through a sieve, reserving the Armagnac and prunes separately. Heat the olive oil in a large saucepan over medium-high heat. Cook the pheasant legs, thighs, necks, wing tips, and carcasses, turning frequently, for 10 to 15 minutes, or until golden brown on all sides. Add the onion, shallots, and garlic and cook for 2 minutes more. Deglaze with the reserved Armagnac, then add the chicken stock. Add the thyme sprigs, parsley, and peppercorns and bring to a boil. Decrease the heat to maintain a simmer and cook, skimming occasionally, for 45 minutes. Strain the sauce through a fine-mesh sieve into a bowl and set aside.

FOR THE POTATO PANCAKES: Grate the potatoes using the coarse shredding disk of a food processor. Then fit the food processor with the metal blade and return the potatoes to the processor. Add the lemon juice, salt, onion, flour, and egg. Pulse just until a loose batter forms, making sure you don't puree the potatoes. The batter should mound but still be loose and slightly liquidy. Stir in a little more flour if it's too loose. To cook the potato pancakes, line a baking sheet with paper towels. Heat olive oil to a depth of $\frac{1}{8}$ inch in a large nonstick skillet over medium-high heat. When the oil shimmers, drop several rounded spoonfuls of the batter, about 2 heaping tablespoons, to form 2-inch pancakes. Cook for about 3 minutes, or until golden on the bottom. Maintain the heat so the oil bubbles around the edges of the pancakes. Turn and cook for another 3 minutes. Transfer the pancakes to the lined baking sheet and set aside. Repeat making pancakes with the remaining batter.

TO COOK THE PHEASANT: Remove the breasts from the marinade and pat dry with paper towels. Heat the 1 tablespoon of the olive oil in a large skillet over medium heat. Add the pheasant breasts, skin side down, cover with parchment paper, and weight them with another pan that just fits inside the skillet. Cook for about 4 minutes, or until the skin is golden and crispy, then turn and cook for another 6 to 8 minutes, or until an instant-read thermometer inserted into the thickest part of the breasts reads 140°F. Decrease the heat to medium-low, drain off the oil, and add the butter. When the butter has melted and begins to foam, spoon it over the pheasant breasts, basting several times. Remove from the heat and keep warm.

TO SERVE

Meanwhile, increase the oven temperature to 375°F. Reheat the potato pancakes in the oven for about 5 minutes, or until warm. Heat the sauce, add the spring onions, and reduce over high heat for about 5 minutes, or until the liquid is syrupy and the onions are tender. Add the Braised Bacon and Bacon Braising Stock and prunes to the sauce and decrease the heat to low. Whisk in the crème fraîche. Heat the remaining 2 tablespoons oil in a large skillet or sauté pan over high heat. Add the spinach and cook, stirring, just until wilted. Drain off the liquid in the pan and season the spinach to taste with salt and pepper. With a slotted spoon, place some of the onions, prunes, and bacon onto each of 4 warm dinner plates. Place a small pile of spinach alongside. Top with the pheasant breasts and spoon the sauce around.

This duck recipe is hearty yet sophisticated. The duck skin is replaced with thin slices of apple wood–smoked bacon, which keeps the duck moist and allows you to stuff the breast with a tempting combination of braised apples and chestnuts. The result of this effort is a neat little package that, when cut, reveals a mosaic of stuffing, that holds all the earthy flavors of fall. Celery root is at its sweetest in the fall and winter and makes a rich, delicate puree, our favorite with the deep flavors of bacon, apples, chestnuts and duck. A reduction of Calvados, the famous apple brandy from France, is added to the sauce and pulls all of these ingredients together.

DUCK BREAST STUFFED WITH APPLES AND CHESTNUTS AND ROASTED IN BACON

CELERY ROOT PUREE AND CALVADOS SAUCE

SERVES 4

ROASTED APPLES

4 tablespoons unsalted butter, melted

¼ cup water

1 tablespoon sugar

½ teaspoon kosher salt

2 Fuji apples, peeled, cored, and each cut lengthwise into 8 wedges

12 to 16 peeled whole chestnuts, fresh or frozen (see Kitchen and Shopping Notes)

2 teaspoons fresh thyme leaves

DUCK BREASTS

4 boneless, skinless duck breast halves (about 6 ounces each), butterflied (see Kitchen and Shopping Notes)

24 thin slices bacon (See Kitchen and Shopping Notes)

¼ cup grape seed or olive oil

CELERY ROOT PUREE

1 (1-pound) celery root, peeled and cut into 2-inch pieces

4 tablespoons unsalted butter

Kosher salt

CALVADOS DUCK SAUCE

2 tablespoons olive oil

1 cup thinly sliced unpeeled Fuji apple (about 1 apple)

¼ cup sliced shallots

2 cloves garlic, crushed

1 cup Calvados or good-quality brandy

6 black peppercorns

2 thyme sprigs

1½ cups Dark Chicken Stock (see Basics, page 230)

KITCHEN AND SHOPPING NOTES

Boneless Long Island or Pekin duck breasts are the perfect size for this recipe; avoid the larger and gamier Muscovy or Moulard breasts because they're just too big to work here. You can find boneless duck breasts in many good butcher shops, as well as by mail order. If you're good with a knife, purchase several ducks when they're on sale and bone them yourself. Use the legs to make confit or for a braised duck dish and use the carcasses to make some flavorful duck stock.

You'll need to butterfly the boneless duck breast halves for this recipe. To butterfly them, first remove the skin, and then, with a sharp knife parallel to the cutting board, make a horizontal cut along the rounded, thinner side of the breast. Spread the breast open so it forms a heart shape (see photo on following page).

Once they're wrapped with the bacon, the breasts can be stored in the refrigerator for up to 8 hours, but any longer and the bacon will begin to cure and discolor the meat. The apple-chestnut mixture can be cooked a day ahead without suffering. Note that it's important for the bacon to be sliced superthin so that it wraps easily around the duck, sticks to itself, and renders quickly, leaving only a crisp trace of flavor. Our first choice is apple wood–smoked bacon (see Sources, page 236), which we buy by the slab and slice on a meat slicer. Lacking a meat slicer, your next best option is to find a butcher who will slice the bacon for you. As a last resort, use good-quality supermarket bacon—just remember the words "thinly sliced."

Fresh chestnuts are one of the delights of fall but are difficult to peel (see Braised Chestnut Soup, page 35). Frozen peeled chestnuts (see Sources, page 237) are a terrific store-bought product; just don't use canned chestnuts because they're too soft and coated with a sweet syrup we find unpalatable.

continued

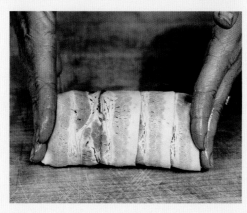

1	4
2	5
3	6

1   Make a horizontal cut along the rounded, thinner side of the breast and spread it open

2   Place 4 roasted apple wedges in the center of the breast and fill in with the chestnuts, using 4 per breast. Fold the breast meat over onto itself to form a roll.

3   Place 4 lengthwise overlapping slices of bacon on a work surface. Place 2 bacon slices perpendicular to the 4 slices, so they overlap by 1 inch to form a cross.

4   Place a duck breast in the center, parallel to the 2 bacon slices

5   Fold the bacon over the duck, then roll it up to form a neat package

6   Sear the duck breast on the seam side of the bacon first

METHOD

butterflying, stuffing, and wrapping the duck breast

<

FOR THE APPLES: Preheat the oven to 350°F. Combine the butter, water, sugar, and salt in a bowl. Add the apples and toss to coat. Spread the apples out on a rimmed baking sheet and roast, stirring frequently, for 20 minutes. Add the chestnuts and roast for 10 minutes more, or until the apples and chestnuts begin to brown and the butter and water have been absorbed. Remove from the oven, toss with the thyme, and set aside to cool.

FOR THE DUCK BREASTS: Working with 1 breast at a time, spread a butterflied breast, skin side down, on a work surface. Place 4 apple wedges down along the center and fill in between with the chestnuts, using about 4 per breast. Fold the breast meat over onto itself to form a roll. Place 4 lengthwise overlapping slices of bacon on the work surface and place 2 slices perpendicular to the 4 slices so they overlap by 1 inch to form a cross (see photo 3). Place a duck breast in the center, parallel to the 2 bacon slices, fold the bacon over the duck, then roll it up to make a neat package. Repeat with the remaining breasts and bacon. Refrigerate for up to 8 hours.

To cook the duck, increase the oven temperature to 375°F. Heat the oil over medium heat in a large ovenproof sauté pan. Carefully place the bacon-wrapped duck breasts in the pan and cook on all sides for about 6 minutes to render and brown the bacon. Drain off most of the fat from the pan and put into the oven to finish the cooking, about 15 minutes for medium-rare. Remove the pan from the oven and let the duck breasts rest for 5 to 8 minutes.

FOR THE CELERY ROOT PUREE: Put the celery root into a large saucepan with generously salted water to cover and add 2 tablespoons of the butter. Bring to a boil, decrease the heat to maintain a simmer, and cook for about 20 minutes, or until the celery root is soft when pierced with a knife. Drain, then transfer the celery root to a blender with the remaining 2 tablespoons butter. Puree until smooth and season with salt if necessary. Set aside for up to 1 hour at room temperature and rewarm before serving.

FOR THE DUCK SAUCE: Heat the olive oil in a saucepan over medium-high heat. Add the apple, shallots, and garlic and cook for about 6 minutes, or until they begin to caramelize. Add the Calvados, increase the heat to high, and cook until almost all the liquid has evaporated. Add the peppercorns, thyme, and chicken stock and simmer for 25 to 30 minutes, or until thickened to the consistency of heavy cream. Strain the sauce through a fine-mesh sieve into a small saucepan. Refrigerate for up to 2 days and reheat before serving.

TO SERVE

Place a ½-cup mound of celery root puree in the center of 4 warm dinner plates and spread out with the back of a spoon into 4-inch circles. Trim off about ¼ inch from the ends of each duck breast, and then cut each breast crosswise in half. Place 2 pieces of duck in the center of the celery root puree, and spoon over a little sauce. Drizzle some of the remaining sauce around the puree.

PAN-ROASTED SQUAB

HAZELNUT PANCAKES, GRAPE AND KUMQUAT RELISH, FOIE GRAS SAUCE

SERVES 4

RED GRAPE AND KUMQUAT RELISH

½ cup seedless red grapes, halved

½ cup tangerine segments (see Kitchen and Shopping Notes, page 70)

¼ cup thinly sliced kumquats

¼ cup candied hazelnuts (see Basics, page 228), coarsely chopped

1 tablespoon honey

1 tablespoon champagne vinegar

½ teaspoon chopped fresh rosemary leaves

¼ cup olive oil

HAZELNUT PANCAKES

2½ tablespoons hazelnut paste (see Sources, page 237)

1 cup whole milk

1 large egg

1 cup self-rising flour

1 teaspoon kosher salt

¼ teaspoon baking powder

¾ cup candied hazelnuts (see Basics, page 228), coarsely chopped

FOIE GRAS SAUCE

4 squab (about 1 pound each)

2 tablespoons olive oil

2 tablespoons minced shallots

2 thyme sprigs

12 black peppercorns, cracked

¼ cup Madeira

4 cups Dark Chicken Stock (see Basics, page 230)

¼ cup whole red seedless grapes

2 ounces foie gras, cleaned, deveined, and cut into ½-inch pieces

Kosher salt and freshly ground black pepper

SQUAB

Reserved boned squabs

Kosher salt and freshly ground black pepper

2 tablespoons grapeseed or olive oil

2 tablespoons unsalted butter or olive oil

Baby arugula or watercress, cleaned, for garnish

Squab is, without a doubt, our favorite meat to eat and cook. We love it prepared simply—pan-roasted and served with a bitter green salad, garlic crostini, and pan drippings—or dressed to the nines with foie gras or truffles for a wine dinner or multicourse tasting menu. Cooked to medium-rare is the only way to enjoy squab. One could make an argument for the long, slow braise in the Italian style, but for us, when cooked beyond rosy pink, the red meat of this lush little bird becomes dull and livery. For this cold-weather dish, we've chosen a red grape and kumquat relish that lends a nice tart contrast to the rich squab meat and velvety foie gras sauce. As for the hazelnut pancakes, they're just plain good.

continued

KITCHEN AND SHOPPING NOTES

Don't be intimidated by these little birds. Think of them as small, dark meat chickens. Fresh squab is widely available by mail order and from specialty butchers. If you're lucky enough to live near an Asian market, you will likely find squab with their head and feet still attached—so much the better for the sauce. And if you're really lucky, you'll also get them with their livers. Arguably the squab livers are the best part when seasoned with salt and pepper, quickly seared, and served next to the squab on the plate. Count on one squab per person.

We realize most people don't have bits and pieces of foie gras in their kitchens, but thankfully D'Artagnan mail order (see Sources, page 236) saves the day with preportioned slices of foie gras.

METHOD

FOR THE GRAPE AND KUMQUAT RELISH: Toss the grapes, tangerine segments, kumquats, and hazelnuts together in a bowl and set aside. Just before serving, whisk the honey, vinegar, rosemary, and olive oil in another bowl and then toss with the grape mixture.

FOR THE HAZELNUT PANCAKES: Stir together the hazelnut paste, milk and egg in a bowl until smooth. Sift the flour with the salt and baking powder and fold into the milk mixture to make a smooth batter. You want a batter that is neither too runny nor too thick; it should easily drop off a spoon into a pan and form a round pancake. The pancake batter can be made up to 3 hours ahead and refrigerated. Stir in the chopped hazelnuts just before cooking the pancakes.

FOR THE FOIE GRAS SAUCE: Bone the squab by carefully cutting down along either side of the breastbone and scraping down either side of the rib cage to free the breast and legs. Cut down the backbone to halve the squabs. Cut off the 2 first joints of the wings and trim all the meat of any ragged edges. Set the halved and boned squabs aside in the refrigerator. Heat the olive oil in a large saucepan over medium-high heat. Lightly brown the squab bones, wings, and trimmings, stirring to color on all sides. Pour off and discard all but 1 tablespoon of the fat. Add the shallots, thyme sprigs, and peppercorns and cook until the vegetables have softened and begin to brown, 6 to 8 minutes more. Add the Madeira and reduce the liquid by two-thirds. Add the chicken stock, bring to the boil, then decrease the heat to maintain a simmer. Add the grapes and cook for 45 minutes, skimming once or twice. Strain through a fine-mesh sieve, return the liquid to the saucepan, and reduce to 1 to 1¼ cups, continuing to skim it occasionally as it reduces. Let the liquid cool slightly, then strain it into a blender. With the machine running, carefully and slowly add the foie gras, piece by piece, until the sauce is smooth and pale. Season to taste with salt and pepper and strain again through a fine-mesh sieve into a clean saucepan. Set aside and keep warm.

TO COOK THE SQUAB AND HAZELNUT PANCAKES: Preheat the oven to 400°F. Season the squab generously with salt and pepper. Heat the oil in a large ovenproof skillet over high heat until it shimmers. Carefully add the squab, skin side down. To ensure the skin is crisp and a rich mahogany brown (like we love), place a piece of parchment paper on top of the squab, then place another pan just large enough to fit inside on top to weight the squab down. Cook for about 2 minutes, then put the weighted pan into the oven for 2 to 3 minutes if you prefer your squab on the rare side, 4 to 5 minutes if you want it more done. Remove the weight, turn the squabs over, and cook for 2 to 3 minutes more. Remove from the oven and let the squabs rest in the pan for 5 minutes while you cook the pancakes.

Stir the chopped hazelnuts into the pancake batter. Heat a large nonstick skillet over medium heat. When hot, add the 2 tablespoons butter, let it heat for 30 seconds or so, and drop 6 mounds of batter, 1 tablespoon each, into the pan, leaving a little space between them. Cook for 2 to 3 minutes, or until golden brown on the bottom, then flip over and brown on the other side. Remove the pancakes to a warm plate and set aside while you cook the remaining batter. (The cooked pancakes become tough and dry if they sit too long, so they should be served as soon as possible.)

TO SERVE

Place 2 or 3 pancakes on each of 4 warm dinner plates. Arrange 2 squab halves on top of the pancakes and spoon some sauce around. Dot the sauce and spoon the remainder of the relish over the squab. Garnish with baby arugula.

There is a lot more to cooking than getting to the end of the recipe.

RABBIT TWO WAYS

LEGS FRIED IN A PARMESAN CRUST
AND ROASTED LOINS WRAPPED IN SMITHFIELD COUNTY "PROSCIUTTO"
FAVA BEANS, ENGLISH PEAS, AND MINT

SERVES 4

RABBIT LEGS

4 rabbit hind legs (see Kitchen and
    Shopping Notes)
Kosher salt and freshly ground
    black pepper
1 cup all-purpose flour
4 large egg whites
1 cup fine dried bread crumbs
    or panko (Japanese bread
    crumbs)
1 cup freshly grated good-quality
    Parmesan cheese
2 teaspoons chopped fresh
    flat-leaf parsley leaves
1 teaspoon chopped fresh
    thyme leaves
Extra-virgin olive oil

RABBIT LOINS

4 rabbit loins (saddles, see Kitchen
    and Shopping Notes)
Kosher salt and freshly ground
    black pepper
2 teaspoons chopped fresh
    thyme leaves
4 very thin large center-cut slices
    Smithfield County "prosciutto"
    (see Kitchen and Shopping
    Notes)
2 tablespoons extra-virgin olive oil

FAVA BEANS AND
ENGLISH PEAS

4 tablespoons extra-virgin olive oil
1 tablespoon aged balsamic vinegar
1 cup shelled fava beans (see Basics,
    page 229)
1 pound English peas, shelled (about
    1 cup shelled)
Kosher salt and freshly ground
    black pepper
1 tablespoon julienned fresh
    mint leaves
1 tablespoon finely sliced
    fresh chives
2 teaspoons julienned fresh
    basil leaves
1 tablespoon unsalted butter

Although we've included this recipe in the poultry chapter, let's reject the common notion that rabbit—and indeed all lean white game meats, including frog legs and rattlesnake—tastes like chicken. We prefer to think of rabbit as neither chicken nor game but as a delicate and tender vehicle for flavor.

For this dish, we wanted contrasting tastes and textures, so we used different techniques for the different rabbit parts. In one recipe, the leg meat is removed from the bone, flattened slightly, and then panfried in aromatic olive oil until it's crispy yet fork-tender. In the other recipe, the boneless loins are wrapped in air-cured ham to protect their lean meat from the heat of the oven, then roasted until succulent and heady with the aromas and flavors of fresh thyme and salty ham. These two preparations tasted side by side are a revelation and well worth the effort, but be aware that you'll be spending a fair amount of time in the kitchen. Consider making them one at a time—each is a stand-up dish on its own.

KITCHEN AND SHOPPING NOTES

All domestic rabbits sold today are farm-raised. Unlike their wild hare "cousins," they possess a fine-grained texture and delicate flavor, but because they're so lean and are often cooked without the protection of their skin, care needs to be taken during cooking to ensure they don't become dry.

continued

When you go to the market, it's usual to buy a whole rabbit; they're classified in the same vernacular as chicken. For instance, a 2- to 3½- pound rabbit is called a fryer, while a rabbit weighing 4 pounds and up is called a roaster. A roaster is great if you are preparing a big braised casserole for a potluck. For individual servings, however, where you want each portion to be the same size (a great concern for restaurants), you want a fryer rabbit that's at least 2½ but not over 3 pounds. Anything smaller, say a 2-pounder, doesn't have much meat on it and, frankly, looks really sad on the plate.

Ask your butcher to bone the rabbit for you. When completed you will have 2 nice big, meaty hind legs, 2 kind of skinny legs (good for braising, stock, or southern-fried rabbit), 2 loins, 2 racks, 2 dubious belly flaps (we've made rabbit bacon but don't recommend it), 1 gorgeous liver, 2 delicious kidneys, and bones for stock. The point being that you will have many bits and pieces with which to get creative. Don't be too quick to dismiss the value of learning the skills involved in preparing your ingredients (such as boning a rabbit); an intense involvement in the whole process is deeply satisfying. There is a lot more to cooking than getting to the end of the recipe.

It is unconventional to use extra virgin olive oil for frying or sautéing, but it pays off here in extra flavor dividends. For a walk on the wild side try clarified butter, different but equally delicious.

There are some special ingredients we've specified in this rabbit recipe. We're delighted with the rebirth of American artisanal hams and urge you to investigate producers such as Johnston Farms in North Carolina or the Bay Area's own Hobbs, who make many styles of dry-cured hams that are similar to Italian prosciutto. Imported Spanish serrano and Iberico hams, and Italian Parma or San Daniele prosciutto are widely available and will certainly work. (Just make sure the slices are as wide and long as possible.) While good-quality air-cured hams are interchangeable, we've not found anything that compares with aged artisan-made balsamic vinegar or *aceto balsamico tradizionale di Modena,* worth every dear penny you pay for it. Keep in mind, however, that this *antico condimento* (antique condiment), which is aged 25 years or more (called *extra-vecchio,* meaning extra-old), is consumed one drop at a time, and even a tiny bit will have a flavorful impact on anything it graces.

METHOD

FOR THE RABBIT LEGS: The easiest boning method is to cut the meat completely away from the bone. But for a nicer presentation at the restaurant, we open the leg to remove the thigh bone and french the shin bone or drumstick, scraping away any sinew. Place the boneless meat between 2 pieces of lightly oiled plastic wrap or parchment and gently pound it until it is ¼ inch thick (as close to the bone as possible, so the meat cooks evenly) like you would for scaloppine. Repeat with the remaining legs. Generously season both sides of the legs with salt and pepper, then line up 3 shallow bowls. Put the flour in the first bowl, the egg whites in the second, and then combine the bread crumbs, Parmesan, parsley, and thyme in the third and season with salt and pepper. Lightly beat the egg whites and set a wire rack over a baking sheet nearby. Dip each rabbit leg into the flour, shaking off any excess, then into the egg, and finally into the flour-Parmesan mixture, patting the coating on both sides to make sure the legs are evenly coated. Place the legs on the rack and refrigerate until ready to cook, up to 3 hours ahead.

FOR THE RABBIT LOINS: Basically you are going to combine the 4 boneless loins into a small roast. Place the rabbit loins on a work surface; season them with salt, pepper, and sprinkle with 1 teaspoon of the thyme. Lay out the prosciutto slices, 2 slices lengthwise and 2 slices crosswise, so they roughly form a cross. Sprinkle with the remaining 1 teaspoon thyme. Place the rabbit in the center of the prosciutto, which should extend beyond the rabbit. Bring the ends of the top 2 slices of prosciutto up and over the rabbit, then fold the remaining slices over and around the loin to form a nice tight package. Place the rabbit, seam side down, on a plate for at least 2 hours or even better, wrap it in plastic and refrigerate overnight.

TO COOK THE RABBIT LOINS: Preheat the oven to 350°F. Heat an ovenproof skillet or sauté pan large enough to accommodate the wrapped roast over medium heat. Add the oil and when it's hot, add the rabbit and cook until the prosciutto just begins to color. Using tongs, turn the roast as needed and cook for 5 to 6 minutes total, or until golden on all sides. Put the pan into the oven for 6 minutes. Remove the rabbit from the oven, transfer to a cutting board, and let rest for at least 5 minutes. Start cooking the rabbit legs when you put the rabbit loins into the oven, so they're ready to serve at the same time.

TO COOK THE RABBIT LEGS: Have a baking sheet lined with paper towels ready nearby. Pour oil to a depth of $\frac{1}{8}$ inch into a large skillet or sauté pan and heat over medium heat. When the oil begins to shimmer, add the rabbit. Do not crowd the pan; the legs should not be touching. Cook, turning once, for 6 to 8 minutes total, or until golden brown on both sides, reducing the heat if the crust begins to burn. Transfer the legs to the paper towels to drain. These are best served right away because the crust will soften and separate from the meat as they cool.

FOR THE FAVA BEANS AND PEAS: When the rabbit legs are just about finished, lightly whisk 2 tablespoons of the olive oil with the balsamic vinegar in a small bowl. Heat the remaining 2 tablespoons olive oil in a sauté pan over medium-high heat until barely warm. Add the fava beans, peas, and a splash of water to help them heat through, then season with salt and pepper. Toss the vegetables until they're hot, then add the mint, chives, basil, and butter. Remove the pan from the heat when the butter has melted.

TO SERVE

Divide the rabbit legs among 4 warm dinner plates and place a spoonful of the vegetables next to the legs. Trim a tiny slice off the ends of the rabbit loin roast, slice it into 4 equal medallions, and lean a medallion against the vegetables on each plate. Drizzle the balsamic mixture around the medallions.

MEAT

FENNEL-ROASTED PORK TENDERLOIN AND PORCINI-PORK SAUSAGE WRAPPED IN PANCETTA

WHITE AND GREEN BEANS WITH GARLIC CONFIT, PORK-PORCINI JUS

SERVES 4

NATURAL PORK JUS

2 tablespoons grape seed oil

1 small onion, halved and sliced

Reserved pork tenderloin tail ends,
    cut into 1-inch pieces (see
    Kitchen and Shopping Notes)

2 ounces dried porcini mushrooms,
    soaked in hot water for
    15 minutes and drained

3 thyme sprigs

2 cloves garlic, lightly crushed

1 tablespoon sherry vinegar

¼ cup dry sherry

2 cups Dark Chicken Stock (see
    Basics, page 230)

2 tablespoons heavy cream

PAN-ROASTED PORK TENDERLOIN

2 pork tenderloins (¾ to 1½ pounds
    each), tail ends trimmed and
    reserved (see Kitchen and
    Shopping Notes)

1 teaspoon Fennel Rub (see Basics,
    page 231)

1 teaspoon Porcini Powder (see
    Basics, page 234)

Kosher salt and freshly ground
    black pepper

1 tablespoon olive oil

PORCINI-PORK SAUSAGE WRAPPED IN BACON

¾ pound Porcini-Pork Sausage
    (see Basics, page 233)

8 thin slices bacon or pancetta

2 tablespoons olive oil

1 cup French beans (*haricots verts*),
    ends trimmed, beans cut into
    1-inch lengths

Garlic Confit and Gigande Bean
    Fondue (see Basics, page 232)

Pork tenderloin makes an ideal small roast, although two of this cut's finer attributes—leanness and mild flavor—require a bit of culinary acumen. To balance the tenderloin's leanness, we like to serve it with rich homemade pork sausage patties wrapped in pancetta, and to give the tenderloin a little flavor boost, we coat it in an aromatic mixture of fennel pollen and porcini mushroom powder. Tender, creamy gigande beans and slender, sweet French beans make this a kind of sophisticated "pork and beans" dish with color and crunch.

KITCHEN AND SHOPPING NOTES

It's almost impossible—and actually silly—not to make a big batch of sausage, so here are a few suggestions for the 3 pounds of sausage you'll have left over. It can be stuffed into casings and frozen or made into what we call IQF (individually quick-frozen) patties. It's a wonderful basic recipe, which has served us well when added to a stuffing, pasta sauce, or braised or sautéed greens.

Try to choose tenderloins that have nearly identical weights so they will cook in the same amount of time. Natural pork will yield the most delicious results, but if you're buying conventional pork, check the package or ask your butcher if the pork has been "enhanced," which means it has had salt or water added to make it juicier. Injected pork has a slightly spongy texture and an odd flavor. Pork tenderloin is a great vehicle for flavor but needs to be liberally seasoned—don't be afraid to salt it generously. Trim off about 3 inches from the tail ends of the tenderloins, which gives you 2 pieces of meat with fairly equal diameters, ensuring they'll cook more evenly. Save the tails for the sauce.

METHOD

FOR THE PORK JUS: Heat the grape seed oil in a large saucepan over high heat. Add the onion and pork and cook for 5 to 7 minutes, or until golden brown. Add the mushrooms, thyme sprigs, and garlic and cook for 1 minute more, stirring a few times. Add the sherry vinegar, then the sherry and reduce to a syrup. Add the chicken stock and bring to a simmer, stirring to prevent the vegetables from sticking. Tip the pan slightly to one side so you can more easily skim off the impurities as they gather. Simmer for about 20 minutes, or until the sauce has reduced and thickened. Strain through a fine-mesh sieve into a smaller saucepan and skim again. Bring to a boil over medium-high heat and whisk in the cream. Skim and continue to cook for 5 minutes, testing several times for the right consistency. A bit of sauce spooned onto a small plate should slowly spread, rather than run. Conversely, an overreduced sauce will be bitter and its complex flavors diminished. Set the sauce aside and keep warm.

FOR THE SAUSAGE WRAPPED IN BACON: Form the sausage into 4 patties, each about 3 inches wide and ¾ inch thick. (We like to pack the sausage mixture into 3-inch round cutters or ring molds.) Wrap the circumference of the patties with the bacon slices. Cover and refrigerate for several hours or overnight.

FOR THE PORK TENDERLOIN: Preheat the oven to 400°F. Coat the tenderloins with the Porcini-Fennel Powder and season with salt and pepper. Heat the olive oil in a large ovenproof skillet or sauté pan over medium-high heat. Place the tenderloins in the pan with room between them. Cook for about 5 minutes, or until browned on all sides, then put the pan in the oven. Roast for 5 to 8 minutes, or until the temperature on an instant-read thermometer reads 140° to 145°F when inserted into the center of the roasts. Remove the pan from the oven and transfer the pork to a platter to rest for 5 to 10 minutes.

While the pork is resting, lower the oven temperature to 350°F. Heat a large ovenproof nonstick skillet over medium heat. Add the olive oil and, using tongs, first sear the sausages on the side where the bacon overlaps so it seals. Then turn the sausages to brown the bacon on all sides. Next, cook on the flat sides for about 2 minutes per side, or until golden. Put the pan in the oven for 6 minutes, or until the sausage is cooked through. (Make a small cut in the center of a sausage to see that no pink remains.)

TO SERVE

Blanch the French beans in a saucepan of boiling water until just tender and remove to a bowl of ice water. Drain and set aside. Heat the Garlic Confit and Gigande Bean Fondue in a skillet until warm. Mix in the French beans. Slice each tenderloin into 6 equal pieces. Place a spoonful of the beans and garlic confit in the center of each of 4 warm dinner plates. Place a sausage on top. Place 3 slightly overlapping slices of the tenderloin next to the beans, keeping everything in a tight compact area in the center of the plate. Drizzle the pork jus over the pork and sausage.

CIDER-BRINED BERKSHIRE PORK LOIN CHOP

BACON, POMEGRANATE, AND PISTACHIO RELISH, SHAVED BRUSSELS SPROUTS, AND CIDER JUS

SERVES 4

BRINED PORK CHOPS

3 cups hot (150°F) water
¼ cup kosher salt
½ cup packed brown sugar
1 cup apple cider
2 tablespoons crushed black
    peppercorns
2 tablespoons Dijon mustard
1 bunch thyme
1 tablespoon chopped fresh
    rosemary leaves
4 double-cut center loin
    Berkshire pork chops
    (10 to 12 ounces each)
Kosher salt and freshly ground
    black pepper
3 tablespoons olive oil

BRAISED BACON

½ pound slab bacon, cut into
    ¼-inch dice
½ cup water
2 tablespoons unsalted butter,
    melted

CIDER SAUCE

1 tablespoon olive oil
¼ cup sliced shallots
2 cloves garlic, sliced
½ cup apple cider
5 thyme sprigs
6 black peppercorns
Reserved liquid from braising bacon
½ cup Dark Chicken Stock (see
    Basics, page 230)

POMEGRANATE RELISH

2 tablespoons pistachio oil
2 tablespoons olive oil
1 tablespoon balsamic vinegar
1 tablespoon pomegranate
    molasses (see Kitchen and
    Shopping Notes)
¼ cup pomegranate seeds (see
    Kitchen and Shopping Notes)
¼ cup finely diced (¼-inch) celery
Reserved braised bacon
¼ cup pistachios, toasted (see
    Basics, page 234)
Kosher salt and freshly ground
    black pepper

BRUSSELS SPROUTS

2 tablespoons olive oil
2 tablespoons minced shallots
1 pound Brussels sprouts, ends
    trimmed, outer leaves
    removed, and very thinly
    sliced on a mandoline
¼ to ½ cup water
4 tablespoons unsalted butter,
    cut into ½-inch pieces
Kosher salt and freshly ground
    black pepper

Our fondness for center-cut pork loin chops followed us from L'Avenue to Boulevard, but in our L'Avenue days the pork we were supplied was always lean, and the chops—even generously cut ones—were often dry. We weren't willing to give up on this wonderful cut of meat, so we began brining our chops to return some tenderness, moisture, and flavor. Over the last few years, marbled pork has made a comeback, thanks to Iowa Farms, organized by Bill Niman, and heritage breeds, such as Berkshire (also known as Kurobuta), that have become more widely available. Though these heritage breeds have made brining unnecessary, we still like the extra flavor that brining adds. Where we once brined our pork for up to 3 days, we've now shortened the brining time to 6 hours, which provides the meat with just a hint of sweetness and delivers a beautifully caramelized chop. This pork chop may be as close as we've ever come to a signature dish.

continued

Finding a source for Berkshire pork or other heritage breeds can be a challenge, but once you've tasted the meltingly tender and flavorful pork of decades past, you'll want to bug you local butcher to make it readily available. Ask your butcher what kind of pork he sells and where it comes from. Believe it or not, this is how positive change happens in the food-supply chain. How do you think mesclun mixes, mâche, and arugula ended up next to the iceberg lettuce in almost every grocery store in America?

Texture plays a really important role in any dish. In the relish, the jewel-like seeds of the pomegranate are visually appealing, but they're really there to provide a crunchy sweetness that complements the pork. To get the amount of pomegranate seeds required for this recipe: Cut the pomegranate crosswise in half. Hold one of the halves over a bowl with the cut side facing the bowl. Bang the fruit with the back of a wooden spoon, which should release most of the seeds almost entirely intact. We can't recommend any substitutes for fresh pomegranate seeds, except maybe Champagne grapes, or their dry version, Zante currants. If you omit, them you'll end up with a tasty, though less visually appealing relish.

Pomegranate molasses is made by reducing pomegranate juice to a syrup and is widely available in Middle Eastern markets or by mail order (see Sources, page 237).

Brussels sprouts is another vegetable we look forward to seeing every fall, and we serve them with meat, poultry, and fish, but they are really wonderful with pork. Our favorite preparation is Brussels sprouts shaved thinly on a mandoline, sautéed in a little olive oil until crisp-tender, and liberally seasoned with salt and pepper.

METHOD

TO BRINE THE PORK CHOPS: Combine the water, salt, and brown sugar in a large bowl or glass measuring cup, stirring until the salt and sugar dissolve. Add the cider, peppercorns, mustard, thyme sprigs, and rosemary. Refrigerate the brine until cold, then put the chops in a large zippered bag and pour the brine over. Seal the bag, pressing out as much air as possible. Place the bag in a bowl (just in case it leaks), or just place the brine in a bowl and add the pork chops. Let the chops brine in the refrigerator for 4 to 6 hours.

FOR THE BACON: Preheat the oven to 325°F. Spread the bacon out in a small rimmed baking sheet or baking dish. Add the water and butter to the pan, place in the oven, and braise, stirring often, for 20 to 30 minutes, or until the bacon is slightly rendered and soft. Using a slotted spoon, transfer the bacon to a plate and strain any liquid in the pan through a fine-mesh sieve into a small bowl. Reserve the braising liquid for the sauce and the bacon for the relish. The bacon and the braising liquid can be refrigerated for up to 2 days.

FOR THE CIDER SAUCE: Heat the olive oil in a saucepan over medium heat. Add the shallots and garlic and cook for about 5 minutes, or until golden. Add the cider and simmer until almost all of the liquid has evaporated. Add the thyme sprigs, peppercorns, reserved bacon liquid, and chicken stock and simmer for 20 to 30 minutes, skimming several times to remove impurities and ensure a clear sauce. When the liquid has reduced and thickened, strain it through a fine-mesh sieve into a small saucepan or container. Refrigerate for up to 2 days and rewarm before serving.

FOR THE POMEGRANATE RELISH: Whisk the pistachio oil, olive oil, balsamic vinegar, and pomegranate molasses together in a small bowl until blended. Stir in the pomegranate seeds and celery. The relish can be made up to 1 hour ahead to this point, but the reserved bacon and pistachios should be added right before serving.

TO COOK THE PORK CHOPS: Preheat the oven to 375°F. Remove the pork chops from the brine, wipe off the herbs, and pat the chops dry with paper towels. Season the chops lightly with salt and pepper (they will pick up salt from the brine). Heat the olive oil in a large ovenproof skillet or sauté pan over medium heat until the oil shimmers. Add the pork chops and cook for 2 to 3 minutes, or until golden. Turn the chops over and cook for another minute or so. (Don't be too aggressive with the heat because brining quickens the browning process and the chops will burn if the heat is too high.) Put the pan into the oven for 10 to 15 minutes, or until the temperature on an instant-read thermometer reads 140° to 150°F. Let rest for 5 to 10 minutes, during which time the internal temperature of the pork will rise 5°F. You want the final temperature to be no more than 155°F; there will be just a hint of pink in the pork.

FOR THE BRUSSELS SPROUTS: Heat the olive oil in a sauté pan over medium-high heat until it shimmers. Add the shallots and Brussels sprouts and cook, stirring occasionally, for 3 minutes. Add ¼ cup of the water and the butter and cook for about 5 minutes, or until most of the liquid has evaporated and the Brussels sprouts are tender but haven't lost their bright color, adding another ¼ cup water if necessary. Season to taste with salt and pepper.

TO SERVE

Meanwhile, to finish the relish, warm the bacon in a small skillet and stir into the pomegranate relish along with the pistachios. Place equal portions of the Brussels sprouts on each of 4 warm dinner plates and top with a pork chop. Spoon the sauce over the chops and around the plates. Finish with a generous plop of relish on top of the pork.

LAMB PORTERHOUSE CHOP STUFFED WITH BROCCOLI RABE AND MELTED GARLIC

POTATO "RISOTTO"

SERVES 6

LAMB STUFFING

2 bunches broccoli rabe (rapini)

¼ cup peeled cloves garlic

⅓ cup olive oil

½ cup panko (Japanese bread crumbs)

Leaves from 1 bunch flat-leaf parsley

½ cup mascarpone or cream cheese

1 teaspoon finely grated lemon zest

Kosher salt and freshly ground pepper

POTATO "RISOTTO"

1 pound Yukon Gold potatoes (about 4 medium)

2 cups heavy cream

2 tablespoons unsalted butter

1 onion, finely diced (about 1 cup)

Kosher salt and freshly ground black pepper

LAMB

6 porterhouse lamb chops, each 2 inches thick

Kosher salt and freshly ground black pepper

Reserved lamb stuffing

2 tablespoons olive oil

MEAT JUS

2 tablespoons olive oil

1 onion, coarsely chopped (about 1 cup)

5 cloves garlic, lightly crushed

½ cup dry white wine

1 cup Dark Chicken Stock (see Basics, page 230)

3 thyme sprigs

Kosher salt and freshly ground black pepper

We adore this little lamb roast. Double-cut lamb porterhouse chops, stuffed with savory dark greens and cooked to rosy pink perfection, is a very satisfying combination, especially when paired with the decadently creamy potato "risotto."

We must pause here in reverence and credit the amazingly creative Michel Richard for potato "risotto." It's a wonderful twist on risotto, where tiny cubes of potato are soaked in cream and cooked using some of the same techniques as you would use for a classic risotto. Over the years this dish has evolved, and we are not sure Michel would even recognize this version of his recipe, but we consider it a tribute to his playful genius.

continued

KITCHEN AND SHOPPING NOTES

To stuff these little roasts, you must have the true porterhouse chop: a nice large loin side with a prominent, not skimpy, fillet side. You will most likely have to ask your butcher to get these cut extra-thick (2 inches) for you (see Sources, page 236).

We use the very common restaurant technique of first cooking the meat on top of the stove to brown it and then putting it into the oven to finish cooking. But in this recipe, instead of keeping the chops flat in the pan the usual way, the chops are placed so they "stand up" on their T-bones. This allows the air to circulate around them with the bones serving like little racks. The chops also cook more evenly and aren't overbrowned on one side or the other.

Broccoli rabe is a favorite of ours because of its peppery green leaves and sweet little meaty broccoli-like florets. But there are other dark greens that will work as well if broccoli rabe isn't unavailable. Consider one of the dark green kales or Swiss chard; we have even been known to combine large leafy spinach together with broccoli, which we cook until very tender.

METHOD

FOR THE LAMB STUFFING: Strip the leaves from the stems of the broccoli rabe, cut off the florets, and set aside. Cook the stems in a saucepan of boiling water until tender, then drain and immerse in a bowl of ice water. Drain again, squeeze tightly to remove as much water from the stems as possible, and roughly chop. Put the garlic in a small microwave-safe container and add the olive oil. Microwave on HIGH for 2 minutes, or until the garlic cloves are soft when pierced with the tip of a small knife. Drain the garlic into a sieve, reserving the garlic-flavored oil for another use. Put the panko and parsley leaves in a food processor fitted with the metal blade and pulse until the crumbs turn green. Scrape the mixture into a bowl and set aside. Put the reserved broccoli rabe leaves and florets into the food processor along with the chopped stems (no need to clean the food processor bowl). Process until the greens are pureed, then add the mascarpone and pulse several times, just until combined. Add the rapini-mascarpone mixture, lemon zest, and garlic to the panko mixture and stir well to combine. Season to taste with salt and pepper. Set aside or refrigerate for up to 2 days

FOR THE POTATO "RISOTTO": With a sharp chef's knife or mandoline, cut the potatoes into uniform $\frac{1}{8}$-inch-thick slices. Stack the slices, several at a time, cut into $\frac{1}{8}$-inch-thick julienne strips, and then into $\frac{1}{8}$-inch dice. As you cut each stack of potatoes, immerse them in the cream in a bowl. When all the potatoes are cut, cover the bowl and set aside for at least 2 hours or refrigerate overnight. Melt the butter in a large saucepan over medium heat. Add the onion and cook until soft and translucent, about 6 minutes. Drain the potatoes through a fine-mesh sieve placed over a bowl, reserving the cream. Add the potatoes to the onion in the saucepan and pour in enough of the reserved cream to cover and separate the potatoes. Heat the cream almost to a boil, then reduce the heat to very low. Slowly simmer the potatoes in the cream, stirring frequently, for about 10 minutes, or until the potatoes yield to the bite but still keep their shape. Remove from the heat, season with salt and pepper, and set aside for up to 2 hours. Reheat before serving, either over low heat on top of the stove or in a microwave in a microwave-safe container.

TO STUFF AND COOK THE LAMB: Preheat the oven to 375°F. With a boning knife, separate the meat from both sides of the T-bone of a chop, leaving the meat attached at the top of the T. Season the meat all over with salt and pepper. Firmly press about ¼ cup of stuffing onto each side of the bone and then replace the meat. Wrap kitchen twine around the perimeter of the chop, circling it twice, and tie securely. Repeat with the remaining chops and stuffing.

Heat a large ovenproof sauté pan over high heat. Add the oil, heat for a few seconds, and add the lamb chops. Using tongs, turn the chops to brown them on all sides, beginning with the fatty edges. Transfer the chops to a plate and discard the fat in the pan. Return the chops to the pan and stand them up on their T-bones (so the meat is not touching the pan). Put the pan into the oven and roast the chops for 15 minutes, or until the temperature on an instant-read thermometer reaches 130°F (for medium-rare). Remove from the oven, cover with a clean kitchen towel, and let rest for at least 15 minutes before serving.

FOR THE MEAT JUS: While the chops are in the oven, heat the olive oil in a saucepan over medium heat. Add the onion and garlic and cook, stirring, for about 8 minutes, or until golden brown. Add the white wine, increase the heat, and cook for about 5 minutes, or until the liquid has thickened and is almost syrupy. Add the chicken stock and thyme. Simmer for about 15 minutes, or until the jus coats the back of a spoon. Add any accumulated lamb juices to the jus before serving.

TO SERVE

Cut the strings from the lamb chops. Reheat the potato risotto if necessary and place a scoop of it in the center of each of 6 warm dinner plates. Nestle a lamb chop into the risotto and then spoon the jus around the edges.

VEAL CHOPS STUFFED WITH PORCINI MUSHROOMS AND ASIAGO CHEESE

ROASTED FINGERLING POTATOES, TOMATOES, SAGE, PANCETTA, AND ARUGULA

SERVES 4

STUFFED VEAL CHOPS

8 fresh porcini mushrooms (about
⅓ pound)

4 tablespoons olive oil

4 tablespoons unsalted butter

10 fresh whole sage leaves

1 (6- to 8-ounce) piece Asiago or
Montasio cheese

4 bone-in center-cut veal rib chops
(about 10 ounces each),
bones frenched

Kosher salt and freshly ground
black pepper

½ cup dry sherry, vermouth, or
dry white wine

1 cup Dark Chicken Stock (see
Basics, page 230)

ROASTED FINGERLING POTATOES

8 medium fingerling potatoes
(2½ to 3 inches long)

4 cloves garlic, thinly sliced

4 small sage leaves

⅓ cup Light Chicken Stock (see
Basics, page 230)

¼ cup heavy cream

3 tablespoons olive oil

Kosher salt and freshly ground
black pepper

4 Roma tomatoes, peeled, halved,
and seeded

4 (⅛-inch-thick) slices pancetta

3 cups arugula

Extra-virgin olive oil

Aged balsamic vinegar

Kosher salt and freshly ground
black pepper

Big, thick, juicy veal chops are an extravagance these days, and we've added to the bill by stuffing the chops with fresh porcini, our favorite mushrooms. The combination of these two ingredients plus the molten Asiago cheese makes an exquisite mouthful worth taking out a loan for. In combination with all of the other ingredients, the fingerling potatoes become a rustic yet luxurious accompaniment to the veal chops. The cream turns them bubbly brown, the pancetta and sage impart meaty and earthy flavors, and the roasted Roma tomatoes add a splash of bright color and just the right touch of acidity.

KITCHEN AND SHOPPING NOTES

Today there are often two choices at the market or butcher shop when it comes to veal, milk-fed or grass-fed, and there is a noticeable difference between the two. Milk-fed is more tender and succulent, and grass-fed is more full flavored and deeply colored. The choice comes down to personal preference, so we encourage you to seek out and try both kinds. What's really important in this recipe is the thickness of the chops. Ask for chops that are at least 1½ to 2 inches thick. Any thinner and you won't be able to stuff them, and they'll dry out and become tough when they're roasted in the oven after sautéing. The final step of basting the chops with butter and sage is another technique we like to use to layer on more flavor. Be sure to let the chops rest before serving to allow the juices to be reabsorbed into the meat; an essential step when cooking any large chop or roast.

Fingerling potatoes come in numerous varieties, from yellow to purple fleshed, from waxy to dry. At the restaurant, we often use French or banana fingerlings, or occasionally we walk on the wild side and use huckleberry or all-red potatoes. For this recipe, any waxy potato will do but, again, the thickness is important. You're layering several different ingredients together and you want them all to finish cooking at the same time.

METHOD

TO STUFF THE VEAL CHOPS: Cut off the porcini stems and halve them lengthwise. Heat 1 tablespoon of the olive oil with 1 tablespoon of the butter in a large skillet over high heat until the butter melts and the foam begins to subside. Add the porcini caps and stems and sauté for 2 minutes. Add 8 of the sage leaves and cook for 2 minutes more. Remove from the heat, let cool, then cover and refrigerate for about 30 minutes, or until the mushrooms and sage leaves are well chilled. Cut the piece of cheese into $\frac{1}{4}$-inch-thick slices about the same size as the mushrooms. Top 4 of the mushrooms with 1 or 2 slices of cheese (to cover the mushroom) and 2 sage leaves. Top with the remaining 4 mushrooms to form a "sandwich."

Using a small, sharp paring knife, make a small incision into a veal chop where the meat meets the rib bone "handle." Carefully work the knife into the center of the chop to make a pocket, taking care not to cut through the sides of the chop. Insert a mushroom sandwich into the pocket and press the meat to enclose it. Secure the pocket opening with a toothpick. Repeat with the other chops. Set aside or cover with plastic wrap and refrigerate for up to 8 hours.

FOR THE FINGERLING POTATOES: Preheat the oven to 375°F. Slice $\frac{1}{8}$ inch off 2 opposite long sides of the potatoes to expose the flesh and give them a flat surface. Toss the potatoes with the garlic, sage, chicken stock, cream, and olive oil in a large bowl. Season with salt and pepper. Spread the potatoes, along with the cream mixture, cut side down and in a single layer, on a rimmed baking sheet or in a shallow roasting pan and nestle the tomatoes in between the potatoes. Lay the pancetta slices across the top. Roast for 15 minutes. Using a spatula, turn over anything that looks dry and roast for another 8 to 10 minutes, or until tender. Remove from the oven and set aside. The potatoes can be made up to an hour ahead and reheated in a 375°F oven for 5 minutes before serving.

TO COOK THE VEAL CHOPS: Increase the oven temperature to 400°F. Heat the remaining 3 tablespoons olive oil in a large ovenproof skillet or sauté pan over medium-high heat. Season the chops with salt and pepper and place in the pan. Cook for 2 to 3 minutes per side, or until golden, then, using tongs, hold the chops upright to brown the fatty edges. Put into the oven and roast for 12 to 15 minutes, or until the meat is still slightly pink when cut into near the bone and the temperature reads 130°F on an instant-read thermometer. About 2 minutes before you think the chops are done, add 1 tablespoon of the butter and the 2 sage leaves to the pan. Return the pan to the oven and when the chops are done baste them with the melted sage-butter mixture. Transfer the chops to a platter and pour out any fat and the sage leaves. Set the pan over medium-high heat, add the sherry, and reduce by two-thirds. Add the chicken stock and reduce again by half. Add the remaining 2 tablespoons butter, whisking until melted and smooth.

TO SERVE

Arrange the potatoes in the center of 4 warm dinner plates. Top with a veal chop, and drizzle with a little of the pan sauce. Toss the arugula with a little olive oil and vinegar and mound on the chops. Season to taste with salt and pepper.

For us, one of the great pleasures of dining out is finding a dish on a menu that we would never, ever think of preparing at home.

VEAL, VEAL, VEAL

ROASTED TENDERLOIN, VEAL OSSO BUCO, AND VEAL CHEEK RAVIOLI

SERVES 6

**BRAISED VEAL CHEEKS
AND VEAL OSSO BUCO**

6 (2- to 3-ounce) veal cheeks

6 Bobby veal shanks (see Kitchen
and Shopping Notes)

Kosher salt and freshly ground
black pepper

4 tablespoons olive oil

1 small onion, finely diced

1 carrot, peeled and finely diced

1 celery rib, finely diced

1 tablespoon tomato paste

1 bay leaf

2 flat-leaf parsley sprigs

1 thyme sprig

2 cups dry white wine

4 cups Dark Chicken Stock (see
Basics, page 230)

½ head garlic (cut crosswise), root
end trimmed and loose papery
outer skin removed

VEAL TENDERLOIN

1 whole veal tenderloin (1½ pounds)

Kosher salt and freshly ground
black pepper

12 thin slices pancetta

**LEMON AND
PARMESAN RELISH**

¼ cup lemon segments (see Kitchen
and Shopping Notes, page 70)

¼ cup (⅛-inch) diced Parmigiano-
Reggiano Cheese

1 teaspoon finely chopped shallots

¼ cup pine nuts, toasted (see
Basics, page 234)

1 teaspoon chopped fresh
flat-leaf parsley

VEAL CHEEK RAVIOLI

Braised veal cheeks

1 recipe Pasta Dough (see Basics,
page 233)

¼ cup Creamed Spinach (see
Basics, page 229)

2 tablespoons olive oil

¾ cup Beurre Fondue (see Basics,
page 228)

For us, one of the great pleasures of dining out is finding a dish on a menu that we would never, ever think of preparing at home. Assembling all of the ingredients, strategizing advance prep, cooking each dish, and then having everything ready to plate at the same time can take away your will to live, or maybe just your will to eat. Veal, Veal, Veal is just that sort of dish; three different—and somewhat complicated—preparations of veal, each with its own unique flavor, texture, and cooking technique.

The ravioli is so spectacular it's often found as a starter on our menu. Osso buco occupies a niche in the comfort food zone. Our method for this succulent braise is classic but the diminutive size of the veal shank and the perky lemon and Parmesan relish makes this dish special. As for the last part of the trio, the veal fillet is all about tenderness, but since tender doesn't always translate into flavor, pancetta slices wrapped around the veal tenderloin comes to the rescue of this very lean meat.

Although it may be the culinary equivalent of a graduate thesis, this is the kind of plate we love to serve at the restaurant. But fortunately for the home cook, while all three recipes combine beautifully, individually they command the center of any plate.

KITCHEN AND SHOPPING NOTES

In order to serve all three veal dishes on one plate, it's important that each preparation is less than entrée size. For the veal osso buco, we use the shanks of what's called Bobby veal: cut from very young animals, which have smaller bones and make perfect little servings. Although Bobby veal is available by mail order (see Sources, page 236) or can be special ordered through butchers, as a substitute, you could use front-leg shanks, or serve just a few pieces from one or two large hind shanks. One time-saving step in the recipe is that the veal shanks and cheeks can be braised at the same time in the same liquid.

Our pasta dough recipe makes more than you'll need for the ravioli. We suggest you divide the dough in half, roll out one-half for the ravioli squares, and then roll out the other half and cut it into fettuccine. Keep the fettuccine for up to 2 days in the refrigerator and use for another meal. You'll also only need ¼ cup creamed spinach and our recipe in Basics makes 2¼ cups. You can quarter the Basics recipe.

METHOD

FOR THE VEAL CHEEKS AND SHANKS: Preheat the oven to 350°F. Trim the veal cheeks of any tough excess connective tissue and season the veal cheeks and shanks with salt and pepper. In a casserole dish that can hold the veal shanks and cheeks snugly, heat 2 tablespoons of the olive oil over medium-high heat. Using tongs to turn them, cook the shanks for 7 to 10 minutes, or until golden brown on all sides, then transfer to a plate and set aside. Add the veal cheeks to the pan and brown on both sides, for 6 to 8 minutes, decreasing the heat if necessary to prevent scorching. Transfer the cheeks to the plate with the shanks.

Pour off and discard the fat from the casserole and add the remaining 2 tablespoons olive oil. Add the onion, carrot, celery, and tomato paste and sauté for about 6 minutes, or until softened and just beginning to color. Add the bay leaf and parsley and thyme sprigs and cook for 2 minutes more. Add the wine, increase the heat to high, and reduce the liquid by half. Add the chicken stock and garlic and bring to a simmer. Return the shanks and cheeks (plus any accumulated juices) to the casserole. Cover and bake, turning the shanks and cheeks over once, for 1 to 1½ hours, or until very tender when pierced with a fork.

Remove the casserole from the oven. Carefully lift the meat out and place on a plate. Strain the pan liquid through a fine-mesh sieve into a large bowl. Discard the vegetables and skim off any fat. Add the shanks and cheeks to the liquid in the bowl, cover loosely, and refrigerate overnight.

FOR THE VEAL TENDERLOIN: Liberally season the veal with salt and pepper. Lay the pancetta slices on a work surface with the long sides slightly overlapping. Place the tenderloin at one end of the pancetta and roll up. This can be done up to 6 hours in advance and refrigerated.

FOR THE LEMON AND PARMESAN RELISH: Cut the lemon segments in half crosswise and combine with the cheese and shallots in a bowl. (The pine nuts and parsley are stirred in just before serving, so the nuts stay crunchy and the parsley stays green.)

continued

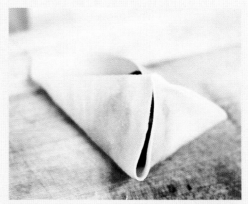

1	4
2	5
3	6

1   Place 1 heaping tablespoon of creamed spinach in the center of the pasta square and top with a veal cheek

2   Trim the veal cheek to fit the ravioli if necessary

3   Bring the 4 corners up and over the filling

4   Form a pyramid

5   Tightly press together all the edges to form a tight seal

6   To make a decorative edge, trim the edges with pinking shears or a scalloped pasta cutter

making the ravioli

<

FOR THE RAVIOLI: Remove the veal cheeks from the braising liquid and set aside. Measure out ½ cup of the braising liquid and pour into a small sauté pan. Return the shanks and the remaining braising liquid to the refrigerator. Reduce the ½ cup liquid by two-thirds, until almost a syrup. Add the veal cheeks and turn in the liquid several times to glaze them. Set aside to cool.

Divide the pasta dough in half. Wrap one of the pieces in plastic and save it for another time (see Kitchen and Shopping Notes). With a pasta machine set on its widest roller setting, run the dough through once. Fold the dough crosswise into thirds and run through once more. Continue feeding the dough through the rollers, decreasing the setting on each pass, until you get to the next to thinnest (number 2) setting. Cut the dough into 6 (4½-inch) squares. Sprinkle each square with a little flour, then stack them and cover with a damp towel to keep them from drying out while you fill the ravioli.

To make the ravioli, place 1 heaping tablespoon of creamed spinach in the center of one of the pasta squares. Top with 1 veal cheek (trim the cheek to fit in the ravioli if necessary) and moisten the edges of the pasta square with water. Bring the 4 corners up and over the filling to form a pyramid. Tightly press all the edges together to form a tight seal. Lay the ravioli on its side and, using a scalloped pasta cutter, trim the edges, turning the ravioli as needed, to create a decorative finish. Place the ravioli on a baking sheet dusted with flour and make the rest of the ravioli with the remaining pasta squares and veal cheeks. Refrigerate the ravioli for up to 6 hours before cooking.

TO SERVE

About 1 hour before you want to serve the dish: Preheat the oven to 350°F. Remove any solid fat from the top of the cold braising liquid. Transfer the shanks and the braising liquid to an ovenproof dish. Cover and bake, turning the shanks occasionally, for 30 to 45 minutes, or until heated through. Transfer the shanks from the braising liquid to a plate or cutting board. Pour the braising liquid through a fine-mesh sieve into a small saucepan. Return the shanks to the baking dish, spoon some of the braising juices over the shanks, and keep warm in the oven. Bring the remaining braising liquid to a simmer. Reduce the liquid by half and keep warm.

Meanwhile, bring a large pot of generously salted water to a boil for the ravioli. While the water heats, heat the 2 tablespoons olive oil in an ovenproof sauté pan over medium heat. Add the veal tenderloin to the hot oil and brown on all sides. Put into the oven for 10 to 15 minutes, or until an instant-read thermometer inserted into the center of the roast reads 125° to 130°F. Let the roast rest for 5 to 10 minutes while you cook the ravioli.

Have the Beurre Fondue warming in a small skillet over low heat. With a slotted spoon, gently lower the ravioli, one at a time, into the boiling water and cook for about 3 minutes, or until tender with a little "tooth." Using the slotted spoon, carefully transfer the ravioli to the warm Beurre Fondue.

Place 2 generous slices of veal tenderloin on each of 6 warm dinner plates. Nestle a ravioli and veal shank next to the tenderloin. Spoon some braising liquid over everything and top the veal tenderloin and shank with some relish. (Any leftover braising liquid can be frozen for later use.)

FIRE-ROASTED ANGUS BEEF FILET

SWEET WHITE CORN AND CHANTERELLES, BLUE CHEESE FRITTERS, HEIRLOOM TOMATOES

SERVES 4

WHITE CORN AND CHANTERELLES

½ pound fresh chanterelle
    mushrooms

2 tablespoons olive oil

2 tablespoons unsalted butter

1½ cups sweet white corn kernels
    (from 3 small or 2 medium
    ears corn)

1 teaspoon chopped fresh
    thyme leaves

Kosher salt and freshly ground
    black pepper

BLUE CHEESE FRITTERS

¾ cup cake flour

3 tablespoons cornstarch

2 teaspoons baking powder

1 cup beer

Kosher salt and freshly ground
    black pepper

5 ounces Fourme d'Ambert,
    Cambozola or other firm
    blue cheese or double-
    cream cheese

2 cups canola oil, for frying

ROASTED-TOMATO BEEF JUS

2 tablespoons olive oil

¼ cup sliced shallots

2 cloves garlic, sliced

4 Oven-Roasted Tomatoes (see
    Basics, page 232), cut into
    large pieces

½ cup dry red wine

2 cups Rich Beef Stock (see
    Basics, page 231)

2 tablespoons unsalted butter

Kosher salt and freshly ground
    black pepper

HEIRLOOM TOMATOES

8 large heirloom tomatoes (any color)

Best-quality extra-virgin olive oil,
    for drizzling

Kosher salt and freshly ground
    black pepper

BEEF FILET

2 tablespoons olive oil

4 (6- to 8-ounce) Angus beef filets

Kosher salt and freshly ground
    black pepper

HERB SALAD

1 cup mixed fresh herbs, such as
    flat-leaf parsley, chives, basil,
    tarragon, thyme, celery leaves,
    and chervil

¼ cup extra virgin olive oil

1 tablespoon Champagne vinegar

Fire-roasted filet mignon is without a doubt our most popular main course, which is a little disappointing to us because, frankly, filet mignon is boring. We prefer the more flavorful but less tender cuts like bavette, New York strip, and rib eye. When we do put more challenging cuts of beef on the menu, after a few disappointments we return to the steadfast and true Angus filet mignon because, to some extent, tenderness has taken precedence over taste, following the theory that if you can "cut it with a fork," it must be the best. While not in full agreement, we have to admit that when we tested this recipe, we found that the Angus filet was tender as well as irresistibly delicious when generously seasoned and flavored by the grill.

We especially liked cutting into the blue cheese fritters and allowing their warm, gooey centers to flow over the filet, making the dish truly divine. The cubes of heirloom tomatoes, with their bold colors and acidic flavors, complement one of our favorite combinations: sweet white corn with fresh chanterelle mushrooms. This is a perfect dish for summer when tomatoes are at their peak, corn is at its sweetest, and cooking outdoors seems like the natural thing to do.

continued

KITCHEN AND SHOPPING NOTES

Beef from the Black Angus breed is known for its marbling, rich flavor, and tenderness. Look for the Certified Black Angus (CAB) label or check with your butcher to assure its quality. While all CAB beef is superior, we also like to buy natural Angus beef, which is raised humanely without antibiotics or supplemental hormones (see Sources, page xxx).

The tomatoes for this dish are cut into large cubes, and while they make a dramatic presentation, you end up with quite a bit of waste. So save the tomato trimmings for salads, or freeze them and use to flavor soups and sauces.

In terms of the timing for this dish, heat the oil for the fritters and prepare your grill for the beef. You can either cook the meat first and then fry the fritters, or do them simultaneously (or, better yet, enlist the help of a "grill chef"). The fritters will stay hot for at least 10 minutes while you plate the food.

METHOD

FOR THE CORN AND CHANTERELLES: Wipe the chanterelles clean with a damp kitchen towel and trim off the very bottom of the stems. Peel the stems, then cut the mushrooms lengthwise into $\frac{1}{4}$-inch-thick slices. Heat the olive oil in a saucepan over medium heat. Add the chanterelles and sauté for 3 to 4 minutes, or until they soften and begin to brown lightly around the edges. Decrease the heat to medium-low and add the butter. When the butter has melted, add the corn and cook, stirring a few times, for 4 to 5 minutes, or until the corn is just tender but still has a little crunch. Add the thyme and season to taste with salt and pepper. Set aside for up to 4 hours.

FOR THE FRITTERS: Whisk the flour, cornstarch, and baking powder together in a small bowl. Gently stir in the beer until just mixed and slightly lumpy. Season with a pinch each of salt and pepper. Divide the cheese into 4 pieces and shape into balls. Refrigerate the fritter batter and the cheese separately for up to 4 hours before frying.

FOR THE TOMATO BEEF JUS: Heat the olive oil in a saucepan over medium heat. Add the shallots and garlic and cook for about 5 minutes, or until lightly golden. Add the tomatoes and cook for about 5 minutes, or until they begin to caramelize. Add the red wine, increase the heat, and reduce until the liquid has almost evaporated. Add the beef stock and bring to a simmer. Decrease the heat to maintain a low simmer and cook, skimming frequently, for 20 to 30 minutes, or until reduced by two-thirds. Strain through a fine-mesh sieve, and whisk in the butter until melted and smooth. Season to taste with salt and pepper and set aside for up to 1 hour. Or, refrigerate for up to 2 days, whisking in the butter just before serving.

FOR THE HEIRLOOM TOMATOES: Cut the tomatoes into large cubes, 1½ to 2 inches square. If the tomatoes are large you may be able to get 2 cubes per tomato. Drizzle with a little olive oil, sprinkle with salt and pepper, and set aside for up to 1 hour.

TO COOK THE BEEF FILETS AND FRITTERS: Heat the canola oil in a large saucepan or deep fryer to 350°F on a deep-fry thermometer. Line a plate with paper towels. Prepare a barbecue for direct-heat grilling, or if you're cooking the beef indoors, preheat the oven to 400°F. Rub both sides of the filets with olive oil and season liberally with salt and pepper. Oil the grill, then sear the filets on both sides. Cook until the temperature reaches 125° to 130°F (medium-rare) on an instant-read thermometer. Alternatively, cook the beef in a lightly oiled hot skillet or sauté pan until browned on both sides and finish the cooking in the oven for about 5 minutes, or until the desired temperature is reached. Let rest for 5 minutes before serving.

While the meat is cooking fry the fritters: Dip the cheese into the batter until coated and carefully lower the fritters, 3 or 4 at a time, into the hot oil. Cook for about 2 minutes, turning with a slotted spoon so they cook evenly on all sides, then with the spoon transfer to the paper towels to drain.

TO SERVE

Warm the corn-chanterelle mixture and the beef jus. Make the herb salad by lightly dressing the herbs with olive oil and vinegar. Place a spoonful of the vegetables off to one side of each of 4 warm dinner plates. Arrange 3 or 4 of the tomato cubes next to the corn mixture, and if the tomatoes haven't been seasoned, drizzle them with olive oil and sprinkle with salt and pepper. Place a filet on top of the corn mixture, and top with a fritter. Heap a mound of herb salad over the tomatoes and fritter.

NEW YORK STRIP ROASTED IN AN HERBED SALT CRUST

CREAMED MORELS WITH AGED MADEIRA ON TOAST

SERVES 16

HERBED SALT CRUST

4 cups kosher or coarse sea salt

2 cups water

2 large egg whites

¼ cup chopped garlic

¼ cup chopped fresh thyme leaves

2 tablespoons chopped fresh
    flat-leaf parsley leaves

1½ tablespoons chopped fresh
    rosemary leaves

2 tablespoons freshly ground
    black pepper

5 to 6 cups all-purpose flour

CREAMED MORELS

6 ounces small dried morel
    mushrooms, or 2 pounds
    small fresh morels (see Kitchen
    and Shopping Notes)

3 tablespoons unsalted butter

6 tablespoons minced shallots

2 cups aged dry Marsala wine

4 cups heavy cream

1 tablespoon chopped fresh
    thyme leaves

NEW YORK STRIP

1 whole New York strip (11 or
    12 pounds), cleaned of all sinew
    and trimmed (see Kitchen and
    Shopping Notes)

Kosher salt and freshly ground
    black pepper

¼ cup olive oil

1 large egg yolk

2 tablespoons water

16 (½-inch-thick) slices good-quality
    French bread or brioche

½ cup (1 stick) unsalted butter, at
    room temperature

Watercress sprigs or baby arugula,
    for garnish

Cooking in a salt crust is a time-honored technique in which meat, fish, or poultry is encased and roasted in a simple pastry made of flour, salt, and water. The crust, which acts like a vessel, is discarded; it simply serves to preserve moisture, ensure even cooking, and season the meat. In this recipe, the sea salt, thyme, and rosemary we've added to the basic flour-water mixture imparts flavor as well as aroma, and after roasting the crust is opened to reveal a perfectly cooked, top to bottom medium-rare, juicy New York strip.

This is a marvelous dish to prepare for entertaining, since most of the work is done ahead. The sight of this roast resting in its speckled brown crust along with the fantastic fresh herb aromas has everyone eagerly anticipating dinner. Try this recipe in the spring when morel mushrooms are in season along with the first-of-the-season asparagus. It's difficult to imagine anything better.

continued

1	4
2	5
3	6

1   Remove the sinew

2   Cut away the "chain"

3   The steak should be clear of all
    gnarly bits

4   Trim away the fat cap and fascia

5   Cut off the nerve end and save the
    triangle steak

6   Split the steak in half lengthwise

For this recipe you'll have to purchase a whole New York strip. A whole New York ranges in size from 11 to 14 pounds and will weigh about 6 to 8 pounds after you remove all the fat, silver skin, and sinew, and then trim it into a neat, uniform, and completely "nude" piece of meat (see photos, previous page). It may seem like a daunting project, but look at it as an excellent opportunity to hone your butchering skills.

We've written this recipe to serve 16 people, but the meat can easily be cut into smaller portions to serve fewer people by simply cutting off a few steaks from the vein or rump end before trimming the whole strip. To serve 16 to 18 people generously, you need to end up with 6 or 7 pounds of meat, 4 or 5 pounds for 12 people, and 2 or 3 pounds for 6 people; the serving size ultimately depending on the appetites of your guests. (You need to decrease the recipe for the crust as well for fewer servings.) The trimmings can be used to enrich a beef sauce and any nice pieces of leftover meat can be sliced or cubed to use in a stir-fry or sauté. We recommend that you clean and trim the New York a day ahead to give it plenty of time to rest and recuperate from the ordeal.

The surest way to ruin this dish is to remove the meat from the crust before it has finished resting. It's absolutely essential for the meat to rest in the crust for 30 minutes after its roasted so that the juices can be reabsorbed into the meat, making it tender and juicy. Also, make sure you remove the meat from the oven when it's rare, because it will continue to cook in the salt crust and come up to medium-rare during its rest. Make a salad—another perfect accompaniment—peel the asparagus, play charades, but above all be patient. Note that the salt crust needs to rest for at least 2 hours before wrapping the meat but can be held in the refrigerator for up to 24 hours.

If you're lucky enough to find fresh morels during the spring, by all means use them in place of the dried. Just follow the recipe, but omit soaking the morels and instead sauté them separately in olive oil and add them to the reduced sauce. When choosing fresh morels for this recipe, we prefer the fingertip size because they make for more pleasant eating and presentation. See Kitchen and Shoping Notes, page 100 for directions on cleaning them. (A better use for large morels is as impressive appetizers or side dishes, stuffed and baked with creamed spinach.)

METHOD

FOR THE SALT CRUST: Combine the salt, water, egg whites, garlic, thyme, parsley, rosemary, and pepper in the bowl of an electric mixer and beat on medium speed until well mixed. Mix in 5 cups of the flour until the dough is firm and feels slightly dry and stiff, like play dough, adding in additional flour if necessary. Continue to beat for 2 minutes. At this point the dough should be smooth and firm, but not sticky. Add in more flour if necessary. Divide the dough in half, shape each piece into a square, and wrap in plastic wrap. Refrigerate for at least 2 hours or up to overnight.

continued

FOR THE MORELS: Soak the dried morels in boiling water to cover in a small bowl for 30 minutes. Drain the mushrooms into a sieve placed over a small bowl. Strain the morel liquid through a coffee filter into a small saucepan, then reduce over high heat to ¼ cup. Melt 1 tablespoon of the butter in another small saucepan over medium heat. Add the shallots and cook for about 2 minutes, or until softened. Stir in the morels and Marsala and bring to simmer. Decrease the heat to low and cook for about 10 minutes, or until the Marsala has almost evaporated. Add the reduced morel liquid and the cream and cook for about 30 minutes, or until the sauce reduces enough to coat the mushrooms. The sauce should coat the back of a spoon. Whisk in the remaining 2 tablespoons butter until melted and smooth, add the thyme, and season with salt and pepper. Set aside.

FOR THE BEEF: Remove the dough from the refrigerator and bring to room temperature. With a knife held parallel to the work surface, cut the meat lengthwise in half. Pat the meat dry with paper towels and season liberally on all sides with salt and pepper. Heat the olive oil in a large skillet over medium-high heat and sear 1 of the pieces of meat for 2 to 3 minutes on each side. Repeat with the other piece of meat. Set aside to cool to room temperature.

Meanwhile, preheat the oven to 375°F and line a heavy rimmed baking sheet with parchment paper. Whisk the egg yolk and water together in a small bowl and set aside. Lightly dust the work surface with flour. Roll out 1 piece of the dough into a 14-by-18-inch rectangle and place one of the seared filets in the center. Carefully lift up the long sides of the dough to enclose the meat, overlapping the edges and pressing them together. Bring up the short ends and press them together to make a sealed package. Place seam side down on the prepared baking sheet. Brush the dough with the egg wash. Repeat with the remaining dough and piece of meat. Put the baking sheet in the oven and bake for 20 to 25 minutes, or until an instant-read thermometer inserted into the center of the filets reaches 120°F. Remove from the oven and let rest for 30 minutes. Leave the oven on.

About 10 minutes before serving, using a round cutter, cut the bread slices into 3- or 4-inch rounds. Spread both sides of each bread round with the softened butter, place the slices on a small baking sheet, and toast in the oven, turning once, until golden on both sides.

TO SERVE

Warm the creamed morels in a small saucepan over low heat. Remove the beef from the crusts and carve each filet into 8 generous slices. Place a toasted bread slice in the center of each of 16 warm dinner plates and nap with the creamed morels. Place a beef slice on top and moisten with a little more sauce. Garnish each with a clump of watercress.

"STEAMSHIP" SHORT RIBS BOURGUIGNON

SERVES 4

BEEF SHORT RIBS

4 pieces center-cut flanken-style
    beef chuck short ribs (about
    1 pound each)

Kosher salt and freshly ground
    black pepper

2 tablespoons olive oil

1 thick slice apple wood–smoked
    bacon, cut into ½-inch pieces

1 small onion, chopped

1 carrot, peeled and chopped

1 celery rib, chopped

8 button mushrooms, halved

4 unpeeled cloves garlic

4 flat-leaf parsley stems

4 to 6 thyme sprigs

1 bay leaf

¼ cup red wine vinegar

2 cups dry red wine

6 cups Dark Chicken Stock (see
    Basics, page 230)

4 tablespoons unsalted butter,
    cut into bits, for rewarming
    the short ribs

CARROT MOUSSELINE

4 cups diced (½-inch) carrots
    (about 10 carrots)

1 cup water

½ cup (1 stick) unsalted butter

2 teaspoons kosher salt

1 teaspoon sugar

Freshly ground black pepper

PEARL ONIONS

1 tablespoon olive oil

16 to 20 red or white pearl onions
    or 12 cipollini onions, peeled,
    root ends intact

¼ cup braising liquid

2 tablespoons unsalted butter

Kosher salt and freshly ground
    black pepper

BUTTON MUSHROOMS

2 tablespoons olive oil

12 to 16 small to medium button
    mushrooms

1 tablespoon unsalted butter

2 cloves garlic, crushed

1 thyme sprig

Kosher salt and freshly ground
    black pepper

2 tablespoons braising liquid

ROASTED GERMAN BUTTERBALLS

8 to 10 small German Butterball,
    Yukon Gold, or Yellow Finn
    potatoes, turned (2 to 3 ounces
    each, see Kitchen and
    Shopping Notes)

½ cup water

Kosher salt and freshly ground
    black pepper

1 tablespoon unsalted butter

GARNISH

Braised Bacon (see Basics, page
    228)

Coarse sea salt and freshly ground
    black pepper

Chervil sprigs, for garnish

There is no finer choice for braising than beef short ribs. This well-marbled cut becomes exquisitely tender when cooked slowly. It's also an absolute fact that meat cooked on the bone has the best flavor and produces a superior sauce. Our recipe employs the classical wisdom of slowly braising beef, along with mushrooms and herbs, in a big red wine. We use a large center-cut three-rib piece of meat for each serving, but to give this dish a slightly updated and sophisticated presentation, two of the bones and the tough connective tissue are removed. The meat is then wrapped and tied around the remaining bone, creating what we call the "steamship" effect. It's an unusual and dramatic way to serve the short ribs and makes eating them pure pleasure.

continued

Traditionally the side vegetables would be cooked with the meat in the braise, but here once the diced vegetables have flavored the braising juices, they are strained out. Instead, the side vegetables are cooked separately, but we use the braising sauce to flavor and glaze them. This extra step produces perfectly cooked vegetables that don't have to be fished out of the braise for serving.

There are several kinds of short ribs: chuck, plate, and rib, and each can be cut in three basic ways: English style, flanken style, or Hawaiian style. For this recipe, ask for ribs from the chuck and have them cut flanken style. Chuck ribs are usually the meatiest with the best ratio of fat and meat to bone.

The crucial step here, and in fact in all braising, is the browning or caramelizing of the meat, which is what gives braises their deep, rich flavor. It's important not to rush this step; all the surfaces of the meat need to be slowly browned over medium heat. If the temperature is too high the meat could burn, and any burned bits not discarded will turn the braising juices bitter. Also, overcrowding the ribs in the pan will steam rather than brown the meat, and you will be unable to achieve a nicely caramelized surface. Conversely, do not allow a thick crust to form on the meat; as appealing and tasty as this may seem, it will become a dull, tasteless coating after braising.

We like to salt the ribs (about $\frac{1}{2}$ teaspoon per pound) and refrigerate them for at least 3 hours or up to a day ahead, then let them come to room temperature for an hour before cooking so they cook more evenly. (All meats cook more evenly if they start out at room temperature.) When it comes to browning, it's important to use medium heat.

The real key to successful braising is low, slow cooking, the only path to ideally tender, succulent meat. Many cooks assume that cooking in liquid automatically ensures the meat will be moist, but braising at too high a temperature or for too long results in dry, stringy meat. Cook the short ribs gently and for only as long as it takes for them to become fork-tender. Braising them a day or two in advance is a good idea, because the flavor develops and improves overnight and it is easier to remove the fat when solidified. As with all short ribs, when the meat is perfectly cooked the bones will fall off; just push them back in before serving.

If you can't find German Butterball potatoes, use Yukon Gold or Yellow Finns. Choose large potatoes so they can be "turned." Turning potatoes is a skill that takes practice, but once mastered it requires little more time than peeling. To turn the potatoes, first quarter them. Using a paring knife, cut the potatoes into football shapes with 7 sides, cutting from top to bottom. Sound impossible? Then start by shaping 4 sides and work your way up to 7—have fun and don't worry too much about the shape of the potato, just make sure they are similar in size so they cook evenly.

continued

creating the
"steamship"

>

METHOD

FOR THE SHORT RIBS: Place the ribs on a work surface, meat side down. With a small, sharp knife, remove the bones from the ribs and set aside. Trim away any membrane and excess fat from the boned rib. Clean 4 of the bones with a sharp knife by scraping off the sinew and fascia. Set aside the 4 cleaned bones. Season the meat with salt and pepper. Place a cleaned bone in the center of each rib (see photo 4). Roll the meat around the bone. Wind a length of butcher's twine a couple of times around the rib and tie it off. Season the outside of the roll with more salt and pepper. Repeat with the remaining ribs. Push the rib bones down into the roll for browning.

Preheat the oven to 375° F. Heat the oil in a casserole dish (large enough to fit the ribs in 1 layer) over high heat until it shimmers but isn't smoking. Put in the ribs, decrease the heat to medium-high, and brown them on all sides, carefully turning with tongs, 15 to 20 minutes total. If the oil begins to smoke, decrease the heat a little. Transfer the short ribs to a plate and discard the oil. Heat about 1 tablespoon of oil to the casserole dish and brown the reserved bones (this will add a lot of flavor to your sauce). Remove the bones from the casserole dish and reserve. Add the bacon, onion, carrot, celery, mushrooms, and garlic and cook, stirring occasionally, until the vegetables have softened and just begun to turn golden, 5 to 8 minutes. Add the parsley stems, thyme sprigs, and bay leaf and cook for 3 to 5 minutes more. Add the red wine vinegar and cook until the liquid has almost evaporated, being careful not to let the vegetables scorch. Add the red wine and reduce by three quarters. Return the short ribs and the reserved bones to the casserole dish and pour in enough chicken stock to just barely cover the meat. Bring to a simmer and put the casserole dish in the oven. Bake, covered, for 2 to 2½ hours, until the ribs are fork-tender. Handling the ribs gently, transfer them to a platter. Strain the braising liquid through a fine-mesh sieve into a bowl and discard the solids. Let the liquid sit for a few minutes so the fat accumulates on the surface (tossing in a few ice cubes will speed the process), then skim off and discard the fat. With a pair of tongs, pull up the center bone from each rib to create the "steamship."

Reserve 1 cup of the braising liquid for glazing the vegetables and pour the rest into a saucepan. Reduce over medium heat by half, skimming the sauce frequently. Clean the casserole, return the ribs, and pour the reduced braising jus through a fine-mesh sieve over the ribs. Let the meat cool in the liquid so the juices get reabsorbed. The ribs can be refrigerated for up to 3 days.

continued

1	4
2	5
3	6

1 Place the ribs on a work surface, meat side down. With a small, sharp knife remove all three bones from the ribs.

2 Choose 1 bone and clean it. Use the remaining bones for the sauce.

3 Rib with bones removed

4 Place a bone in the center of the rib

5 Roll the rib tightly around the bone

6 Wind a length of butcher's twine around the rib and tie it off

FOR THE CARROT MOUSSELINE: Put the carrots into a saucepan with the water, bring to a boil, then decrease the heat to maintain a low simmer. Cover and cook for about 15 minutes, or until the carrots are very tender. Drain the carrots into a sieve placed over a bowl and reserve the liquid. Put the carrots into a blender with the butter, salt, and sugar and process, adding enough of the reserved liquid to make a smooth puree. Season to taste with more salt if necessary and freshly ground pepper. Set aside or refrigerate and reheat before serving.

FOR THE PEARL ONIONS: Heat the oil in a small skillet over medium heat. Add the onions, cover, and cook, shaking the pan occasionally, for 6 to 8 minutes, or until the onions are lightly golden. Add the butter and braising liquid, bring to a simmer, and cook for 4 to 6 minutes, or until the onions are tender but not falling apart. Season with salt and pepper and set aside.

FOR THE MUSHROOMS: Heat the oil in a skillet over high heat. Add the mushrooms and cook, shaking the pan only once or twice (to prevent the mushrooms from releasing too much liquid), for 4 or 5 minutes, or until you can hear them "singing" and they begin to brown. Add the butter, garlic, and thyme, decrease the heat to medium, and cook, using a spoon to baste the mushrooms with the butter, for about 2 minutes longer. Season with salt and pepper, stir in the braising liquid, then combine with the onions in the pan.

FOR THE POTATOES: Place the potatoes in a small casserole dish, add the butter and water, and season with salt and pepper. Bake in the 375°F oven, stirring once or twice, for 20 to 30 minutes, or until they begin to turn golden brown and are fork-tender.

TO SERVE

Lower the oven temperature to 350°F. Cover the casserole with the short ribs with foil and place in the oven for 30 minutes, or until the ribs are heated through. Remove from the oven and baste the ribs with the braising jus. Preheat the broiler. Dot the short ribs with the 4 tablespoons butter, and slide the dish under the hot broiler. When the surface of the ribs starts to caramelize after 3 or 4 minutes, slide them out, spoon some sauce on top, and slide them back under the broiler until the sauce and meat are sizzling.

Reheat the vegetables if necessary. Set the ribs in the center of 4 warm dinner plates, and remove the butcher's twine from the ribs. Spoon the carrot mousseline into a soft oval mound next to the meat, and arrange an equal amount of each vegetable to the side with the bacon. Drizzle some sauce on the ribs and around the vegetables. Season with sea salt and pepper and garnish with chervil.

More is definitely more!

NEW YEAR'S EVE VENISON CHOP "ROSSINI"

VENISON, FOIE GRAS, TOAST, CREAMED SPINACH, TRUFFLE SAUCE,
AND SHAVED BLACK TRUFFLES

SERVES 4

VENISON CHOPS

4 (6-ounce) venison chops
4 cloves garlic
4 tablespoons olive oil
4 medium-thin slices prosciutto
Freshly ground black pepper
8 thyme sprigs
Kosher salt
4 tablespoons unsalted butter, cut
    into 4 pieces

TRUFFLE SAUCE

¼ cup ruby port
¼ cup Madeira
1½ cups Rich Beef Stock (see
    Basics, page 231)
1 ounce fresh, canned, or frozen
    truffles (see Kitchen and
    Shopping Notes), diced
4 tablespoons unsalted butter,
    cut into 5 or 6 pieces
¼ teaspoon black truffle oil
Kosher salt and freshly ground
    black pepper

TOAST

4 (½-inch-thick) slices rustic
    sourdough bread
1 tablespoon extra-virgin olive oil
Kosher salt and freshly ground
    black pepper
1 clove garlic, halved

FOIE GRAS

½ pound fresh grade A foie gras,
    sliced into 4 equal portions (see
    Kitchen and Shopping Notes,
    page 78)
Coarse sea salt and freshly ground
    black pepper
1 teaspoon grape seed oil

CREAMED SPINACH

(see Basics, page 229)

2 to 4 ounces fresh black truffles,
    for shaving over the dish

Occasionally we embrace the concept that less is more, but on New Year's Eve "More is definitely more!" Divinely decadent tournedos Rossini—filet mignon, foie gras, and truffles—have always been a standard on our New Year's menu; it seems to be the one dish we just can't remove. In addition to using the classic filet mignon, we've also served tournedos Rossini substituting charred rare ahi tuna for the beef. But perhaps our all-time favorite variation is venison chop Rossini. Believe it or not, apart from the sauce, the recipe is easily put together; basically it's just one luxury item piled on top of another. If the sauce is going to prevent you from trying this recipe, drizzle the finished dish with yet another luxury item: *aceto balsamico,* which is absolutely delicious and requires no extra work. At the restaurant, we grill the venison and foie gras over a hot fire, which adds another flavor dimension, but we've written the recipe for a standard oven.

continued

KITCHEN AND SHOPPING NOTES

The biggest challenge of this recipe is in obtaining the ingredients, but all you need to do is plan ahead. There are many mail-order sources as well as specialty markets that carry them. Farm-raised venison is available year-round. Venison has a rich and robust flavor but is extremely lean and should not be cooked beyond medium-rare; overcooked venison is dry, gamey, and will leave you disappointed (to say the least). Because fat equals flavor, foie gras makes the perfect complement to the lean venison and helps carry the flavor of the truffles as well.

Spend the extra money for grade A foie gras; it's much easier to slice into the ¾- to 1-inch-thick portions needed in order to achieve a crisp exterior during sautéing. If the thought of working with fresh foie gras scares you, consider purchasing a well-made foie gras terrine (see Sources, page 236), which you only have to slice and shave truffles over. Unfortunately, there's nothing on earth that can substitute for the aroma or flavor of fresh truffles. As the composer Rossini (for whom this dish is named) said, "The truffle is the Mozart of mushrooms." We have found, however, that if fresh truffles are unavailable or prohibitively expensive, frozen truffles (see Sources, page 237) will work in the sauce. Just double the amount of truffles specified for the sauce, and skip the shaved fresh truffles for the top. Keep in mind, however, that this dish is meant to be one big indulgence.

METHOD

FOR THE VENISON CHOPS: Peel and halve the garlic cloves. Using ½ garlic clove for each chop, rub both sides of each chop with the cut side of the garlic and drizzle with 2 tablespoons of the olive oil. Wrap a slice of prosciutto around the circumference of each chop, and tie a piece of kitchen twine around each chop to secure the prosciutto. Lightly season on all sides with pepper and place in a shallow baking dish. Crush the thyme sprigs with your hands to release the essential oils and place a sprig on top and under each chop, along with the garlic. Set aside for 2 hours or refrigerate up to overnight.

FOR THE TRUFFLE SAUCE: Combine the port and Madeira in a saucepan and reduce over medium heat until it's thick and syrupy. Add the beef stock and reduce until thick enough to coat the back of a spoon (you should have about ¾ cup). Strain through fine-mesh sieve into a bowl and return to the saucepan. Set aside or refrigerate in a covered container for up to 2 days.

FOR THE TOAST: Using a round cutter, cut 2½-inch rounds from the bread slices. Brush both sides with the olive oil and sprinkle with salt and pepper. Toast in a hot oven or under a broiler just until beginning to color. Very, very lightly rub the cut side of the garlic over both sides of the toasts and set aside for up to 2 hours.

TO COOK THE FOIE GRAS AND VENISON CHOPS: Preheat the oven to 450°F. Season the foie gras with plenty of salt and pepper. Heat the grape seed oil in a heavy ovenproof skillet over high heat until almost smoking. Carefully place the foie gras in the pan and cook for about 2 minutes, or until dark golden brown. Turn over and put the pan into the oven for 3 minutes. To check for doneness, pick up a slice; if it bends, it's done. Set aside and keep warm while you cook the venison.

Remove the thyme sprigs and garlic from the venison chops and reserve. Heat the remaining 2 tablespoons olive oil in an ovenproof skillet or sauté pan over high heat until it shimmers. Season the chops generously with salt and carefully set them into the hot pan. Using tongs to turn them, sear the chops on all sides for about 6 minutes, or until they're evenly and heavily browned. Put the pan into the oven for 8 minutes, turning the chops once halfway through. Remove from the oven and put the garlic and thyme back on the chops. Place a piece of the butter on each chop and set aside in a warm place for a few minutes until the butter melts. Spoon the melted butter over the chops and remove the twine.

TO SERVE

Finish the sauce. Bring the sauce to a boil, then lower the heat to a simmer and add the diced truffle. Swirl in the butter a little at a time until it's fully incorporated. Add the truffle oil, season to taste with salt and pepper, and keep warm. Warm the spinach in a small saucepan and place a spoonful in the center of each of 4 warm dinner plates. Place a warm toast round on top of the spinach, then spoon the remaining spinach on each toast (remember we said a *pile* of luxury ingredients). Top with a venison chop and nap with the sauce. Place the foie gras on the sauced venison and, finally, using a truffle slicer or mandoline, rain truffles generously over all.

DESSERTS

WHOLE-APPLE CRISP

. . . .

RUM RAISIN ICE CREAM, CIDER CARAMEL SAUCE

. . . .

SERVES 4

RUM RAISIN ICE CREAM

1½ cups dried whole stemmed Red
    Flame seedless grapes (see
    Sources, page 237)
¾ cup dark rum
7 large egg yolks
¾ cup granulated sugar
2 cups whole milk
2 cups heavy cream

CRISP TOPPING

1½ cups all-purpose flour
1 cup chopped pecans, toasted
    (page 234)
¾ cup old-fashioned rolled oats
⅔ cup packed brown sugar
¼ cup maple sugar
¾ cup (1½ sticks) cold unsalted
    butter, cut into 12 tablespoons
1 teaspoon kosher salt

**APPLES AND
CARAMEL SAUCE**

2 cups natural apple juice or cider
½ cup (1 stick) unsalted butter
1 cup packed light brown sugar
4 Golden Delicious, Fuji, or Granny
    Smith apples, peeled, cored
    and left whole
¼ cup heavy cream

Karen Shaw and Jennifer Holbrook were the opening pastry chefs at Boulevard. These talented women possessed the unique ability to create desserts in large quantities that not only satisfied the demands of a busy restaurant but retained an undeniably homemade quality that is usually only possible when recipes are produced in small batches.

We wanted an apple crisp that wasn't just baked in individual dishes or spooned from a large hotel pan onto a plate, and Karen's brilliant response was to caramelize whole apples, then bake them covered in crisp topping. Baking the apples whole gives them a silky smooth texture and a more elegant shape, while the caramel contributes another delectable layer of flavor. With the simple addition of cream to the caramel, a lovely sauce is created, which is ultimately drizzled over the boozy rum raisin ice cream.

This dessert has all the flavors of home, enhanced by a pastry chef's skills and knowledge of taste, texture, and presentation.

KITCHEN AND SHOPPING NOTES

When Karen made this dessert, it looked like a large snowball covered in crisp topping. But when we tested the recipe, frankly, we couldn't keep the topping from sliding off the baked apples (it seems Karen took that secret with her when she left). Our modification was to stuff the whole apples into ring molds and then pat on the topping before baking.

The proper apple is essential to this dish. Choose a baking apple that holds its shape and doesn't cook down into a pile of mush or explode. We've had success with Golden Delicious, Fuji, and Granny Smith apples and are hesitant to recommend apples we haven't worked with. If the apples do "explode" and fall apart, just pack them into the ring molds and cover with them with the topping; no one will know the difference.

Rum raisin ice cream is a favorite of ours, and here it's given a new twist with the addition of dried Red Flame grapes, which have a lighter, fresher flavor and a cool appearance.

The source we've found for this raisin is Fresh and Wild in Washington State (see Sources, page 237). These dried grapes are sold on the stem, which is unusual; they also make a festive addition to a cheese plate. Dried currants and sultanas are fine substitutes, but be sure to warm them in the dark rum; it is an important step that plumps the raisins and keeps them moist in the ice cream.

METHOD

FOR THE ICE CREAM: Combine the raisins and rum in a small saucepan and bring to a simmer. Immediately remove the pan from the heat and let the raisins cool in the pan. Strain through a sieve into a bowl, reserving the raisins and rum separately. Combine the egg yolks and granulated sugar in the bowl of an electric mixer fitted with the paddle attachment and beat until a ribbon forms when the beaters are lifted. Meanwhile, heat the milk and cream together in a saucepan until little bubbles begin to appear around the edge. Whisk some of milk-cream mixture into the yolk-sugar mixture, then whisk the yolk mixture into the saucepan and cook over low heat, stirring constantly, until the custard coats the back of a spoon (when you draw your finger across the back of the spoon, there should be a visible trail that doesn't immediately flow back together). Strain through a fine-mesh sieve into a container, add the reserved rum, and chill thoroughly, at least 2 hours. Freeze according to the ice cream maker's instructions, then stir in the reserved raisins. The frozen ice cream should be stored in a tightly covered plastic or stainless-steel container. For the best flavor and texture, let it soften slightly at room temperature before serving.

FOR THE CRISP TOPPING: Put all the ingredients in the bowl of an electric mixer fitted with the paddle attachment and mix on low speed until well combined but pieces of butter are still visible. Set aside or refrigerate in a covered container for up to 1 week.

FOR THE APPLES AND CARAMEL SAUCE: Preheat the oven to 350°F. Cook the apple juice in a small saucepan over high heat until reduced to 1 cup. Transfer to a glass measuring cup and set aside. Combine the butter and brown sugar in the same saucepan (no need to clean it) and bring to a boil over high heat. Decrease the heat to medium and cook, stirring occasionally, until the brown sugar and butter melt and the mixture turns a rich brown, about 5 minutes (taking care it doesn't burn). Slowly stir in the reduced apple juice, then remove from the heat. Put the apples into a small baking dish (so they fit snugly) and pour the caramel over. Bake for 15 minutes, turn the apples over, and bake for another 15 minutes, or until a toothpick can be inserted easily. Remove from the oven and let cool to room temperature.

Place 4 (2½-inch) ring molds on a small rimmed baking sheet that has been lined with parchment paper. Remove the apples from the caramel, pour the caramel into a small saucepan, and stir in the cream until blended. Bring to a boil, then immediately remove from the heat and set aside. Nestle the apples into the ring molds and top each with an equal amount of crisp topping, patting lightly to form an even layer. At this point the apples can be refrigerated for up to 8 hours before being baked.

TO SERVE

Preheat the oven to 350°F. Bake the apples for 15 to 20 minutes, or until warmed through and the topping is golden. Using a spatula, transfer the apples with the ring molds to 4 dessert plates or shallow bowls. Lift off the ring molds, place a scoop of the ice cream next to each apple, and drizzle caramel sauce over all.

CHOCOLATE CHERRY SHORTCAKES

OLD-FASHIONED VANILLA ICE CREAM AND CHERRIES JUBILEE

SERVES 8

CHOCOLATE CHERRY BISCUITS

2 cups self-rising flour

½ cup Valrhona or other Dutch-
    processed cocoa powder (see
    Sources, page 237)

½ cup sugar, plus additional
    for dipping

¼ teaspoon kosher salt

1 cup dried Bing cherries or dried
    sour cherries

1 cup Valrhona (or other premium)
    bittersweet chocolate chips
    or nickel-size pieces chopped
    bittersweet chocolate

2 cups heavy cream

6 tablespoons unsalted butter,
    melted

CHERRIES JUBILEE

3 cups fresh Bing cherries,
    halved and pitted

⅓ cup plus 2 tablespoons kirsch

½ cup sugar

3 tablespoons freshly squeezed
    lemon juice

½ cup brandy

2 tablespoons unsalted butter

OLD-FASHIONED VANILLA ICE CREAM

1 vanilla bean

2 cups heavy cream

1 cup whole milk

⅔ cup sugar

5 large egg yolks

We're delighted by the slightly retro idea of cherries jubilee, which we've updated and refreshed to take advantage of gorgeous California Bing cherries. The warm cherries jubilee, served with these naughty biscuits, is the ideal chocolate-and-cherry moment. The only possible way to improve on this moment is to bring the chocolate biscuits to the table just baked, when their chocolate aroma and ethereal texture are at their finest. Once you've tasted them hot from the oven, it will be hard to serve them any other way.

KITCHEN AND SHOPPING NOTES

Every brand of chocolate has its own distinct flavor, texture, and color. Most pastry chefs are devoted to certain chocolate brands and develop recipes using their favorites. Because these biscuits are almost pure chocolate, their flavor depends completely on the chocolate you use. When it comes to cocoa, as far as we're concerned Valrhona sets the standard. However, whichever brand of cocoa you use, make sure it's Dutch-processed, which neutralizes the chocolate's natural acidity and provides the cocoa with a darker, more chocolaty flavor.

Bittersweet chocolate chips are essential and, again, we recommend Valrhona. They make bittersweet chocolate *pistoles,* which are like large chocolate chips that we find are easier to measure and melt. For these shortcakes, we just put the whole pistoles right into the mix with the dried ingredients. If you can't find *pistoles* (see Sources, page 237), cut a block of semisweet chocolate into nickel-size pieces.

continued

When we first opened Boulevard, these double chocolate–cherry shortcakes made everyone's pants fit a little tighter. Racks of them, just out of the oven and devilishly full of molten chocolate, became our morning-coffee nemesis.

We like using big, meaty dried Bing cherries in the biscuits, but dried sour cherries are a good substitute.

The biscuits recipe yields 9 biscuits, 8 dessert servings plus an extra biscuit for the cook. They may be made 4 hours ahead and rewarmed before serving.

METHOD

FOR THE BISCUITS: Preheat the oven to 400°F. Stir the flour, cocoa, sugar, and salt together in a large bowl until well combined, then stir in the dried cherries and chocolate chips. Add the cream and stir until the mixture comes together into a somewhat stiff dough. Turn out onto a clean cutting board and, with your hands, press the dough into a 6-inch square about 2 inches thick. With a long, thin knife, cut the dough into 9 (2-inch) squares. Dip the tops of the biscuits into the melted butter and then into sugar, pressing lightly so it adheres. Place the biscuits 2 inches apart on an ungreased baking sheet. Bake for about 15 minutes, or until they're light gold and spring back when pressed lightly. Set aside at room temperature for up to 4 hours.

FOR THE CHERRIES JUBILEE: Combine the cherries and the ⅓ cup kirsch in a bowl and let macerate for 30 minutes, tossing occasionally. Put half of the cherries, the sugar, and lemon juice into a saucepan and simmer over medium heat for about 5 minutes, or until the liquid begins to thicken. Remove from the heat, add the brandy and, averting your face, carefully ignite the brandy with a long match. Let burn for about 1 minute to burn off the alcohol, then extinguish the flame by covering the pan. Remove the lid and continue to simmer the cherry mixture until it reduces to a syrup. With a slotted spoon, transfer the cherries to a bowl and reserve. Add the remaining 2 tablespoons kirsch to the syrup and set aside or refrigerate for up to 2 days (along with the reserved cherries in a separate container).

FOR THE ICE CREAM: Split the vanilla bean in half lengthwise and scrape the seeds into a saucepan. Add the vanilla-bean pod, cream, milk, and sugar and cook over low heat, stirring occasionally, for about 3 minutes. Whisk the sugar and egg yolks in a small bowl just to combine them, then whisk in some of the warm milk mixture until blended. Stir the sugar and egg-yolk mixture into the saucepan and cook over low heat, stirring constantly, until the custard coats the back of a spoon (when you draw your finger across the back of the spoon, there should be a visible trail that doesn't immediately flow back together). Strain through a fine-mesh sieve into a container and chill thoroughly, at least 2 hours. Freeze according to the ice cream maker's instructions. The frozen ice cream should be stored in a tightly covered plastic or stainless-steel container. For the best flavor and texture, let it soften slightly at room temperature before serving.

TO SERVE

Preheat the oven to 350°F. Split the biscuits and put into the oven for about 5 minutes, or until warmed through. Heat the cherry syrup in a small skillet over medium heat, add the reserved cherries and the butter, and swirl the pan until the butter has melted and combined with the syrup. Center a warm biscuit bottom on 8 dessert plates or shallow bowls and put equal spoonfuls of the cherries and their syrup on each, reserving a cup or so. Place on a biscuit top, followed by a scoop of ice cream. Dollop the remaining cherries and syrup around or to the side of the biscuits.

MANJARI CHOCOLATE TRUFFLE TART WITH SALTED CARAMEL ICE CREAM

SERVES 12

BRITTANY SALT CARAMEL ICE CREAM

2⅓ cups whole milk

2 cups heavy cream

8 large egg yolks

½ teaspoon *fleur de sel*

1¼ cups sugar

⅛ teaspoon cream of tartar

SALTY CLEAR CARAMEL

2¼ teaspoons *fleur de sel*

1½ cups sugar

½ teaspoon cream of tartar

2 tablespoons light corn syrup

CHOCOLATE TART DOUGH

1 cup (2 sticks) butter

½ cup plus 1 tablespoon sugar

1 egg yolk

1 egg

2¼ cups flour

½ cup unsweetened Dutch-processed cocoa powder

¼ teaspoon salt

MANJARI CHOCOLATE TRUFFLE FILLING

12 ounces Valrhona Manjari chocolate, chopped

1½ cups heavy cream

CHOCOLATE GLAZE

½ cup (1 stick) butter

6 ounces extra-bitter chocolate, chopped

1 tablespoon light corn syrup

2 tablespoons water

Sleek and elegant, this is a very grown-up dessert. It's pure indulgence, with nothing between you and the chocolate, except for a fleeting escape to the salted caramel ice cream. We love the use of salt in these two confections as it brings out a surprising savory side to both the caramel and the chocolate. Like red lipstick and pearls, this chocolate and caramel dessert makes a strong statement without a lot of frills and fluff.

KITCHEN AND SHOPPING NOTES

We tasted this tart made with eight different chocolates and finally decided on the Manjari Single Estate Chocolate from Valrhona. Manjari's intense chocolate flavor is perfect in this silky, smooth tart. The tart dough recipe is enough to make two 9-inch tarts, so we recommend you freeze half of the dough and save it for another use. It's important to use *fleur de sel*. We find its flavor and texture incomparable in the salted caramel ice cream.

METHOD

FOR THE BRITTANY SALT CARAMEL ICE CREAM: In a large saucepan, heat the milk and cream over medium-high heat, just until little bubbles begin to appear around the edge. Set aside. In a medium bowl, whisk together the yolks with the salt and set aside. Place the sugar and cream of tartar in a heavy medium saucepan and stir in enough water to just moisten the mixture so it resembles damp sand. Using a pastry brush dipped in water, wipe down the sides of the pan to remove sugar crystals. Cook over medium heat until it turns the color of straw. Decrease the heat slightly and cook until the caramel turns deep gold. Remove from the heat and carefully whisk in the warm milk/cream mixture. Return to the heat and whisk until thoroughly combined. Slowly ladle half of the caramel/cream mixture into the yolks and sugar, stirring continuously with the whisk, until it's well combined. Strain through a fine-mesh sieve into a bowl, stir a few times, and chill for at least 2 hours. Freeze and store according to the ice cream maker's instructions.

continued

FOR THE SALTY CLEAR CARAMEL: In a small bowl, combine the salt with ⅓ cup hot water and stir until dissolved. Set aside. Combine the sugar, cream of tartar, and corn syrup in a heavy medium saucepan and cook over medium heat until it's the color of light straw. Decrease the heat slightly and swirl the pan so it cooks evenly. Remove from the heat and carefully stir in the dissolved salt water. Return to the heat and continue stirring until the sugar mixture is thoroughly combined and as viscous as honey. Cool and store at room temperature for up to 1 week.

FOR THE CHOCOLATE TART DOUGH: In an electric mixer fitted with a paddle attachment, mix the butter and sugar on medium-low speed until combined. Add the egg yolk and continue to mix until combined, then add the whole egg, again mixing until combined. In a large bowl, sift together the flour, cocoa powder, and salt. Add dry mixture to the egg/sugar mixture. Mix on low speed just until the dough comes together. Remove the dough from the bowl and without kneading it, shape into a flat disk 1-inch thick. Wrap the dough in plastic wrap and refrigerate for at least ½ hour or up to 5 days.

TO ASSEMBLE THE TART: Allow the dough to reach room temperature for 20 minutes before rolling. Cut the dough in half and make 1 tart shell, freezing the remainder of the dough for a later use. On a lightly floured surface, roll out the dough with a rolling pin while applying light pressure. Rotate the dough in quarter turns, applying slightly more pressure with the rolling pin each time. Continue in this manner until dough is evenly ⅛ to ¼-inch thick and about 12-inches in diameter. Carefully roll dough onto the rolling pin, place over a 9-inch tart pan, and gently unroll dough. Press dough into the pan with your fingertips. Cut off excess dough using a paring knife or roll the rolling pin over top of the filled form and remove excess pieces. Chill the tart shell for at least 15 minutes. Preheat the oven to 350° F. Line the tart shell with parchment paper. Fill with dried beans or pie weights and bake for 25 minutes. Remove the beans or pie weights and check for doneness. Touch the dough and if it is wet or has a lot of give, bake it for an additional 5 to 10 minutes (without the weights), but be careful because chocolate scorches easily. Remove from the oven and set aside to cool.

FOR THE MANJARI CHOCOLATE TRUFFLE FILLING: Place the chocolate in a medium heatproof bowl. Heat the cream in a small saucepan until little bubbles appear around the edge then pour the cream over the chocolate, stirring continuously until the chocolate is melted and appears smooth and shiny. Immediately pour the filling into the baked and cooled tart shell and, using an offset spatula, spread it out evenly. Refrigerate until the filling is set, about 3 hours.

FOR THE CHOCOLATE GLAZE: Melt the butter, chocolate, corn syrup, and water in a medium bowl over barely simmering water. When the chocolate has melted, stir until all the ingredients are combined and the glaze appears smooth. Remove from the heat. You can refrigerate for up to 5 days and rewarm until it's pourable. Pour the warm glaze onto chilled tart, tipping the tart shell to spread glaze evenly. Tap the tart on a hard surface to help smooth the glaze and to release any air bubbles. Refrigerate until glaze is set, about 30 minutes.

TO SERVE

About 30 minutes before serving, have a pitcher of warm water, a large chef's knife, and clean towel at the ready. Drizzle 12 dinner plates with a little salty caramel. Slice the tart into 12 equal wedges, first dipping the knife in the warm water and then wiping it clean after each cut. Place the tart wedges on the plates and let them sit for 30 minutes so they warm up slightly. When you're ready to serve, scoop two scoops of ice cream off to one side. Sprinkle both the tart and ice cream with a little *fleur de sel*.

Jennifer Holbrook's signature dessert—and everyone's most requested birthday surprise— this white chocolate–banana cream pie always takes the cake.

WHITE CHOCOLATE-BANANA CREAM PIE

SERVES 6

PIE DOUGH

1½ cups all-purpose flour

½ cup (1 stick) unsalted cold butter

1 teaspoon sugar

⅓ cup heavy cream

4 ounces bittersweet chocolate

WHITE CHOCOLATE
PASTRY CREAM

2 cups whole milk

½ vanilla bean

½ cup plus 2 tablespoons sugar

¼ cup cornstarch

6 large egg yolks

2 tablespoons unsalted butter,
    cut into 4 pieces

6 ounces white chocolate, chopped

2 ripe bananas

WHIPPED CREAM

1 cup heavy cream

2 tablespoons sugar

¼ vanilla bean, halved lengthwise
    and seeds scraped

BRÛLÉED BANANAS

2 ripe bananas

⅓ cup sugar

HOT FUDGE SAUCE

(see Basics, page 232)

Dark chocolate curls or
    shavings (see Kitchen and
    Shopping Notes)

It's difficult to improve on a good, old-fashioned classic like banana cream pie, but adding white chocolate to the pastry cream actually intensifies the vanilla and banana flavors. Finely tuned to please the inner child in all of us, it will be impossible to put your spoons and forks down until every bite has been eaten.

KITCHEN AND SHOPPING NOTES

Never a fan of soggy desserts, Jennifer always painted a layer of dark chocolate onto the inside of a pie shell to prevent any moisture from messing up her crisp crust.

While it may seem unnecessary, dicing the bananas guarantees that you will get the same amount of banana in every bite. Be sure to choose bananas that have just barely begun to freckle.

The simplest way to make shavings of chocolate is by dragging the blade of a large chef's knife across the smooth (back) side of a chocolate bar or block. Use the shavings right away, or use the knife blade to transfer them to a plate (the heat of your hands can melt them). Chocolate curls are prettier, but they take a little more practice to master. To make curls, you'll need a large professional-size (5-pound) bar of chocolate and either a warm place in your kitchen, such as near the oven, or a lamp you can put directly over the chocolate to warm it. Place the bar of chocolate near the heat source for 5 to 10 minutes, just long enough for it to soften without melting. Hold a large chef's knife with both hands and, using moderate pressure, scrape the blade across the chocolate at a 90-degree angle, using one long pulling motion. You want curls that are not cracked or brittle, so soften the chocolate a little longer if necessary. Repeat warming the bar and scraping until you think you have enough curls. Put the curls on a baking sheet or plate away from heat for up to a few hours ahead, or store wrapped on a baking sheet for up to 1 month.

For this recipe you'll need 6 individual 10-ounce (4½ inch) pie tins or plates (see Sources, page 237).

METHOD

FOR THE PIE DOUGH: Preheat the oven to 350°F. Using an electric mixer fitted with the paddle attachment, mix the flour, butter, and sugar together on low speed until it resembles coarse meal. Add the cream and mix until the dough just comes together and forms a ball. Remove from the bowl and flatten the dough into a disk. Wrap in plastic and let rest in the refrigerator for 15 minutes. On a lightly floured work surface, roll the dough out into a ¼-inch-thick circle. Cut out 6 circles slightly larger than your pie tins and ease a dough circle into each tin, pressing it into the corners and crimping the edges to form a decorative old-fashioned flute. Line the dough with aluminum foil and fill with dry beans or pie weights. Bake the pie shells for 15 to 20 minutes, or until the edges are golden. Remove from the oven and let cool on wire racks. Melt the chocolate in a small bowl set over a small saucepan of simmering water (make sure the bottom of the bowl does not touch the water). Using a pastry brush, paint the insides of the cooled pie shells with the melted chocolate and set aside.

FOR THE PASTRY CREAM: Combine the milk and vanilla bean in a saucepan and bring to a simmer over medium heat. Whisk the sugar, cornstarch, and egg yolks together in a bowl until smooth, then slowly ladle in the warm milk, whisking constantly. Pour the mixture back into the saucepan and cook over medium heat, whisking, until the mixture has thickened to a puddinglike consistency. Whisk in the butter and white chocolate until they're completely melted and smooth. Strain through a fine-mesh sieve into a bowl and press plastic wrap directly onto the surface to prevent a skin from forming. Refrigerate for at least 4 hours and up to 3 days.

To assemble the pies, cut the bananas into ¼-inch cubes and fold into the cold pastry cream. Remove the pie shells from the tins, and fill with the banana cream, dividing it evenly, and smoothing the tops with the back of a spoon or offset spatula. Refrigerate for 1 hour or up to 1 day.

FOR THE WHIPPED CREAM: Using an electric mixer fitted with the whisk attachment, whip the cream, sugar, and vanilla-bean seeds on medium speed until the cream forms firm peaks. Refrigerate for up to 1 hour. If the cream separates before using, gently rewhip with a hand whisk.

TO SERVE

Just before serving, cut the 2 bananas diagonally into ¼-inch-thick slices (figure on about 6 slices per serving). Spoon a pool of fudge sauce on each of 6 dessert plates and place a pie on top of the sauce. Place a fan of banana slices next to each pie and sprinkle the bananas with the sugar. Using a butane torch, caramelize the bananas, being careful not to scorch the pies. Top each pie with a dollop of whipped cream and a shower of chocolate curls.

CARROT CAKE WITH CREAM CHEESE FILLING

CANDIED WALNUT ICE CREAM, CREAM CHEESE ICE CREAM, CARROT SORBET

SERVES 12

CARROT CAKE

1⅓ cups all-purpose flour

1¾ teaspoons ground cinnamon

1½ teaspoons baking powder

¾ teaspoon baking soda

¾ teaspoon kosher salt

1 cup grape seed or other flavorless
vegetable oil

1 cup packed dark brown sugar

¾ cup granulated sugar

3 large eggs

¾ teaspoon vanilla extract

4 large carrots (about ¾ pound
total weight), peeled and
finely grated

CREAM CHEESE FILLING

1 pound cream cheese (preferably
natural, see Kitchen and
Shopping Notes), at room
temperature

1 cup sifted confectioners' sugar

¾ teaspoon vanilla extract

CARROT SHERBET

1 cup organic carrot juice (see
Kitchen and Shopping Notes)

1 cup plus 2 tablespoons light
corn syrup

1 cup whole milk

2 tablespoons vodka

CANDIED WALNUT
ICE CREAM

1½ cups heavy cream

1½ cups whole milk

1 cup Candied Walnuts (see Basics,
page 228)

8 large egg yolks

¾ cup granulated sugar

CREAM CHEESE ICE CREAM

1 cup whole milk

Pinch of kosher salt

6 large egg yolks

¾ cup granulated sugar

1 cup plus 2 tablespoons (10 ounces)
natural cream cheese (see
Kitchen and Shopping Notes),
at room temperature

¾ cup sour cream

½ teaspoon vanilla extract

WALNUT CARAMEL

2 cups granulated sugar

1 tablespoon light corn syrup

1¼ cups heavy cream

1½ cups walnuts, blanched, toasted
(see Basics, page 234), and
finely chopped

1 teaspoon walnut oil

CANDIED CARROTS

2 cups granulated sugar

1 cup water

2 carrots, peeled and julienned

Moist, crumbly and delicious, the simple truth is carrot cake is our favorite excuse to eat cream cheese frosting. Hardly considered a suitable dessert for white tablecloth dining, Nancy Pitta has certainly gone beyond the carrot cake cliché with this dazzling remake: multiple layers of cake and cream cheese frosting, candied walnut ice cream, cream cheese ice cream, and the biggest surprise of all, carrot sherbet . . . how sweet it is!

KITCHEN AND SHOPPING NOTES

Carrots play a very important role in this dessert, and it's no surprise that using the sweetest, most flavorful carrots truly matters here. Optimally, use organic carrots with a bright orange color, and squeeze the juice right before making the sorbet. An alternative is to buy the juice freshly squeezed from a local juice bar. Odwalla is a good-quality mass-market juice.

continued

The cream cheese you use for the ice cream must be natural, meaning without stabilizers, which would make the ice cream gummy. If you can't find natural cream cheese, skip the ice cream all together; however, the stabilizers in packaged cream cheese (the kind in the foil wrapper) don't seem to affect the filling at all.

Don't be tempted to add walnuts to the cake, as they would make it impossible to slice the cake into thin layers, and the layers are what make this cake distinctive. If you just *have* to have nuts in your carrot cake, sprinkle the walnuts over the layers after frosting them.

Take your time when cutting the cake; don't be tempted to slice it until it is completely cooled. Refrigerating the cake overnight makes it much easier to slice.

METHOD

FOR THE CARROT CAKE: Preheat the oven to 350°F. Spray a 9-by-12-inch rimmed baking sheet with nonstick cooking spray and line the pan with parchment paper. Spray the parchment and set aside. Sift together the flour, cinnamon, baking powder, baking soda, and salt into a bowl and set aside. Whisk the oil, sugars, eggs, and vanilla together in a large bowl until combined. Add the flour mixture and whisk until no streaks of flour are visible. Using a rubber spatula, stir in the grated carrots and then scrape into the prepared pan. Bake for 25 to 30 minutes, or until a tester inserted near the center of the cake comes out nearly clean with just a few moist crumbs. Let cool completely in the pan on a wire rack.

FOR THE CREAM CHEESE FILLING: In the bowl of an electric mixer fitted with the paddle attachment, beat the cream cheese on medium speed until smooth. Mix in the confectioners' sugar on low speed, stopping once to scrape down the sides of the bowl. Add the vanilla and beat on medium speed until the filling is free of lumps.

FOR THE SHERBET: Combine all the ingredients in the canister of an ice cream maker and freeze according to the manufacturer's instructions.

FOR THE CANDIED WALNUT ICE CREAM: Heat the cream and milk in a saucepan just until small bubbles appear around the edge, then add the walnuts. Remove from the heat, cover, and let steep for 30 minutes. Whisk the egg yolks and granulated sugar in a bowl until blended. Strain the cream mixture through a sieve into another saucepan and discard the walnuts. Whisk some of the walnut-infused cream into the yolk mixture, then whisk the yolks into the saucepan. Cook over low heat, stirring constantly, until the custard coats the back of a spoon (when you draw your finger across the back of the spoon, there should be a visible trail that doesn't immediately flow back together). Strain through a fine-mesh sieve into a container and chill thoroughly, at least 2 hours. Freeze according to the ice cream maker's instructions. The frozen ice cream should be stored in a tightly covered plastic or stainless-steel container. For the best flavor and texture, let it soften slightly at room temperature before serving.

FOR THE CREAM CHEESE ICE CREAM: Heat the milk and salt in a saucepan just until small bubbles appear around the edge. Whisk the egg yolks and granulated sugar in a bowl until blended, then whisk in some of the warm milk. Stir the yolk mixture into the saucepan and cook over low heat, stirring constantly, until the custard coats the back of a spoon (when you draw your finger across the back of the spoon, there should be a visible trail that doesn't immediately flow back together). Whisk in the cream cheese, sour cream, and vanilla until blended and smooth. Strain through a fine-mesh sieve into a container and chill thoroughly, at least 2 hours. Freeze according to the ice cream maker's instructions. The frozen ice cream should be stored in a tightly covered plastic or stainless-steel container. For the best flavor and texture, let it soften slightly at room temperature before serving.

FOR THE WALNUT CARAMEL: Combine the granulated sugar and corn syrup in a heavy saucepan and stir in enough water to moisten the mixture so it resembles damp sand. Cook over medium heat until it turns the color of straw, using a pastry brush dipped in water to wipe down the sides of the pan to remove any sugar crystals. Decrease the heat slightly and cook, swirling the pan constantly, until the caramel turns a deep gold. Remove from the heat and carefully whisk in the cream (be careful as the hot mixture will bubble up and splatter). Return to the heat and whisk until thoroughly combined. Stir in the walnuts, and when the caramel is completely cool, stir in the walnut oil. Store in a tightly covered container in the refrigerator for up to 1 week.

FOR THE CANDIED CARROTS: Combine $1\frac{1}{2}$ cups of the granulated sugar and the water in a small saucepan, bring to a boil, and add the carrots. Cook for 1 minute, then strain through a fine-mesh sieve into a bowl, pressing down on the carrots to remove the excess moisture. Spread the carrots out on paper towels and let cool completely. Put the remaining $\frac{1}{2}$ cup sugar in a small, shallow bowl. Working with a few pieces of carrot, toss them in the sugar until they're evenly coated. Spread the carrots out on a rimmed baking sheet or a plate and coat the remaining carrots in the same way. Wrap in plastic and keep at room temperature for up to 2 days.

TO ASSEMBLE THE CAKE: Invert the carrot cake onto a cutting board and peel off the parchment. Using a serrated knife, cut the cake lengthwise in half. Slice each half into 3 thin layers so you end up with 6 layers. Soften the cream cheese filling slightly in a microwave so that it's spreadable (or leave it at room temperature). Place a sheet of parchment on the work surface and, using 2 wide spatulas (so the thin layer doesn't break), lift up 1 of the cakes layers and place on the parchment. With an offset spatula, evenly spread about $\frac{1}{2}$ cup of the cream cheese filling over the layer. Repeat the filling and layering, ending with a cake layer. Press down lightly on each layer as it's added so that the cake will be firm and compact. Transfer the filled layers with the parchment to a baking sheet and put in the refrigerator to firm up, about 2 hours. Using a serrated knife to get clean cuts, cut the cake crosswise on the diagonal into alternating triangles that are 1 inch wide at their base. You should have 24 triangles.

TO SERVE

Warm the walnut caramel and drizzle it decoratively onto 6 dessert plates. Place 2 cake triangles on each plates, 1 triangle long side down and the other short side down. Place 2 small scoops of cream cheese ice cream and 1 scoop of walnut ice cream together in a group, then place a scoop of carrot sherbet on top. Garnish with the candied carrots.

HEATHER HO'S LEMON MERINGUE ICEBOX CAKE

SERVES 12

GRAHAM CRACKER CRUST

1½ cups graham cracker crumbs

4 tablespoons unsalted butter, melted

LEMON CURD

6 large eggs

6 large egg yolks (reserve the whites for the meringue)

¼ cup finely grated lemon zest (from about 4 large lemons)

1 cup freshly squeezed lemon juice

¾ cup sugar

1 cup (2 sticks) cold unsalted butter, cut into ½-inch pieces

CARAMEL CREAM

1¼ cups heavy cream

1⅓ cups (11 ounces) cream cheese, softened

¾ cup caramel sauce (see Bittersweet Chocolate Cake, page 215)

LEMON CREAM

1 cup heavy cream

Lemon curd

MERINGUE

6 large egg whites (from the lemon curd)

2 cups sugar

About ¾ cup caramel sauce (see Bittersweet Chocolate Cake, page 215)

We had two wonderful roller-coaster years with Heather Ho at the helm of Boulevard's pastry department; her energy and creativity inspired us all—she was truly a force of nature. Heather returned to New York City as the pastry chef at Windows on the World, where her career tragically ended on September 11, 2001, in an irresolvable and heartbreaking way.

This lemon icebox cake became one of Heather's signature desserts, although it barely scratched the surface of her talents. The unexpected combination of tart lemon and rich caramel, topped with spiky brûléed meringue and fresh huckleberry sauce, is as good to look at as it is to eat.

KITCHEN AND SHOPPING NOTES

To our amazement, Heather always made her own graham crackers, a complex and thankless task from which you will be spared; go ahead and buy them. As with all icebox cakes, these individual cakes freeze extremely well and are the most delicious when still half frozen. This recipe can be made as one big cake, but Heather's special touch was to pipe a caramel center into each cake; a delicious detail difficult to achieve in anything other than individual molds.

To make the individual cakes, you'll need 12 metal ring molds, each 2 inches high and 2½ inches in diameter. These little metal rings are invaluable for preparing small desserts and are just the right size for individual servings. You could also use plastic PVC pipe, which can be purchased at hardware stores in different diameters and can be cut to any length. But unfortunately, this particular dessert can be a little tricky to release from a PVC mold because, unlike metal ring molds, you can't use a torch to heat them.

Small butane torches are readily available in cookware shops and are really handy to have in the kitchen; not only do they easily warm the sides of molds to release cold desserts, but they also make quick work of caramelizing sugar or meringue. The caramel cream and lemon curd can be made ahead and refrigerated for up to 5 days. The caramel needs to be rewarmed to a pourable consistency before using.

METHOD

FOR THE GRAHAM CRACKER CRUST: Preheat the oven to 350°F. Spread the graham cracker crumbs on a rimmed baking sheet and toast for about 7 minutes, or until they just start to take on color. Transfer the crumbs to a bowl and stir in the melted butter with a fork or your fingers until evenly moistened. Set aside.

FOR THE LEMON CURD: Whisk the eggs, egg yolks, lemon zest and juice, and sugar together in a bowl until well combined. Set over a saucepan of simmering water (make sure the bottom of the bowl does not touch the water). Cook, stirring constantly with a wooden spoon or heatproof rubber spatula, for 10 to 15 minutes, or until the mixture becomes thick and custardlike. Remove the bowl from the heat and whisk in the butter, one piece at a time, until melted and smooth. Strain the curd through a fine-mesh sieve into a clean bowl and immediately cover with plastic wrap, pressing it down on the surface to prevent a skin from forming. Refrigerate until ready to use, up to 3 days.

FOR THE CARAMEL CREAM: Whisk the cream in a bowl until it holds a soft peak and set aside. Using an electric mixer fitted with the paddle attachment, beat the cream cheese until smooth. Heat the caramel sauce over a saucepan of barely simmering water or in the microwave on HIGH for 1 minute, or until it's pourable but not too warm. Add the caramel sauce to the cream cheese and beat until thoroughly combined. Fold the whipped cream into the cream cheese–caramel mixture just until blended. Spoon the caramel cream into a pastry bag fitted with a ½-inch plain tip and refrigerate for up to 1 hour before assembly.

FOR THE LEMON CREAM: Whisk the cream just until it holds a stiff peak. Fold in the lemon curd until it's thoroughly combined and no streaks remain. Spoon the lemon cream into a pastry bag fitted with a ½-inch plain tip and refrigerate until assembling, up to 1 hour.

TO ASSEMBLE THE DESSERT: Line a small rimmed baking sheet with parchment paper. Place 12 (2½-inch-diameter) ring molds on the sheet and lightly spray the insides of the molds with nonstick cooking spray. Sprinkle 1½ tablespoons of the graham cracker crumb mixture onto the parchment inside each mold and press down to make a flat crust.

Spoon 1½ cups of the lemon curd into a pastry bag fitted with a ⅜-inch plain tip and pipe a thin layer onto the crusts. Pipe a layer of caramel cream about ¾ inch thick on top of the lemon curd. Sprinkle with a thin layer of graham cracker crumbs. Pipe a ½-inch-thick ring of lemon cream just along the inside edges of the molds, and spoon about 1½ teaspoons of the caramel sauce into the centers.

Make the meringue by whisking the egg whites with the sugar in a bowl (or the bowl of a stand mixer) set over a saucepan of simmering water (make sure the bottom of the bowl does not touch the water). Whisk until the egg whites are warm and the sugar has dissolved, about 3 minutes. Remove the bowl from the heat. Using the whisk attachment of the electric mixer set on medium-high speed, beat until the mixture forms stiff peaks. Top each icebox cake with an equal amount of meringue. Using the back of a spoon, pull up the meringue to form whimsical peaks. Freeze the molds for at least 6 hours; for longer storage, cover the frozen molds with plastic wrap and freeze for up to 1 week.

TO SERVE

About 1 hour before serving, transfer the icebox cakes to the refrigerator to soften slightly. Warm the remaining caramel sauce and drizzle in a decorative pattern on each of 12 dessert plates. Release the icebox cakes from their molds by briefly heating the sides of the molds with a butane torch, or run a small, sharp knife around the insides and lift the molds off the cakes. Using the torch, lightly brown the meringues. Alternatively, brown them under a broiler. Transfer the cakes to the plates and serve immediately.

BITTERSWEET CHOCOLATE CAKE

CARAMEL CORN ICE CREAM AND CARAMEL SAUCE

SERVES 6

CARAMEL CORN ICE CREAM

3 ears supersweet white corn

4 cups heavy cream

⅛ teaspoon kosher salt

10 large egg yolks

1 cup granulated sugar

CARAMEL POPCORN

12 cups unsalted popped popcorn
(from ½ cup kernels)

1¼ cups packed dark brown sugar

¾ cup (1½ sticks) unsalted butter

⅓ cup dark corn syrup

½ teaspoon kosher salt

CARAMEL SAUCE

2 cups granulated sugar

1 tablespoon light corn syrup

1¼ cups heavy cream

CHOCOLATE CAKE

¾ cup (1½ sticks) unsalted butter,
cut into 12 pieces

7 ounces bittersweet (61%)
chocolate, chopped

¼ cup cake flour

1 tablespoon unsweetened cocoa
powder

¼ teaspoon kosher salt

5 large eggs, separated

½ cup granulated sugar

⅓ cup packed dark brown sugar

⅛ teaspoon cream of tartar

This dessert is worth your weight in caramel corn, which is a good thing because you'll have enough leftover caramel corn from this recipe to take as a gift to the neighbor who always feeds your cat when you're away. We were unable to resist the temptation to take supersweet white corn and turn it into ice cream. When Nancy Pitta first made this luscious white corn ice cream we wanted to pair it with wild blueberries, but in our hearts we knew we would be the only two people eating it. Fortunately, Nancy was wise enough to know that a bittersweet chocolate cake would lead people to this unusual ice cream, just in case the caramel corn wasn't enough.

We think this chocolate cake is destined to become one of your favorites. Light and fine textured yet full of intense chocolate flavor, it's everything a chocolate cake should be, and so we return to it time and time again. The combination of crunchy caramel corn, velvety corn ice cream, and "your new best friend chocolate cake" makes a delicious and unusual dessert that will surprise and delight your guests.

continued

These small chocolate cakes are made in 10-ounce ramekins, but because they're so thin, they can quickly overcook. They're done when the centers are dark and still soft; to be on the safe side, remove them from the oven a little before you think they're done, when the centers still jiggle a bit. By the time they cool, they should be perfect.

The best popcorn is made from kernels that are fresh and popped in a hot-air popper. You can use unsalted microwave popcorn, but the quality varies by brand. If you're using a hot-air popper, make a tent out of plastic wrap that extends from the mouth of the popper to the bowl to prevent the corn from jumping out. Make sure you sort through the popped corn and discard any unpopped kernels before combining it with the caramel.

METHOD

FOR THE CARAMEL CORN ICE CREAM: With a chef's knife, cut the corn kernels from the cobs and put them into a large saucepan. Cut the cobs into 2-inch pieces and add to the saucepan along with the cream and salt. Bring the cream to a boil, remove from the heat, then cover and let steep for 45 minutes. Strain the mixture through a fine-mesh sieve and return to the saucepan. Heat over medium heat just until little bubbles begin to appear around the edge. Whisk the egg yolks and granulated sugar together in a bowl until smooth. Slowly ladle about half of the corn-cream mixture into the yolk mixture, whisking constantly until well combined. Pour the yolk-cream mixture into the saucepan and whisk to combine. Cook over medium heat, stirring with a rubber spatula so that you can scrape the bottom and corners of the pan, until the mixture thickens and coats the back of the spatula (when you draw your finger across the back of the spatula, there should be a visible trail that doesn't immediately flow back together). Strain again through a fine-mesh sieve into the heatproof container and chill thoroughly, at least 2 hours. Freeze according to the ice cream maker's instructions. The frozen ice cream should be stored in a tightly covered plastic or stainless-steel container. For the best flavor and texture, let it soften slightly at room temperature before serving.

FOR THE CARAMEL POPCORN: Preheat the oven to 250°F. Remove any unpopped kernels from the popcorn, and put the popcorn into a large heatproof bowl. Combine the brown sugar, butter, corn syrup, and salt in a heavy saucepan and cook over medium heat until the butter and sugar have melted, stirring once or twice to make sure all the sugar has melted. Bring to a boil, then immediately pour over the popcorn. Using a rubber spatula, quickly and thoroughly mix until the popcorn is evenly coated, making sure to scrape down the sides of the bowl to get all the caramel. Turn out onto a lightly oiled rimmed baking sheet and bake for 45 minutes, stirring the mixture every 15 minutes or so. Remove from the oven, give it one more stir, and set aside to cool. Once cool, the caramel corn should be dry and crisp. Store at room temperature in an airtight container for up to 3 days.

FOR THE CARAMEL SAUCE: Combine the granulated sugar and corn syrup in a heavy saucepan and stir in enough water to moisten the mixture so it resembles damp sand. Cook over medium heat until it turns the color of straw, using a pastry brush dipped in water to wipe down the sides of the pan to remove any sugar crystals. Decrease the heat slightly and cook, swirling the pan constantly, until the caramel turns a deep gold. Remove from the heat and carefully whisk in the cream (be careful as the hot mixture will bubble up and splatter). Return to the heat and whisk until thoroughly combined. Pour into a heatproof container and set aside to cool. The caramel can be stored in the refrigerator for up to 1 week.

FOR THE CHOCOLATE CAKE: Increase the oven temperature to 325°F. Spray 6 (10-ounce) ramekins well with nonstick cooking spray or generously brush with melted butter. Place the ramekins on a rimmed baking sheet and set aside. Heat the butter and chocolate in a bowl set over a saucepan of barely simmering water (making sure the bottom of the bowl doesn't touch the water) until melted and smooth. Remove from the heat. Let the bowl sit over the water until ready to use. Sift the flour, cocoa powder and salt into a bowl and set aside. Whisk the egg yolks with the sugars in a large bowl until smooth, then add the melted chocolate-butter mixture, whisking constantly until thoroughly combined. Whisk in the flour mixture until well blended.

In the large bowl of an electric mixer fitted with the whisk attachment, beat the egg whites with the cream of tartar until soft peaks form (be careful not to whip them to stiff peaks). Using a rubber spatula, stir one-third of the whites into the chocolate mixture to lighten it, then fold in the remaining whites just until no white streaks remain. Divide the batter among the prepared ramekins. Bake for about 12 minutes, or until the centers are dark but still slightly soft when pressed (see Kitchen and Shopping Notes). Remove from the oven, let cool completely, then unmold the cakes onto a wire rack. The cakes are best eaten the day they're made but can be made several hours in advance.

TO SERVE

Increase the oven temperature to 350°F. Heat the chocolate cakes on a baking sheet for 5 minutes, or until warm. Rewarm the caramel sauce in a small bowl set over simmering water or in the microwave. Pour the warm caramel into a squeeze bottle and decorate 6 dessert plates with caramel. Place a warm cake in the center of each plate, top with a scoop of ice cream, and drizzle with a little more caramel. Scatter caramel corn around the plates, on top of the cake, and over the ice cream.

CHOCOLATE TEMPTATION

. . . .

CHOCOLATE PANNA COTTA, CHOCOLATE TOFFEE CRUNCH

. . . .

SERVES 6

CHOCOLATE BROWNIES

1¾ cups cake flour

2 tablespoons unsweetened
    cocoa powder

1½ teaspoons kosher salt

1½ cups (3 sticks) unsalted butter

6 ounces unsweetened (100%)
    chocolate, chopped

3 ounces bittersweet (61%)
    chocolate, chopped

3 cups sugar

6 large eggs

1½ teaspoons bourbon or dark rum,
    or 1 teaspoon vanilla extract

CHOCOLATE PANNA COTTA

1½ teaspoons unflavored gelatin

1½ cups plus 2 tablespoons
    heavy cream

2½ ounces bittersweet (61%)
    chocolate

⅓ cup mascarpone cheese

2½ tablespoons sugar

¼ teaspoon kosher salt

CHOCOLATE LACE TUILES

½ cup plus 1½ tablespoons all-
    purpose flour

¼ cup unsweetened cocoa powder

¼ teaspoon kosher salt

½ cup (1 stick) unsalted butter

½ cup sugar

5 tablespoons light corn syrup

1 teaspoon vanilla extract

MACADAMIA NUT TOFFEE

½ cup sugar

¼ cup water

1 tablespoon light corn syrup

4 tablespoons unsalted butter, cut
    into 4 pieces

⅛ teaspoon kosher salt

⅛ teaspoon vanilla extract

½ cup macadamia nuts, toasted
    (see Basics, page 234) and
    finely chopped

MANJARI CHOCOLATE TOFFEE CRUNCH

6 ounces milk chocolate, chopped

1 ounce bittersweet (61%)
    chocolate, chopped

8 ounces Manjari chocolate (see
    Sources, page 237)

1 cup crushed or chopped (¼ inch)
    vanilla wafers

½ cup finely chopped macadamia
    nut toffee

1 cup heavy cream

HOT FUDGE SAUCE

(see Basics, page 232)

Macadamia nut toffee, for garnish
    (optional)

Some people plan their meals around dessert, while others simply surrender to temptation. Decadent and delicious, two desserts are always better than one. Here we are doing just that (admittedly easy for professional kitchens): pairing two fabulous chocolate desserts when really either would be completely satisfying on its own. Like a Fudgesicle without the icy bite, the chocolate panna cotta with its brownie bottom would be perfect served next to a pile of fresh summer berries. On its own, the chocolate toffee crunch is like the best candy bar you can imagine. You could also cut it into bite-size pieces and serve as a petit four, or serve it alongside seasonal citrus segments for a simple yet sophisticated dessert. It is tempting to make just one or the other, but we think it's worth the effort to serve these chocolate desserts together and experience the different tastes and textures.

KITCHEN AND SHOPPING NOTES

Extra-bitter chocolate is a term usually reserved for chocolate that has at least 61% or more cocoa and less sugar. It's mainly used in restaurants, but you can find it from mail-order sources and in specialty food stores.

continued

The brownies are dense and rich, not cakelike at all. Check the baking time carefully and remove from the oven when a skewer comes out almost clean with just a few moist crumbs attached.

Note that the batter for the tuiles can be made up to 1 week ahead, but once baked, the tuiles keep for only 3 days.

METHOD

FOR THE BROWNIES: Preheat the oven to 350°F. Spray a 9-by-12-inch rimmed baking sheet with nonstick cooking spray. Line the bottom with parchment paper and spray the parchment. Set out the 6 (2-ounce) timbales or ramekins for the panna cotta.

Sift the cake flour, cocoa powder, and salt into a bowl or onto a piece of parchment and set aside. Put the butter and chopped chocolates into a bowl set over a saucepan of simmering water (make sure the bottom of the bowl doesn't touch the water) and heat, stirring occasionally, until the chocolate and butter have melted, then stir in $1\frac{1}{2}$ cups of the sugar and remove from the heat. Whisk the eggs, the remaining sugar, and the bourbon together in a large bowl. Stir in the melted chocolate mixture with a wooden spoon or heatproof rubber spatula, then add the sifted flour mixture and stir until well combined. Pour into the prepared baking pan and place in the oven. The baking time is crucial—begin checking after 30 minutes—a skewer should come out nearly clean with just a few moist crumbs. It may take as long as 45 minutes. Remove from the oven and let cool completely in the pan on a wire rack. With a small, sharp knife, cut out 3 brownies the same size as the diameter of the top of the panna cotta timbales, and then cut them horizontally in half. Cover and set aside or store at room temperature for up to 1 day. Reserve extra brownies for another use.

FOR THE PANNA COTTA: Spray 6 (2-ounce) timbales or ramekins with nonstick cooking spray and set aside. Sprinkle the gelatin over $\frac{1}{4}$ cup of the cream in a small bowl, then stir well and set aside. Heat the remaining cream in a small saucepan over medium heat just until little bubbles begin to appear around the edge, then whisk in the mascarpone, sugar, and salt until combined. Pour over the chopped chocolate, whisking constantly until the chocolate has melted and the mixture is smooth. Set the bowl with the gelatin-cream mixture over a small saucepan of simmering water for a few minutes, stirring occasionally, until the gelatin has completely dissolved (rub a small amount of the mixture between two fingers to check). Whisk the gelatin mixture into the chocolate mixture, then strain through a fine-mesh sieve into a large glass measuring cup. Slowly pour into the prepared timbales, dividing it evenly. Refrigerate for 1 hour, or until they just begin to set up, then press a brownie on the top. (It's easier to place the brownie directly onto the panna cotta when it is in the process of setting up. If it's already firm, however, just before serving, warm the surface with a butane torch and press the brownie firmly onto the top.) Refrigerate for at least 2 hours more, or until firm.

FOR THE TUILES: Sift the flour, cocoa, and salt together into a large bowl or onto a piece of parchment and set aside. In the bowl of an electric mixer fitted with the paddle attachment, beat the butter and sugar together on medium speed until well blended. Beat in the corn syrup and vanilla, decrease the speed to low, and add half of the flour mixture, mixing until combined. Mix in the remaining flour mixture until combined. Refrigerate the batter, covered, for at least 1 hour or for up to 1 week.

Preheat the oven to 350°F. Let the tuile batter come to room temperature. Place a nonstick baking liner on a baking sheet. Using a small offset spatula, spread the batter on the prepared sheet into a rough rectangle ¹⁄₁₆ inch thick. Bake for about 6 minutes, or until the batter stops bubbling. Remove from the oven and immediately, while the tuile is still warm and pliable, use a knife or pizza cutter to cut into rectangles about 1½ by 2½ inches. Using a spatula, and working quickly while the tuiles are still warm, transfer them to a flat plate or baking sheet. If the tuiles cool and become stiff, return the pan to the oven for a minute or two before continuing. Store at room temperature in an airtight container for up to 3 days.

FOR THE TOFFEE: Line a rimmed baking sheet with a nonstick baking liner or parchment paper, spray with nonstick cooking spray, and place near the stove top. Combine the sugar, water, and corn syrup in a small saucepan and cook over medium heat, stirring, until the temperature reaches 280°F on a candy thermometer (if the liquid is too shallow to insert a thermometer, you may need to tilt the saucepan and check at eye level to get an accurate reading). Decrease the heat to medium-low and stir in the butter, 1 piece at a time, until melted and smooth. Decrease the heat to low and cook, stirring constantly, until the mixture reaches 305°F, watching carefully because it cooks rapidly. At this point the caramel should be thick, viscous, and deep golden brown. Remove the pan from the heat and stir in the salt and vanilla. Pour the toffee out onto the prepared baking sheet and, using oven mitts, quickly tilt the pan to spread it thinly and evenly. Sprinkle the macadamia nuts evenly over the toffee and set aside to cool for at least 1 hour. Wrap in plastic and store for up to 2 days. To use the toffee, break it up with your hands, then finely chop ½ cup for the toffee crunch. You'll have more than you need for the recipe. Store the rest in an airtight container at room temperature.

FOR THE TOFFEE CRUNCH: Lightly spray a disposable aluminum foil or metal 9-by-6-by-1-inch loaf pan with nonstick cooking spray and place on a rimmed baking sheet. Combine the milk and bittersweet chocolates in 1 small bowl and the Manjari chocolate in another. Set each bowl over a small saucepan of barely simmering water (make sure the bottoms don't touch the water). Heat, stirring a few times, until both batches have melted. Remove from the heat but let the bowls sit over the warm water until ready to use. Combine the vanilla wafers and toffee in a bowl. Set aside. Whip the heavy cream with an electric mixer until it holds a medium peak and set aside.

To make the base for the toffee crunch, add the milk-chocolate mixture to the toffee mixture, mix well, and immediately pour into the prepared loaf pan. With a small offset spatula, spread to an even thickness. Fold the Manjari chocolate into the whipped cream until no white streaks remain, then pour over the chocolate-toffee layer and spread evenly. Lightly tap the loaf pan on the counter to release any air bubbles from the whipped cream and refrigerate for 3 hours, or until the chocolate cream has set.

TO SERVE

About 30 minutes before serving, remove the toffee crunch from the refrigerator. Drizzle some fudge sauce onto each of 12 dessert plates. Unmold each panna cotta by placing it in a bowl of hot water for a few seconds. Invert onto a small plate and, holding the plate and panna cotta together, give it a quick little shake to help it release from the mold. If it doesn't come out, put it back into the water for another second. With a wide spatula, transfer the panna cotta to one of the sauced plates, placing it slightly off-center. To cut the toffee crunch, dip a chef's knife into a tall container of hot water, wipe it dry, and press it down on the toffee with one rocking motion all the way through. Cut the ends just enough to square them, then carefully cut the toffee crunch into 12 (2-by-2½-inch) rectangles. Place a toffee crunch next to each panna cotta. Slip a tuile in between. Top with a piece of toffee.

VANILLA, VANILLA, VANILLA

CRÈME BRÛLÉE, BAVARIAN TIMBALE, ICE CREAM SANDWICH

SERVES 12

VANILLA CRÈME BRÛLÉE

2¼ cups heavy cream

¾ cup whole milk

1 vanilla bean, halved lengthwise,
      seeds scraped

Pinch of kosher salt

9 large egg yolks

½ cup plus 2 tablespoons sugar

CHOCOLATE MAYO CAKE

2 cups all-purpose flour

½ cup plus 2 tablespoons
      unsweetened cocoa powder

½ teaspoon salt

1¼ teaspoons baking soda

¼ teaspoon baking powder

3 large eggs

1⅔ cups sugar

1 cup mayonnaise

1 tablespoon vanilla extract

1⅓ cups water

BAVARIAN CREAM

1 envelope (2½ teaspoons)
      unflavored gelatin

2½ tablespoons cold water

¾ cup whole milk

½ vanilla bean, halved lengthwise,
      seeds scraped

3 large egg yolks

⅓ cup plus 2 tablespoons sugar

1 cup heavy cream

¼ teaspoon vanilla extract

CHOCOLATE SAUCE

Hot Fudge Sauce (see Basics,
      page 232)

¼ cup water

ICE CREAM SANDWICHES

1¼ cups all-purpose flour

¼ cup plus 1½ teaspoons sugar

¼ teaspoon kosher salt

1 vanilla bean, halved lengthwise,
      seeds scraped

½ cup (1 stick) cold unsalted butter,
      cut into ½-inch pieces

Vanilla ice cream (see Chocolate
      Cherry Shortcakes, page 200)

VANILLA SYRUP

1½ cups sugar

1 cup water

2 tablespoons light corn syrup

1 vanilla bean, halved lengthwise,
      seeds scraped

About 1 cup superfine sugar for
      the brûlée topping

Lovely vanilla, the fruit of a delicate orchid. Creamy, smooth, sweet, and mellow in flavor, it isn't just plain old vanilla to us. Simple and pure flavors with different textures and temperatures have made this one of the most popular desserts we've ever served at Boulevard.

Each "vanilla" is a dessert in itself. Serving all three might be considered over the top, but that's exactly the point.

KITCHEN AND SHOPPING NOTES

There are four main areas in the world that produce vanilla, and each possesses different and distinct characteristics. For a really special effect here, try using vanillas of different origins, particularly if you can get your hands on some Mexican vanilla, the "original" vanilla.

Bourbon vanilla is from Madagascar, which exports most of the world's vanilla beans. It is also considered the highest quality and is our own personal favorite. It's rich, sweet, and very aromatic. Mexican vanilla is mellower and has a slightly spicy note, but is hard to come by. Tahitian vanilla, which is grown from a different species of the vanilla orchid, is a bit floral with notes of anise. Indonesia is a large producer of vanilla beans, but their beans don't receive the same acclaim as those from the other three growing regions.

continued

Timbales, French for "kettledrums," which these small molds resemble, are made of stainless or tinned steel and are available in 2-, 4-, and 6-ounce sizes (this recipe uses 2-ounce timbales). The cookies for the ice cream sandwiches are cut using 1½-inch flower-shaped cookie cutters. Any shape of similar size will do; you could cut squares or rectangles, for example.

METHOD

FOR THE CRÈME BRÛLÉE: Preheat the oven to 325°F. Place 12 (4-ounce) ramekins in a baking dish or roasting pan and set aside. Heat the cream, milk, vanilla-bean pod and seeds, and salt in a saucepan over medium heat, just until little bubbles begin to appear around the edge. Remove from the heat, cover, and let steep for 15 minutes. Whisk the egg yolks and sugar together in a bowl until smooth. Slowly ladle the warm vanilla-cream mixture into the yolk mixture, whisking constantly until well combined. Strain through a fine-mesh sieve into a large glass measuring cup (retrieve, rinse, and dry the vanilla pod and save for another use if you like). Meanwhile bring a teakettle of water to a boil. Slowly pour the custard into the ramekins to within ½ inch of the tops. Carefully put the baking dish into the oven. Pour enough boiling water in the baking dish to come halfway up the sides of the ramekins. Cover the baking dish with aluminum foil and crimp the edges to form a tight seal. Bake the custards for 20 to 30 minutes, or until they feel firm but the centers are still a little jiggly. Remove from the oven and, using tongs, transfer the custards to a baking sheet or wire rack to cool.

FOR THE CHOCOLATE CAKE: Increase the oven temperature to 350°F. Spray a 9-by-12-inch rimmed baking sheet with nonstick cooking spray and line with parchment paper. Spray the parchment and set aside. Sift the flour, cocoa, salt, baking soda, and baking powder together into a bowl or onto a piece of parchment and set aside. In the bowl of an electric mixer fitted with the whisk attachment, whip the eggs and sugar on medium speed until the mixture forms a slight ribbon when the beaters are lifted. Add the mayonnaise and vanilla and beat until thoroughly combined. Add one-quarter of the flour mixture and beat on medium-low speed until combined, then add about one-third of the water. Continue alternately adding the remaining flour mixture and water, mixing well after each addition and ending with the flour mixture. Pour the batter onto the prepared baking sheet and spread it evenly. Bake for about 20 minutes, or until a tester inserted into the center comes out clean and the top springs back when lightly pressed. Let the cake cool in the pan for 20 minutes, then invert onto a wire rack and cool to room temperature. Wrap the cake with plastic and store at room temperature for up to 2 days.

FOR THE BAVARIAN CREAM: Spray 12 (2-ounce) timbales with nonstick cooking spray and set aside. Sprinkle the gelatin over the water in a dish, stir well, and set aside. Heat the milk with the vanilla-bean pod and seeds in a small saucepan over medium heat just until little bubbles begin to appear around the edge. Whisk the egg yolks and sugar together in a bowl until smooth. Slowly whisk half of the warm milk into the yolk mixture, then stir back into the saucepan. Cook, stirring, over medium-low heat, for about 2 minutes, or until the mixture just begins to thicken. Remove from the heat, add the softened gelatin and stir until the gelatin has dissolved (rub a bit between your fingers to check).

Strain through a fine-mesh sieve into a bowl and set aside to cool. In the bowl of an electric mixer fitted with the whisk attachment, whip the cream on medium-high speed until it holds a stiff peak. Fold in the cooled but still liquid egg-milk mixture and whisk on low speed until the mixtures are just combined. Pour into the prepared timbales, dividing it evenly, and refrigerate for about 3 hours, or until firm.

To assemble the Bavarian timbales, heat the hot fudge sauce over low heat on the stove or in the microwave on HIGH for 1 minute. Stir in the water and set aside. Cut the chocolate cake into circles the same size as the open end of the timbales, then cut the circles in half horizontally (each layer will be about $\frac{1}{4}$ inch thick) and set aside. Using a melon baller, scoop out a small deep amount of the Bavarian cream and fill the hollow with chocolate sauce. A few at a time, lightly warm the surface of the Bavarian creams with a torch, then press the cake layers onto the cream, making sure there's a good seal. Refrigerate for up to 8 hours before serving.

FOR THE ICE CREAM SANDWICHES: First make the shortbread cookies: In the bowl of an electric mixer fitted with the paddle attachment, stir together the flour, $\frac{1}{4}$ cup sugar, salt, and vanilla seeds (reserve the scraped pod for another use) until just combined. Add the butter and mix on low speed until the dough just begins to come together. Turn the dough out onto a work surface and pat into a thick disk. Wrap with plastic and refrigerate for at least 1 hour or up to 2 days.

Preheat the oven to 350°F. Lightly flour a work surface and roll the dough out $\frac{1}{8}$ inch thick. Using a $1\frac{1}{2}$-inch flower-shaped cutter, cut out 48 cookies and place on an ungreased baking sheet $\frac{1}{2}$ inch apart. Sprinkle the cookies with the $1\frac{1}{2}$ teaspoons sugar and bake for 7 minutes, or until golden. Transfer to a wire rack to cool completely and store in an airtight container for up to 2 days.

To assemble the sandwiches, place a small (2-ounce) scoop of vanilla ice cream on 24 of the shortbread cookies and top with another cookie, pressing down lightly (make sure the "pretty" side of the cookies is facing out). Wrap each sandwich in plastic and freeze for up to 2 days. Let sit out at room temperature for a few minutes before serving.

FOR THE VANILLA SYRUP: Combine the sugar, water, corn syrup, and vanilla bean pod and seeds in a small saucepan over medium heat and cook for about 15 minutes, or until syrupy. Strain through a fine-mesh sieve into a small bowl and return the vanilla-bean pod to the syrup. Cover and set aside at room temperature for at least 2 hours or up to 5 days.

TO SERVE

Sprinkle the crème brûlée with an even $\frac{1}{8}$-inch-thick layer of sugar. Using a butane torch, caramelize the sugar until it's evenly melted and golden brown. (You can also use a broiler, but it needs to be really hot so the custard doesn't soften before the sugar browns. You'll also probably need to rotate the pan to brown them evenly.) Drizzle 12 dessert plates with a decorative ribbon of vanilla syrup. Place 2 ice cream sandwiches and a crème brûlée on each plate. Dip the timbales into a small bowl of warm water, then invert onto a plate. Using a spatula, transfer the Bavarian creams to the serving plates.

BLVD BASICS

AIOLI

Makes about 1 cup

Using a whole egg in this garlic mayonnaise helps to stabilize it, but 2 egg yolks will also work. Another variation is to use 2 tablespoons of Melted Garlic (see page 232) in place of the minced garlic and replace some of the oil with the oil used to make the Melted Garlic.

3 garlic cloves, peeled
Kosher salt and freshly ground black pepper
1 large egg
1 cup olive oil
Freshly squeezed lemon juice to taste

Finely mince the garlic with a little salt until it forms a paste. Put in a small bowl with some pepper and egg and whisk until combined. Slowly whisk in the olive oil, in drops at first and increasing the amount added as the sauce begins to thicken. Season to taste with lemon juice and more salt and pepper if necessary. Aioli keeps in the refrigerator for up to 5 days. Thin out with a little warm water if necessary.

BEURRE FONDUE

Beurre fondue finds many uses in our kitchen: in pasta sauces, for poaching fish, and for drizzling over vegetables. Like a beurre blanc, it's an emulsification of butter, but water is used for the liquid instead of wine or lemon juice. Bring 2 tablespoons water to a boil in a small skillet or saucepan, decrease the heat to low, and whisk in ½-inch cubes of butter, one piece at a time, until they melt and emulsify. You can add as much butter as needed for any recipe—without increasing the amount of water—from 4 tablespoons or up to several pounds. It's so quick and easy to make beurre fondue that we like to make it just before we need it, but it can be kept for an hour or so over a saucepan of warm water.

BRAISED BACON AND
BACON BRAISING STOCK

Preheat the oven to 350°F. Cut ½ pound slab bacon into ½-by-¾-inch pieces (we call these lardons). Put the lardons into a small ovenproof skillet with water to cover. Bring to a boil, reduce the heat, and simmer for 10 minutes. Drain off the water and cook the bacon over medium-high heat until it begins to brown slightly, about 2 minutes. Add 1 cup Dark Chicken

Stock (page 230) and put the pan into the oven for 20 to 30 minutes, or until the bacon looks crispy around the edges. Strain through a sieve, reserving both the stock and the bacon. Skim off the fat from the stock and discard. You should have about ½ cup liquid. Refrigerate the stock and bacon for up to 4 days in separate containers.

BREAD CRUMBS

Put day-old slices of crustless French bread on a baking sheet and place in a 200°F oven for 1 hour to dry. Let cool, tear into large pieces, and pulse in a food processor or blender until medium-coarse crumbs form. Put in a zippered bag and store at room temperature for up to 2 days or freeze for up to 2 months.

CANDIED NUTS

1 cup nuts: walnuts, hazelnuts, or pecans
2 tablespoons corn syrup
2 tablespoons sugar
⅛ teaspoon salt
Freshly ground black pepper

Fill a medium bowl with hot tap water and add the nuts, swish them around, then drain and transfer to another bowl. Add the corn syrup, sugar, salt, pepper and stir. Line a baking sheet with parchment or use a non-stick baking sheet, and spread out the nuts in one layer, being sure to include any of the sugary liquid left in the bowl on the parchment with the nuts. Increase the oven heat to 325° F and cook for 20 to 30 minutes, stirring the nuts a few times, until golden brown and crispy. Remove from the oven and let cool slightly, then break the nuts apart (watch out as they're hot—use rubber gloves). Store in an air-tight container for up to 1 week. They can be chopped into bite-sized pieces for specific recipes.

CRAB SALAD

Makes ¾ cup

¼ pound cooked Dungeness crabmeat, picked over
2 tablespoons mayonnaise
1 teaspoon seeded, very finely diced (⅛-inch)
    jalapeño pepper
1 teaspoon (¼-inch) finely diced celery
½ teaspoon chopped fresh flat-leaf parsley leaves
¼ teaspoon grated lemon zest

Stir all the ingredients together in a small bowl and refrigerate, covered, for up to 1 day.

CREAMED SPINACH (OR GREENS)

Makes about 2¼ cups

2 pounds spinach, stemmed and cleaned
1 tablespoon unsalted butter
1 shallot, minced
½ cup heavy cream
Kosher salt and freshly ground black pepper
Freshly grated nutmeg (optional)

Put the spinach (with the rinsing water still clinging to its leaves) in a large saucepan, Dutch oven, or large, deep skillet. Cook over medium heat, stirring with tongs, until completely wilted (you may need to do this in batches, depending on the size of your pot). Drain in a colander, rinse with cold water, and squeeze out as much water as possible. (We find that pressing the spinach in a potato ricer works well.) Finely chop the spinach. Melt the butter in a skillet over low heat and sauté the shallot for about 2 minutes, or until softened. Add the spinach and cook over medium heat for about 2 minutes, or until the pan is dry. Add the cream and simmer until the cream has thickened slightly. Season to taste with salt, pepper, and nutmeg. If not using immediately, cool the spinach down quickly by putting it into a bowl set over a bowl of ice water and stirring several times until it is cool. (Otherwise, the spinach will turn an unappetizing gray.) Refrigerate for up to 8 hours.

DUCK CONFIT

While duck confit can be purchased by mail order and in many markets these days, it's not difficult to make, though it does take time and advance planning. The hardest part is finding (or accumulating) a fairly large quantity of duck fat, but you can also purchase duck fat in tubs from several mail-order sources (page xxx). Try slow-cooking some cubed potatoes in duck fat and you'll never want to be without it. If you prefer, however, you can use olive oil in place of duck fat. Once you have duck confit around (it keeps in the fridge for up to 6 months), you'll always be prepared for impromptu dinners. (Figure that a 2-pound container equals about 1 quart fat.)

1 cup kosher salt
1 tablespoon freshly ground black pepper
2 teaspoons dried thyme
2 bay leaves, crumbled
Pinch of ground allspice
10 duck legs (with thighs attached)
2 to 3 quarts duck fat or olive oil

Combine the salt, pepper, thyme, bay leaves, and allspice in a large bowl. Add the duck legs and rub them all over with the salt mixture. Cover with plastic wrap and refrigerate for 24 hours. Remove the legs from the salt, rinse well, and pat dry with paper towels.

Preheat the oven to 200°F. Heat the duck fat in a large saucepan over low heat just until it melts. Put the duck legs in a large casserole dish or saucepan that will hold them snugly in 2 layers. Pour enough of the melted fat over the legs to cover them by an inch or so. Heat the casserole dish over medium heat until the fat comes to a very low simmer. Carefully transfer to the oven and bake until the meat has shrunk from the ankle bones and is very tender but not falling apart. Using tongs, transfer the legs to a wire rack set over a shallow baking pan to drain. When cool, transfer the duck to a glass bowl or crock and refrigerate. Strain the duck fat through a fine-mesh sieve into a clean large saucepan and bring to a boil over high heat. Decrease the heat and simmer until all the duck juices have evaporated, skimming the surface as necessary. Remove from the heat and let the fat cool, then pour over the duck legs, making sure they're covered by at least 1 inch of fat. Cover and store in the refrigerator for up to 6 months. Whenever you remove duck legs, make sure the remaining ones are still covered with fat.

FAVA BEANS

1 pound of favas equals about ½ cup shelled beans

To shell fava beans, break open the fur-lined pods and remove the beans. Blanch in boiling water for 1 minute and drop into a bowl of ice water. Using your fingernail or a small paring knife, slit the skin and pop the bean out.

FISH FUMET

Makes about 4 quarts

The key to making a good fish stock (fumet) is to use bones and trimmings from mild-tasting white fish. Also, clean and rinse the bones well to remove any traces of blood, don't let the stock boil, and skim it frequently. Begin tasting it after 15 minutes to see if it's flavorful enough, but don't cook it longer than 40 minutes. If you like a stronger stock, double the amount of bones.

continued

4 pounds bones and heads (gills removed) from
nonoily, white-fleshed fish, such as sole, halibut,
sea bass, or cod
2 tablespoons flavorless vegetable oil
2 onions, coarsely chopped
1 carrot, coarsely chopped
2 celery ribs, coarsely chopped
1 fennel bulb, coarsely chopped (optional)
1 cup dry white wine
4 quarts water
4 flat-leaf parsley sprigs
2 thyme sprigs
20 black peppercorns
1 bay leaf
Kosher salt and freshly ground black pepper

Rinse the bones and heads well and chop up any large bones. Heat the oil in a large stockpot over medium heat. Add the fish bones and heads, onions, carrot, celery, and fennel, decrease the heat to low, and cook for about 5 minutes, or until the vegetables are soft and translucent. Add the wine, increase the heat to high, and cook for 1 minute to cook off the alcohol, then add the water. Bring the liquid to a simmer and cook, skimming off the foam frequently for a few minutes. Add the parsley and thyme sprigs, peppercorns, and bay leaf and decrease the heat to maintain a simmer for 30 minutes. Remove from the heat and strain through a fine-mesh sieve into a large storage container or two, discarding the solids. Season to taste with salt and pepper. Let cool, then refrigerate for up to 3 days, or ladle the stock into small covered containers and freeze for up to 2 months.

LIGHT CHICKEN STOCK

Makes about 12 cups

4 pounds chicken wings
4 pounds chicken legs, backs, and carcasses,
    or use more chicken wings
About 7 quarts water
10 flat-leaf parsley sprigs
1 bay leaf
1 teaspoon black peppercorns
1 large carrot, peeled and coarsely chopped
2 celery ribs, coarsely chopped
1 leek, halved lengthwise, cleaned, and
    sliced ½ inch thick
1 large onion, coarsely chopped

Put the chicken into a large stockpot and cover with the water, adding more if necessary. Bring the water to a boil over high heat and skim off the

foam. Meanwhile, tie up the parsley, bay leaf, and peppercorns in a cheesecloth bag to make a bouquet garni. Add the carrot, celery, leek, onion, and bouquet garni to the pot and bring back to a boil. Skim again and decrease the heat to maintain a simmer. Cook for 2½ to 3 hours, skimming occasionally. Strain through a fine-mesh sieve into a large bowl or two, let cool completely, and skim once more. Refrigerate, covered, for up to 4 days, then bring back to a boil and refrigerate for 2 more days, or freeze for up to 2 months in small containers.

DARK CHICKEN STOCK

Makes about 8 cups

Dark chicken stock is the workhorse of our kitchen, and having some in your fridge is like money in the bank. Actually it's a double chicken stock, meaning that we use a light chicken stock instead of water for simmering the roasted chicken bones. We also cook the stock in the oven instead of on the stove top, which allows the surface of the stock to caramelize further, so it becomes even richer, darker, and more complex. For our recipe testing we used an extra-large roasting pan. If you don't have one, any large-capacity pot with a generous surface area will do (as long as it will fit in your oven and hold all the wings and liquid, of course). If you can't fit all the bones in one layer, use 2 rimmed baking sheets for roasting. You could also make the stock on top of the stove, but it won't become as dark or as rich. A convection oven, if you have one, will roast the bones much more quickly and evenly.

4 tablespoons flavorless vegetable oil
5 pounds chicken wings
1 small carrot, peeled and coarsely chopped
1 celery rib, coarsely chopped
1 large onion, cut into eighths
12 cups Light Chicken Stock (see above)

Preheat the oven to 450°F. Put 2 tablespoons of the oil in a large, deep roasting pan (see note above) and spread the chicken wings in one layer. Roast, turning once or twice, for 45 minutes to 1 hour, or until the wings are golden brown and crispy on all sides. Toss the carrot, celery, and onion in a bowl with the remaining 2 tablespoons oil, then add to the wings in the pan. Roast, turning once or twice with a spatula, for 30 to 45 minutes more, or until the vegetables are golden. Carefully add the stock to the roasting pan, scraping up all the browned bits on the bottom of the pan. Decrease the oven temperature to 375°F and cook, stirring several times, until the chicken is falling off the bone and the stock is dark brown. Remove the pan from the oven and strain the stock through a fine-mesh sieve into a large bowl or container, pressing on the solids to extract as much liquid as possible. Let cool completely and skim off the fat and discard. Refrigerate for up to 4 days, then bring back to a boil and refrigerate for 2 more days, or freeze for up to 2 months in small containers.

RICH BEEF STOCK

Makes about 6 cups

3 to 4 tablespoons vegetable oil

3 pounds (2-inch-thick) beef shanks or
    bone-in chuck steaks

1 unpeeled onion, halved

1 head garlic, halved crosswise

2 celery ribs, cut into 3 or 4 pieces

2 carrots, peeled and cut into 3 or 4 pieces

8 large domestic brown or white mushrooms

5 flat-leaf parsley stems

8 thyme sprigs

2 bay leaves

2 teaspoons tomato paste

8 cups Dark Chicken Stock (see above)

4 cups water

2 teaspoons black peppercorns

Heat 2 tablespoons of the oil in a large skillet over medium-high heat. Brown the meat on all sides, in batches, transferring it as it is ready to a large stockpot. Discard any oil that has blackened and add the remaining oil if necessary. Add the onion and garlic to the skillet, cut sides down. Decrease the heat to medium and cook until the onion and garlic are very deep brown, being careful to avoid burning (the garlic will brown after just a few minutes). Transfer the onion and garlic to the stockpot. Add the celery, carrots, and mushrooms to the skillet and cook for 5 to 7 minutes, or until lightly browned. Add the parsley stems, thyme sprigs, bay leaves, and tomato paste and cook for 2 to 3 minutes, stirring a few times to distribute the tomato paste. Put a cup or so of the chicken stock into the pan and stir, scraping up any browned bits from the bottom of the pan. Transfer the vegetables and any liquid to the stockpot and add the remaining chicken stock and the water. Bring to a boil over high heat and skim off the foam. Decrease the heat to maintain a simmer, add the peppercorns, and cook for 4 to 5 hours, skimming occasionally. Add more stock or water if necessary to keep the bones covered. Strain through a fine-mesh sieve into a large storage container or two, let cool completely, and skim off the fat. Refrigerate for up to 4 days, then bring back to a boil and refrigerate for 2 days more, or freeze for up to 2 months in small containers.

FENNEL RUB

We sprinkle this mixture on fish, poultry, and pork. Combine 3 tablespoons coarse sea salt, 1 tablespoon crushed fennel seeds or fennel pollen, and 1 tablespoon freshly ground black pepper in a small bowl. Store in an airtight container at room temperature, away from heat and light, for up to 4 months.

GIGANDE BEANS

Makes 6 cups

1 pound dried gigande, Italian butter,
    emergo, or cannellini beans

2 onions, cut into 1-inch pieces

2 carrots, peeled and cut into 1-inch pieces

1 celery rib, cut into 1-inch pieces

1 head garlic, halved crosswise

3 flat-leaf parsley sprigs

4 thyme sprigs

2 tablespoons kosher salt

Rinse the beans and put into a large bowl with cold water to cover by 2 to 3 inches. Swish the beans in the water, then scoop out and discard any "floaters"—they never seem to cook properly. Set the beans aside to soak overnight. Drain the beans and put into a large heavy pot or casserole dish with a tight-fitting lid. Add cold water to cover by at least 4 inches and bring to a boil over high heat. Boil for 3 to 4 minutes, then remove from the heat, cover, and let sit for 1 hour. Combine the onion, carrot, celery, garlic, parsley, and thyme in a cheesecloth bag and tie securely. Drain the beans, then return them to the pot along with the cheesecloth bag. Add cold water to cover, bring to a low simmer, and cook until the beans are tender all the way through, but not to the point where they fall apart. The cooking time can vary tremendously, depending on the type of bean and how old they are. It's best to check them every 15 minutes or so to monitor their progress (gigandes usually take about 1 hour). When the beans are done, remove the pot from the heat and stir in the salt. Let the beans cool in their cooking liquid, adding a large handful of ice cubes to speed up the process. When the beans are cool, remove the cheesecloth bag. Discard everything in the bag except for the garlic and reserve the garlic for making the Melted Garlic and Gigande Bean Fondue that follows. Store the beans in the refrigerator in their cooking liquid until ready to use. Squeeze the softened garlic out of their skins and store, covered, in the refrigerator.

GARLIC CONFIT AND GIGANDE BEAN FONDUE

Makes 2 cups

1 cup cooked gigande beans (see above)
¼ cup bean cooking liquid (see above)
Reserved garlic from the bean cooking liquid (see above)
½ cup best-quality extra-virgin olive oil
Kosher salt and freshly ground black pepper

Combine the beans and cooking liquid in a small saucepan and heat over low heat until warmed through. Transfer the warm beans to a blender and add the garlic. Cover the blender but remove the center part of the lid. With the machine running, add the olive oil. Season to taste with salt and pepper.

HOT FUDGE SAUCE

½ cup (1 stick) unsalted butter
½ cup corn syrup
½ cup water
⅓ cup sugar
¼ cup Dutch-processed cocoa powder
4 ounces bittersweet (61%) chocolate, chopped
1 teaspoon vanilla extract
⅛ teaspoon kosher salt

In a medium saucepan, melt the butter with the corn syrup, water and sugar. When the butter has melted, add the cocoa powder and stir with a wooden spoon or rubber spatula to combine. Bring to a simmer and cook for 3 minutes. Remove the pan from the heat. Place the chopped chocolate in a medium heatproof bowl and pour in the hot butter-cocoa mixture. Add the vanilla and salt, and, using a handheld electric mixer or a whisk, mix until combined. Strain through a fine-mesh sieve into a heatproof storage container or bowl and let cool. Cover and refrigerate for up to 2 weeks.

LOBSTER BASICS— COOKING AND CLEANING

For 2 (1- to 1½- pound) lobsters, bring 8 quarts water to a boil over high heat in a stockpot that holds at least 12 quarts. Add ½ cup kosher salt, 1 teaspoon black peppercorns, and 2 bay leaves. Immerse the lobsters in the boiling water, cover, and cook for 8 minutes for 1-pound lobsters, 10 minutes for 1¼-pound lobsters, and 12 minutes for 1½-pound lobsters. (Begin timing as soon as the lobsters go into the pot.) With tongs, remove the lobsters and rinse under cold water

to stop the cooking. Twist off the tails and snap off the claws, then clean the bodies by removing the lungs and sand sacs. Using kitchen scissors, cut down the center on the underside of the tails and pull out the tail meat in one piece (if this doesn't matter, you can cut the tails in half first). Then crack the claws and remove the meat. Save the shells, legs, head, and tomalley for sauce, or freeze them for later use. (Lobster shells and parts are particularly useful for making shellfish stock.)

MELTED GARLIC

This is an easy recipe for melted garlic that we use for all kinds of dishes. It's also great to have on hand if you have some cooked beans and haven't cooked any garlic with them in the pot.

¼ cup peeled cloves garlic
⅓ cup olive oil

Put the garlic into a small microwave-safe container and cover with the olive oil. Microwave on HIGH for 2 minutes, or until the garlic is soft when pierced with the tip of a small knife. Strain the garlic through a small sieve, reserving the garlic and the garlic-flavored oil separately.

OVEN-ROASTED TOMATOES

12 ripe but firm Roma (plum) tomatoes
2 tablespoons extra-virgin olive oil
½ bunch fresh thyme
4 sprigs fresh rosemary
3 sprigs fresh oregano
1 small clove garlic, thinly sliced
Kosher salt and freshly ground black pepper

Preheat the oven to 250°F and line a rimmed baking sheet with parchment paper. Peel the tomatoes using a swivel-bladed peeler (alternatively, cut an X in the bottom of each tomato, blanch in boiling water for 1 minute, then plunge into ice water and slip off the skins). Cut the tomatoes in half lengthwise and place in a bowl. Add the olive oil, thyme, rosemary, oregano, and garlic, season with salt and pepper, and toss until well coated. Place the tomatoes, cut side down, on the prepared baking sheet and lay the herbs on top. Roast for 2 hours, or until the tomatoes have shriveled and darkened. Remove the herbs. Refrigerate in a covered container for up to 5 days.

PASTA DOUGH

Makes 1 pound

2 cups all-purpose flour, plus additional for kneading
1 large egg
6 large egg yolks
1 tablespoon whole milk
1 tablespoon olive oil
2 teaspoons kosher salt

Mound the flour in the center of a clean, dry cutting board. Make a well in the flour and put the egg, egg yolks, milk, oil, and salt in the well. Using a fork, stir the eggs until they're lightly mixed with the other ingredients in the well, then gradually stir in the flour from around the well. As you add the flour, reshape the well with your hands as needed so it remains intact. When most of the flour has been incorporated, mix in the remaining flour until a shaggy mass has formed. Scrape the cutting board clean, then lightly flour the board. Knead the dough for 5 to 10 minutes, or until smooth, a little elastic, and not sticky, adding more flour to prevent the dough from sticking if necessary. Wrap the dough in plastic and let rest at room temperature for at least 30 minutes before rolling it out.

PESTO

Makes about 1 cup

2 cups loosely packed fresh basil leaves, patted dried
1 clove garlic
2 tablespoons pine nuts, toasted (page 234)
1 teaspoon kosher salt
½ cup extra-virgin olive oil
⅓ cup freshly grated Parmesan cheese

Put the basil, garlic, pine nuts, salt, and ¼ cup of the olive oil in a food processor. Process until smooth, scraping down the sides of the bowl once. With the machine running, add the remaining ¼ cup oil in a thin stream until the pesto has thickened. Transfer to a covered container and press a piece of plastic wrap directly onto the surface to prevent the pesto from darkening. Cover and refrigerate for up to 2 weeks, or freeze for up to 3 months. Stir in the Parmesan just before serving.

PORCINI-PORK SAUSAGE

Makes about 3½ pounds

4 tablespoons unsalted butter
½ pound fresh porcini mushrooms, cleaned and
    diced, or 1 cup dried porcini mushrooms (about
    1½ ounces), soaked in hot water to cover for
    15 minutes, drained, and diced
¼ cup finely chopped onion
2 tablespoons chopped garlic
1 tablespoon chopped fresh sage leaves, or
    2 teaspoons dried sage
2 teaspoons chopped fresh thyme leaves, or
    ½ teaspoon dried thyme
2½ pounds lean pork shoulder, cut into strips
    about ¾ inch thick and 6 inches long
½ pound fatback, cut into strips about
    ¾ inch thick by 6 inches long
1 tablespoon kosher salt
1½ teaspoons freshly ground black pepper
¼ teaspoon fennel seeds, ground
Pinch of freshly grated nutmeg
¼ cup chopped fresh flat-leaf parsley leaves
⅓ cup dry white wine

Melt the butter in a large skillet over medium heat. Add the fresh porcini and onion and cook for about 5 minutes, or until the onion is translucent and the mushrooms have softened. (If using dried porcini, add them to the skillet when the onion is translucent.) Add the garlic and cook for 2 to 3 minutes more. Stir in the fresh sage and thyme and set the mixture aside to cool. (If using dried herbs, add them to the pan with the garlic.)

In a large bowl, sprinkle the pork shoulder and fatback with the salt, pepper, fennel, and nutmeg and toss to coat well. Put the meat into the freezer for 15 minutes. Using a meat grinder fitted with a ⅜-inch-holed die, grind the meat and fat together into a large bowl. Add the mushroom-onion mixture, parsley, and wine and stir well to combine. Heat a small skillet and cook a small patty of the mixture, then taste and adjust the salt, pepper, or herbs as necessary. Form the sausage mixture into 8 patties about 2 inches in diameter and ¾ inch thick, or stuff the mixture into casings, if you like. (We like to pack the sausage mixture into 2-inch round cutters or ring molds.) The sausage can be refrigerated for up to 3 days or frozen for up to 2 months.

PORCINI POWDER

Makes about ⅓ cup

1 ounce dried porcini

Grind the porcini in a coffee grinder dedicated to spices or a spice mill to a fine powder. Store in a covered container at room temperature for up to 1 year.

PRESERVED LEMONS

12 to 15 organic lemons (preferably Meyer)
8 cups water
4 cups champagne or white wine vinegar
1 cup sugar
½ cup kosher salt

Wash the lemons well to remove any wax. Make 4 long lengthwise incisions in each lemon, leaving them attached at both ends. Combine the water, vinegar, sugar, and salt in a large saucepan and bring to a boil, stirring to make sure the salt and sugar have dissolved. If using Meyer lemons, add them to the pan and return the liquid to a boil. Remove the pan from the heat, put a heavy plate on top of the lemons to keep them submerged, and set aside until cool. If using regular (Eureka or Lisbon) lemons, add them to the pan and bring to a slow simmer. Put a heavy plate on top of the lemons to keep them submerged and cook for 12 to 15 minutes, or until the skins have softened. Remove from the heat and let the lemons cool in the liquid. Pack the lemons into clean glass jars, making sure they're completely covered with the liquid (if there's not enough liquid, add freshly squeezed lemon juice). Store, covered, in the refrigerator for up to 6 months.

TARTAR SAUCE

1½ cups homemade or good-quality commercial mayonnaise (we use Best Foods, known as Hellmann's east of the Mississippi)
¼ cup finely chopped cornichons
¼ cup finely diced celery
¼ cup capers, drained, rinsed, and finely chopped
2 tablespoons finely diced shallots
2 tablespoons finely chopped fresh flat-leaf parsley leaves
1 tablespoon Dijon mustard
1 teaspoon freshly ground black pepper

Stir all the ingredients together in a small bowl and refrigerate for up to 2 days.

TOASTING NUTS

Toasting nuts before adding them to recipes coaxes out their flavor and adds a little extra crunch. Walnuts tend to be bitter, so first blanch the walnuts by putting them into a sieve and pouring a teakettle of boiling water over them. Pat the nuts dry with paper towels and spread out on a small rimmed baking sheet or in a pie dish. Bake in a preheated 350°F oven, shaking the pan once or twice, for 8 to 12 minutes, or until the nuts are aromatic and lightly browned.

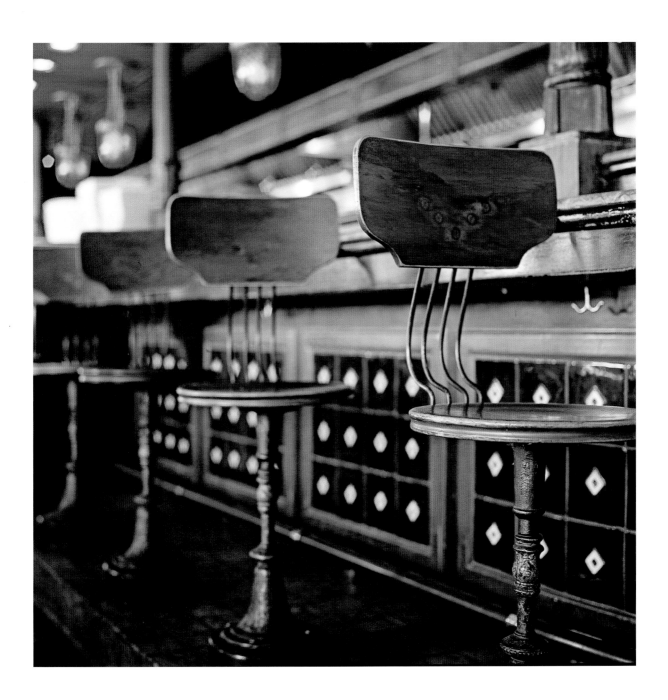

SOURCES

. . . .

Here are the email addresses and phone numbers of our favorite retail mail-order sources for the specialty products we refer to in our recipes. Some of the purveyors sell both retail and wholesale, so you'll have access to many of the same products we use at Boulevard. Today, with the internet, there are very few foodstuffs that *can't* be found and shipped directly to your door, but we recommend that you search out and support local producers for artisanal cheeses, heirloom fruits and vegetables, and organic meat and poultry. If you live near the coasts, locally caught seafood can be substituted in many of our fish recipes. Farmers' markets offer tremendous inspiration to creative cooks (see entry for locations nationwide).

MEATS, POULTRY, AND SEAFOOD

BROWNE TRADING COMPANY
800-944-7848
www.browne-trading.com
Rouget barbet (red mullet), scallops, halibut, snapper, ahi tuna. Although they have a website, you need to call them to order fresh fish, according to its availability.

D'ARTAGNAN
800-327-8346
www.dartagnan.com
Fresh and frozen truffles, duck confit, foie gras, duck, guinea hens, quail, squab, poussin, rabbit, duck fat

FARM-2-MARKET
800-663-4326
www.farm-2-market.com
Mussels, spiny lobster, Dungeness crab, sea scallops

GOLDEN GATE MEAT CO.
415-987-7800
www.goldengatemeatcompany.com
Angus beef, Bobby veal

GREAT-ALASKA-SEAFOOD
866-262-8846
www.great-alaska-seafood.com
Halibut, halibut cheeks

GRIMAUD FARMS
800-466-9955
www.grimaud.com
Duck, guinea hens, pheasants, duck fat

HERITAGE FOODS USA
212-980-6603
www.heritagefoodsusa.com
Wild salmon, pork, oysters

JOHNSTON COUNTY HAMS
919-934-8054
www.countrycuredhams.com
Dry-cured ham (American prosciutto)

MONTEREY FISH MARKET
510-525-5600
www.webseafood.com
Fresh Pacific seafood including Wild Pacific salmon, Dungeness crab, calamari, shrimp, sand dabs

NIMAN RANCH
510-808-0340
www.nimanranch.com
Naturally raised beef, pork, bacon, lamb

NUESKE'S
800-392-2266
www.nueske.com
Bacon

PENN COVE SHELLFISH, LLC
360-678-4803
www.penncoveshellfish.com
Mediterranean mussels

POLARICA
800-426-3872
www.polarica.com
Fresh and frozen truffles, duck confit, foie gras, duck, guinea hens, quail, squab, poussin, pheasant, rabbit, duck fat

PREFERRED MEATS
800-397-6328
www.preferredmeats.com
Beef, Berkshire pork, lamb, apple wood–smoked bacon

TAYLOR SHELLFISH FARMS
360-426-6178
www.taylorshellfishfarms.com
Mediterranean mussels, Dungeness crab

SPECIALTY PRODUCTS AND EQUIPMENT

ADRIANA'S CARAVAN

800-316-0820

www.adrianascaravan.com

Huge international selection of spices, oils, vinegars, fresh and dried mushrooms

BRIDGE KITCHENWARE

212-688-4220

www.bridgekitchenware.com

Extensive selection of professional equipment

THE CHEESE WORKS LTD.

510-769-1150

Distributors of domestic and imported cheeses, plus olives, cured meats, chocolates, and many other specialty foods. Call them for information on local retailers of their products.

CHEFSHOP.COM

877-337-2491

www.chefshop.com

Large selection of food products, including dried gigande and emergo beans, oils, vinegars, spices

CHOCOSPHERE

877-992-4626

www.chocosphere.com

All kinds of chocolate, including Valrhona

DEAN & DELUCA

800-221-7714

www.deandeluca.com

Artisanal oils, vinegars, cheeses, Valrhona chocolate, Johnston country ham, spices

EARTHY DELIGHTS

800-367-4709

www.earthy.com

Fresh and frozen peeled chestnuts, artisanal oils and vinegars, fresh wild mushrooms, foie gras

FARMERS' MARKETS INFORMATION AND LOCATIONS NATIONWIDE

www.ams.usda.gov/farmersmarkets

Produce and other products direct from the source

FRESH AND WILD

P.O. Box 2981

Vancouver, WA 68668

360-737-3652

Call or write regarding wild mushrooms and dried Red Flame seedless grapes

FRIEDA'S

800-241-1771

www.friedas.com

Specialty produce

JACOBS FARM/DEL CABO, INC.

650-879-0580

www.delcabo.com

Cooperative growers of organic tomatoes, fruits, vegetables, herbs

KALUSTYAN'S

800-352-3451

www.kalustyans.com

Huge international selection of spices and condiments, specializing in Middle Eastern foods

KING ARTHUR FLOUR

802-649-3881

www.kingarthurflour.com

Everything a baker could want, including equipment, such as individual pie tins and ingredients such as hazelnut paste.

PCD PROFESSIONAL CUTLERY DIRECT

800-792-6650

www.cookingenthusiast.com

Professional equipment including spiral cutters and torches

PENZEY'S, LTD.

800 741-7787

www.penzeys.com

Spices and herbs

PHIPPS RANCH

650-879-1622

www.phippscounty.com

Dried gigande beans, plus a large selection of organic shelling beans

THE SPANISH TABLE

510-548-1383

www.spanishtable.com

Spanish products, including squid ink, *lomo*, artisanal sherry vinegar, saffron, piquillo peppers, *pimentón*

TIENDA

888-472-1022

www.tienda.com

Spanish products, including *lomo*, piquillo peppers, sherry vinegar, saffron, *pimentón*

URBANI TRUFFLES & CAVIAR

800-889-1928

www.urbanitruffles.com

Fresh and preserved black and white truffles and truffle products

ZINGERMAN'S

888-636-8162

www.zingermans.com

Oils, vinegars, spices, porcini powder, cured meats, olives

INDEX

A

Aioli
  basic, 228
  Soft Saffron Aioli, 14, 16
Almonds
  Almond Pain Perdu, 76, 78–79
  Marcona Almond and Mint Pesto,
    41–43
  toasting, 234
Andouille Gumbo Sauce, 131, 133
Apples
  Apple Cream, 35–36
  Braised Chestnut Soup, 35–36
  Calvados Duck Sauce, 143, 145
  Duck Breast Stuffed with Apples
    and Chestnuts and Roasted in
    Bacon, 143–45
  Endive and Heirloom Apple Salad,
    9–10
  Shaved Apple and Fennel Salad,
    103, 105
  Whole-Apple Crisp, 198–99
Artichokes
  Artichoke Confit, 70–71
  Artichoke Soup, 41–43
  buying, 42
Arugula
  Mediterranean Mussels with
    Panzanella and Arugula, 14–16
  Potatoes Crushed with Garlic, Chiles,
    and Arugula, 96–97
  Warm Arugula and Olive Salad with
    Glazed Walnuts, 134–37
Asiago Cheese, Veal Chops Stuffed with
  Porcini Mushrooms and, 168–69
Asian Pear, Thyme, and Spanish Sherry
  Relish, 80, 84
Asparagus
  Asparagus Vinaigrette, 46, 48
  White Asparagus Salad with
    "Crunchy" Poached Farm Egg,
    11–13
Avocado, Bacon-Wrapped Maine
  Monkfish Stuffed with Lobster and,
  116–19

B

Bacon
  Bacon Braising Stock, 228
  Bacon, Pomegranate, and Pistachio
    Relish, 161–63
  Bacon-Wrapped Maine Monkfish
    Stuffed with Lobster and
    Avocado, 116–19
  braising, 228

Duck Breast Stuffed with Apples
    and Chestnuts and Roasted in
    Bacon, 143–45
  Endive and Heirloom Apple Salad,
    9–10
  Fried Green Tomato and Crispy
    Hama Hama Oyster "BLT,"
    57–59
  Pancetta and Baby Spinach Salad,
    106, 108
  Porcini-Pork Sausage Wrapped in
    Pancetta, 158–59
  Potato, Bacon, and Watercress
    Cakes, 103–4
Banana Cream Pie, White Chocolate–,
  206–7
Banyuls Vinaigrette, 21–22
Basil
  Basil and Tiny Fava Pesto, 60–61
  Basil Oil, 54, 56
  Pesto, 233
  Shrimp and Basil Beignets, 93–95
Bavarian Cream, 223–25
Bavarian Timbales, 223–25
Beans
  Basil and Tiny Fava Pesto, 60–61
  Fava Beans, English Peas, and Mint,
    153, 155
  Garlic Confit and Gigande Bean
    Fondue, 232
  preparing, 229, 231
  Roasted Ratatouille Soup with White
    Beans and Serrano Ham, 33–34
  Shelling Bean Salad, 67–68
  Spring Vegetables, 98, 101
  White and Green Beans with Garlic
    Confit, 158–59
Beef
  Fire-Roasted Angus Beef Filet,
    177–79
  New York Strip Roasted in an Herbed
    Salt Crust, 180–84
  Rich Beef Stock, 231
  "Steamship" Short Ribs Bourguignon,
    185–90
Beignets, Shrimp and Basil, 93–95
Bell peppers
  Provençal Fish Soup, 37–39
  Roasted Ratatouille Soup with White
    Beans and Serrano Ham, 33–34
Beurre fondue
  basic, 228
  Parmesan Beurre Fondue, 51, 53
  Parsley Beurre Fondue, 70–71
Biscuits
  Chocolate Cherry Shortcakes,
    200–202
  Cream Biscuits, 127–29
Bittersweet Chocolate Cake, 215–17
Black Bass, Pan-Roasted, 110–11
Black Pudding, 73–75
Black Truffle Pappardelle, 51–53
Blood Orange Jus, 73, 75

Blood Orange Vinaigrette, 19–20
Blue cheese
  Blue Cheese Fritters, 177–79
  Salt-Roasted Bosc Pear and
    Roquefort Salad, 23–25
Bosc Pear Confit, 76, 79
Bouillabaisse Relish, 37, 39
Braised Chestnut Soup, 35–36
Braised Shellfish Mushrooms, 113–15
Bread
  Almond Pain Perdu, 76, 78–79
  Corn Bread, 131–32
  Creamed Morels with Aged Madeira
    on Toast, 180, 184
  Croutons, 37, 39
  crumbs, 228
  Mediterranean Mussels with
    Panzanella, 14–16
  Spicy Corn Bread Stuffing, 131–32
Brittany Salt Caramel Ice Cream, 203–4
Broccoli Rabe, Lamb Porterhouse Chop
    Stuffed with Melted Garlic and,
    164–67
Brownies, Chocolate, 218, 220
Brussels Sprouts, Shaved, 161–63
Butter, 4
Buttermilk-Brined Fried Little Chickens,
    127–29

C

Cakes
  Bittersweet Chocolate Cake, 215–17
  Carrot Cake with Cream Cheese
    Filling, 208–11
  Chocolate Mayo Cake, 223–24
  Heather Ho's Lemon Meringue
    Icebox Cake, 212–13
Calamari. See Squid
California White Sea Bass Roasted with
    Olives and Basil, 96–97
Calvados Duck Sauce, 143, 145
Candied Carrots, 208, 211
Candied Nuts, 228
Candied Walnut Ice Cream, 208, 210
Caramel
  Caramel Corn Ice Cream, 215–16
  Caramel Cream, 212–13
  Caramel Popcorn, 215–16
  Caramel Sauce, 215, 217
  Cider Caramel Sauce, 198–99
  Salty Clear Caramel, 203–4
  Walnut Caramel, 208, 211
Carpaccio of Fresh Hearts of Palm,
    Cucumbers, and Summer Truffles,
    21–22
Carrots
  Bouillabaisse Relish, 37, 39
  Candied Carrots, 208, 211
  Carrot Cake with Cream Cheese
    Filling, 208–11
  Carrot Mousseline, 185, 190

Carrot Sherbet, 208, 210
Cauliflower
    Cauliflower "Risotto," 110–11
    Cauliflower Soup with Maine Lobster,
        29
Celery Root Puree, 143, 145
Cheddar Dressing, Creamy, 9–10
Cheese. See individual cheese varieties
Cherries
    Cherries Jubilee, 200–202
    Chocolate Cherry Shortcakes,
        200–202
Chestnuts
    Braised Chestnut Soup, 35–36
    Duck Breast Stuffed with Apples
        and Chestnuts and Roasted in
        Bacon, 143–45
    peeling, 35–36
Chicken
    Buttermilk-Brined Fried Little
        Chickens, 127–29
    Dark Chicken Stock, 230–31
    Gravy, 127–28
    Light Chicken Stock, 230
    Roasted Poussin with Spicy Corn
        Bread Stuffing, 131–33
Chocolate
    Bittersweet Chocolate Cake, 215–17
    Chocolate Brownies, 218, 220
    Chocolate Cherry Shortcakes,
        200–202
    Chocolate Glaze, 203–4
    Chocolate Lace Tuiles, 218, 220–21
    Chocolate Mayo Cake, 223–24
    Chocolate Panna Cotta, 218–21
    Chocolate Tart Dough, 203–4
    Chocolate Temptation, 218–21
    Chocolate Toffee Crunch, 218–21
    Hot Fudge Sauce, 232
    Manjari Chocolate Truffle Tart, 203–4
    shavings, 206–7
    types of, 4
Cider
    Cider-Brined Berkshire Pork Loin
        Chop, 161–63
    Cider Caramel Sauce, 198–99
    Cider Sauce, 103, 105, 161, 163
Clams, Steamed, and Chorizo, Pot of,
    121–23
Cod
    Provençal Fish Soup, 37–39
    Roasted True Cod, 106–8
Coriander Risotto, 116, 119
Corn
    Caramel Corn Ice Cream, 215–16
    Caramel Popcorn, 215–16
    Corn Bread, 131–32
    Double Corn Stock, 32
    Single Corn Stock, 31–32
    Spicy Corn Bread Stuffing, 131–32
    Sweet White Corn and Chanterelles,
        177–78
    White Corn Soup, 31–32

Crab
    buying, 48, 56
    Crab Salad, 228
    Dungeness Crab Cake, 46–49
    Little Crab Cake "Soufflés," 31–32
Cream Biscuits, 127–29
Cream cheese
    Caramel Cream, 212–13
    Carrot Cake with Cream Cheese
        Filling, 208–11

    Cream Cheese Ice Cream, 208,
        210–11
    Lemon Cream, 212–13
Creamed Greens, 229
Creamed Morels with Aged Madeira on
    Toast, 180, 184
Creamed Spinach, 229
Creams
    Apple Cream, 35–36
    Bavarian Cream, 223–25
    Caramel Cream, 212–13
    Whipped Cream, 206–7
Creamy Cheddar Dressing, 9–10
Crème Brûlée, Vanilla, 223–25
Crisp, Whole-Apple, 198–99
Croutons, 37, 39
Cucumbers, Carpaccio of Fresh Hearts
    of Palm, Summer Truffles, and,
    21–22

D

Dark Chicken Stock, 230–31
Dark Roux, 131, 133
Dates, Warm Medjool, Stuffed with Goat
    Cheese, 19–20
Desserts
    Bavarian Timbales, 223–25
    Bittersweet Chocolate Cake, 215–17
    Brittany Salt Caramel Ice Cream,
        203–4
    Candied Walnut Ice Cream, 208, 210
    Caramel Corn Ice Cream, 215–16
    Carrot Cake with Cream Cheese
        Filling, 208–11
    Carrot Sherbet, 208, 210
    Chocolate Cherry Shortcakes,
        200–202
    Chocolate Panna Cotta, 218–21
    Chocolate Temptation, 218–21
    Chocolate Toffee Crunch, 218–21
    Cream Cheese Ice Cream, 208,
        210–11
    Heather Ho's Lemon Meringue
        Icebox Cake, 212–13
    Ice Cream Sandwiches, 223–25
    Manjari Chocolate Truffle Tart, 203–4
    Old-Fashioned Vanilla Ice Cream,
        200–202
    Rum Raisin Ice Cream, 198–99
    Vanilla Crème Brûlée, 223–25

White Chocolate–Banana Cream Pie,
    206–7
Whole-Apple Crisp, 198–99
Double Corn Stock, 32
Duck
    Braised Chestnut Soup, 35–36
    Calvados Duck Sauce, 143, 145
    Duck Breast Stuffed with Apples
        and Chestnuts and Roasted in
        Bacon, 143–45
    Duck Confit, 229
Dungeness Crab Cake, 46–49

E

Egg, "Crunchy" Poached Farm, White
    Asparagus Salad with, 11–13
Eggplant
    Melted Eggplant, 93–94
    Roasted Ratatouille Soup with White
        Beans and Serrano Ham, 33–34
Endive
    Endive and Heirloom Apple Salad,
        9–10
    tempering bitterness of, 19

F

Fava beans
    Basil and Tiny Fava Pesto, 60–61
    Fava Beans, English Peas, and Mint,
        153, 155
    preparing, 229
    Spring Vegetables, 98, 101
Fennel
    Artichoke Soup, 41–43
    Bouillabaisse Relish, 37, 39
    Fennel and Leek Relish, 73, 75
    Fennel Confit, 14, 16
    Fennel-Roasted Pork Tenderloin,
        158–59
    Fennel Rub, 231
    Paella Stock, 121, 123
    Provençal Fish Soup, 37–39
    Roasted Ratatouille Soup with White
        Beans and Serrano Ham, 33–34
    Shaved Apple and Fennel Salad,
        103, 105
Fire-Roasted Angus Beef Filet, 177–79
Fish
    Bacon-Wrapped Maine Monkfish
        Stuffed with Lobster and
        Avocado, 116–19
    California White Sea Bass Roasted
        with Olives and Basil, 96–97
    Crispy-Skinned Onaga, 113–15
    Fish Fumet, 229–30
    Jalapeño and Pepper Tartare, 64–65
    Pan-Roasted Black Bass, 110–11

Pan-Roasted Halibut Fillets and Cheeks, 98–101

Pan-Roasted Mediterranean Rouget Barbet, 93–95

Pan-Roasted Wild King or Ivory Salmon, 103–5

Provençal Fish Soup, 37–39

Roasted True Cod, 106–8

Sand Dabs Stuffed with Lobster, 70–71

Shiitake and White Soy Tartare, 64–65

Spicy Red Chile Tartare, 64–65

Trio of Tuna Tartares, 64–65

Foie gras
Foie Gras Sauce, 146, 148
New Year's Eve Venison Chop "Rossini," 193–95
Pan-Seared Foie Gras, 76–79
Quail Stuffed with Foie Gras and Roasted Porcini Mushrooms, 80–84

Fonduta, Parmesan, 11, 13

Fresh Hearts of Palm, 113, 115

Fresh Morel Mushrooms, 98, 100–101

Fried Green Tomato and Crispy Hama Hama Oyster "BLT," 57–59

Fritters, Blue Cheese, 177–79

Frying, tips for, 126

Fudge Sauce, Hot, 232

G

Game hens
Buttermilk-Brined Fried Little Chickens, 127–29
buying, 128

Garlic
Aioli, 228
fresh vs. prepeeled, 4
Garlic Confit and Gigande Bean Fondue, 232
Green Garlic Pesto, 98, 101
Melted Garlic, 232
Potatoes Crushed with Garlic, Chiles, and Arugula, 96–97
Twice-Cooked Potatoes with Garlic Mousseline, 134–37
White and Green Beans with Garlic Confit, 158–59

Gigande beans
Garlic Confit and Gigande Bean Fondue, 232
preparing, 231
Roasted Ratatouille Soup with White Beans and Serrano Ham, 33–34
White and Green Beans with Garlic Confit, 158–59

Glaze, Chocolate, 203–4

Glazed Sweetbreads in Potato Crust, 86–89

Glazed Walnuts, 134, 136–37

Goat cheese
Goat Cheese and Truffle Ravioli, 60–61

Warm Medjool Dates Stuffed with Goat Cheese, 19–20

Grapes
Red Grape and Kumquat Relish, 146, 148
Rum Raisin Ice Cream, 198–99

Gravy, 127–28

Green Garlic Pesto, 98, 101

Greens. See also individual greens
Creamed Greens, 229
tempering bitterness of, 19
Warm Medjool Dates Stuffed with Goat Cheese, 19–20

Green Tomato Vinaigrette, 57, 59

Guinea Hens, Pot-Roasted, 134

H

Halibut Fillets and Cheeks, Pan-Roasted, 98–101

Ham
Roasted Rabbit Loins Wrapped in Smithfield County "Prosciutto," 153–55
Roasted Ratatouille Soup with White Beans and Serrano Ham, 33–34
White Asparagus Salad with "Crunchy" Poached Farm Egg, 11–13

Hazelnuts
Candied Nuts, 228
Hazelnut Pancakes, 146, 148–49
Red Grape and Kumquat Relish, 146, 148

Heather Ho's Lemon Meringue Icebox Cake, 212–13

Heirloom Tomato Carpaccio, 93–95

Heirloom Tomatoes, 177–79

Herb and Lemon Oil, 29

Herb-Roasted Jumbo Prawns, 37, 39

Hot Fudge Sauce, 232

I

Ice cream
Brittany Salt Caramel Ice Cream, 203–4
Candied Walnut Ice Cream, 208, 210
Caramel Corn Ice Cream, 215–16
Cream Cheese Ice Cream, 208, 210–11
Ice Cream Sandwiches, 223–25
Old-Fashioned Vanilla Ice Cream, 200–202
Rum Raisin Ice Cream, 198–99

J

Jalapeño and Pepper Tartare, 64–65

Jus
Blood Orange Jus, 73, 75
Morel Mushroom Jus, 98, 100
Pork-Porcini Jus, 158–59

K

Kabocha Squash Puree, 80, 83, 84

Kumquat and Red Grape Relish, 146, 148

L

Lamb Porterhouse Chop Stuffed with Broccoli Rabe and Melted Garlic, 164–67

Leeks
Artichoke Soup, 41–43
Braised Chestnut Soup, 35–36
Fennel and Leek Relish, 73, 75

Lemons
Heather Ho's Lemon Meringue Icebox Cake, 212–13
Herb and Lemon Oil, 29
Lemon and Parmesan Relish, 171–72
Lemon Cream, 212–13
Lemon Curd, 212–13
Lemon Vinaigrette, 46, 48
Preserved Lemons, 234
segmenting, 70

Lettuce
Fried Green Tomato and Crispy Hama Hama Oyster "BLT," 57–59
Salt-Roasted Bosc Pear and Roquefort Salad, 23–25

Light Chicken Stock, 230

Lisa's Potato Pancakes, 139, 141

Little Crab Cake "Soufflés," 31–32

Lobster
Bacon-Wrapped Maine Monkfish Stuffed with Lobster and Avocado, 116–19
Cauliflower Soup with Maine Lobster, 29
cooking and cleaning, 232
Maine Lobster Tail with John Desmond's Black Pudding, 73–75
Paella Stock, 121, 123
Sand Dabs Stuffed with Lobster, 70–71
Spiny Lobster Paella, 121–23

M

Macadamia nuts
Chocolate Toffee Crunch, 218–21
Macadamia Nut Toffee, 218, 221
toasting, 234

Maine Lobster Tail with John Desmond's Black Pudding, 73–75

Manjari Chocolate Truffle Tart, 203–4

Marcona Almond and Mint Pesto, 41–43

Mashed Potatoes, 127, 129

Mayonnaise
Aioli, 228
Chocolate Mayo Cake, 223–24
Soft Saffron Aioli, 14, 16
Tartar Sauce, 234

Mediterranean Mussels with Panzanella
     and Arugula, 14–16
Melted Eggplant, 93–94
Melted Garlic, 232
Miso Vinaigrette, 64–65
Monkfish, Bacon-Wrapped Maine,
     Stuffed with Lobster and Avocado,
     116–19
Mushrooms
     Braised Shellfish Mushrooms, 113–15
     Creamed Morels with Aged Madeira
          on Toast, 180, 184
     Fresh Morel Mushrooms, 98, 100–101
     Glazed Sweetbreads in Potato Crust,
          86–89
     Morel Mushroom Jus, 98, 100
     Porcini-Pork Sausage, 233
     Porcini Powder, 234
     Pork-Porcini Jus, 158–59
     Quail Stuffed with Foie Gras and
          Roasted Porcini Mushrooms,
          80–84
     Shiitake and White Soy Tartare,
          64–65
     Sweet White Corn and Chanterelles,
          177–78
     Veal Chops Stuffed with Porcini
          Mushrooms and Asiago Cheese,
          168–69
     White Asparagus Salad with
          "Crunchy" Poached Farm Egg,
          11–13
Mussels, Mediterranean, with
     Panzanella and Arugula, 14–16
Mustard Vinaigrette, 103, 105

N

New Year's Eve Venison Chop "Rossini,"
     193–95
New York Strip Roasted in an Herbed
     Salt Crust, 180–84
Nuts. See also individual nuts
     Candied Nuts, 228
     toasting, 234

O

Oil
     Basil Oil, 54, 56
     canola, 4
     grape seed, 4
     Herb and Lemon Oil, 29
     olive, 4
     truffle, 51
Old-Fashioned Vanilla Ice Cream,
     200–202
Olives
     oil, 4
     Warm Arugula and Olive Salad with
          Glazed Walnuts, 134–37
Onaga, Crispy-Skinned, 113–15
Oranges
     Blood Orange Jus, 73, 75

Blood Orange Vinaigrette, 19–20
     segmenting, 70
Osso Buco, Veal, 171–75
Oven-Roasted Tomatoes, 232
Oysters
     Fried Green Tomato and Crispy
          Hama Hama Oyster "BLT,"
          57–59
     shucking, 59
     varieties of, 57

P

Paella
     Paella Stock, 121, 123
     Spiny Lobster Paella, 121–23
Pain Perdu, Almond, 76, 78–79
Palm, hearts of
     buying, 21
     Carpaccio of Fresh Hearts of Palm,
          Cucumbers, and Summer
          Truffles, 21–22
     Fresh Hearts of Palm, 113, 115
Pancakes
     Hazelnut Pancakes, 146, 148–49
     Lisa's Potato Pancakes, 139, 141
Pancetta. See Bacon
Panna Cotta, Chocolate, 218–21
Pan-Roasted Black Bass, 110–11
Pan-Roasted California Pheasant
     Breast, 139–41
Pan-Roasted Crispy-Skinned Onaga,
     113–15
Pan-Roasted Halibut Fillets and Cheeks,
     98–101
Pan-Roasted Mediterranean Rouget
     Barbet, 93–95
Pan-Roasted Squab, 146–49
Pan-Roasted True Cod, 106–8
Pan-Roasted Wild King or Ivory Salmon,
     103–5
Pan-Seared Foie Gras, 76–79
Pan-Seared Monterey Calamari, 54–56
Panzanella, Mediterranean Mussels
     with, 14–16
Parmesan cheese
     Lemon and Parmesan Relish, 171–72
     Parmesan Beurre Fondue, 51, 53
     Parmesan Fonduta, 11, 13
     Rabbit Legs Fried in a Parmesan
          Crust, 153–55
Parsley Beurre Fondue, 70–71
Pasta
     Black Truffle Pappardelle, 51–53
     Goat Cheese and Truffle Ravioli,
          60–61
     Pasta Dough, 233
     Veal Cheek Ravioli, 171–75
Pastry Cream, White Chocolate, 206–7
Pears
     Asian Pear, Thyme, and Spanish
          Sherry Relish, 80, 84
     Bosc Pear Confit, 76, 79
     Salt-Roasted Bosc Pear and
          Roquefort Salad, 23–25

Peas
     Fava Beans, English Peas, and Mint,
          153, 155
     Spring Vegetables, 98, 101
Pecans
     Candied Nuts, 228
     Endive and Heirloom Apple Salad,
          9–10
     Whole-Apple Crisp, 198–99
Pepper, 4
Pesto
     basic, 233
     Basil and Tiny Fava Pesto, 60–61
     Green Garlic Pesto, 98, 101
     Marcona Almond and Mint Pesto,
          41–43
     Pine Nut Pesto, 60–61
Pheasant Breast, Pan-Roasted
     California, 139–41
Pies
     Pie Dough, 206–7
     White Chocolate–Banana Cream Pie,
          206–7
Pine nuts
     Pine Nut Pesto, 60–61
     Pine Nut Relish, 106, 108
     toasting, 234
Pistachios
     Bacon, Pomegranate, and Pistachio
          Relish, 161–63
     toasting, 234
     Warm Medjool Dates Stuffed with
          Goat Cheese, 19–20
Pomegranate
     Bacon, Pomegranate, and Pistachio
          Relish, 161–63
     Warm Medjool Dates Stuffed with
          Goat Cheese, 19–20
Popcorn, Caramel, 215–16
Porcini. See Mushrooms
Pork
     Black Pudding, 73–75
     Cider-Brined Berkshire Pork Loin
          Chop, 161–63
     Fennel-Roasted Pork Tenderloin,
          158–59
     Porcini-Pork Sausage, 233
     Porcini-Pork Sausage Wrapped in
          Pancetta, 158–59
     Pork-Porcini Jus, 158–59
     Seared Sea Scallops, 67–68
Port Vinaigrette, 23, 25
Potatoes
     Glazed Sweetbreads in Potato Crust,
          86–89
     Lisa's Potato Pancakes, 139, 141
     Mashed Potatoes, 127, 129
     Potato, Bacon, and Watercress
          Cakes, 103–4
     Potatoes Crushed with Garlic, Chiles,
          and Arugula, 96–97
     Potato Mousseline, 73, 75
     Potato "Risotto," 164–67
     Roasted Fingerling Potatoes, 168–69
     Roasted German Butterballs, 185,
          187, 190

turning, 187
Twice-Cooked Potatoes with Garlic
    Mousseline, 134–37
Pot of Steamed Clams and Chorizo,
    121–23
Pot-Roasted Guinea Hens, 134–37
Poussin, Roasted, with Spicy Corn
    Bread Stuffing, 131–33
Prawns. See Shrimp and prawns
Preserved Lemons, 234
Prosciutto. See Ham
Provençal Fish Soup, 37–39
Pudding, Black, 73–75

Q

Quail Stuffed with Foie Gras and
    Roasted Porcini Mushrooms,
    80–84

R

Rabbit
    buying, 154
    Rabbit Legs Fried in a Parmesan
        Crust, 153–55
    Rabbit Two Ways, 153–55
    Roasted Rabbit Loins Wrapped in
        Smithfield County "Prosciutto,"
        153–55
Ratatouille Soup, Roasted, with White
    Beans and Serrano Ham, 33–34
Ravioli
    Goat Cheese and Truffle Ravioli,
        60–61
    Veal Cheek Ravioli, 171–75
Red Grape and Kumquat Relish, 146,
    148
Red Wine Sauce, 86, 88
Relishes
    Asian Pear, Thyme, and Spanish
        Sherry Relish, 80, 84
    Bacon, Pomegranate, and Pistachio
        Relish, 161–63
    Bouillabaisse Relish, 37, 39
    Fennel and Leek Relish, 73, 75
    Lemon and Parmesan Relish, 171–72
    Pine Nut Relish, 106, 108
    Red Grape and Kumquat Relish, 146,
        148
    Toasted Walnut Relish, 23, 25
Rice
    Coriander Risotto, 116, 119
    Spiny Lobster Paella, 121–23
Rich Beef Stock, 231
Roasted Fingerling Potatoes, 168–69
Roasted German Butterballs, 185, 187,
    190
Roasted Poussin with Spicy Corn Bread
    Stuffing, 131–33
Roasted Rabbit Loins Wrapped in
    Smithfield County "Prosciutto,"
    153–55

Roasted Ratatouille Soup with White
    Beans and Serrano Ham, 33–34
Roasted Veal Tenderloin, 171–75
Roquefort and Salt-Roasted Bosc Pear
    Salad, 23–25
Rosemary Vinaigrette, 134, 137
Rouget Barbet, Pan-Roasted
    Mediterranean, 93–95
Roux, Dark, 131, 133
Rub, Fennel, 231
Rum Raisin Ice Cream, 198–99

S

Saffron Sauce, 14, 16
Salad dressings and vinaigrettes
    Asparagus Vinaigrette, 46, 48
    Banyuls Vinaigrette, 21–22
    Blood Orange Vinaigrette, 19–20
    Creamy Cheddar Dressing, 9–10
    Green Tomato Vinaigrette, 57, 59
    Lemon Vinaigrette, 46, 48
    Miso Vinaigrette, 64–65
    Mustard Vinaigrette, 103, 105
    Port Vinaigrette, 23, 25
    Rosemary Vinaigrette, 134, 137
    Squid Ink Vinaigrette, 54, 56
    Tomato Vinaigrette, 96–97
Salads
    Carpaccio of Fresh Hearts of Palm,
        Cucumbers, and Summer
        Truffles, 21–22
    Crab Salad, 228
    Endive and Heirloom Apple Salad,
        9–10
    Fennel Confit, 14, 16
    Mediterranean Mussels with
        Panzanella and Arugula, 14–16
    Pancetta and Baby Spinach Salad,
        106, 108
    Salt-Roasted Bosc Pear and
        Roquefort Salad, 23–25
    Shaved Apple and Fennel Salad,
        103, 105
    Shelling Bean Salad, 67–68
    Warm Arugula and Olive Salad with
        Glazed Walnuts, 134–37
    Warm Medjool Dates Stuffed with
        Goat Cheese, 19–20
    White Asparagus Salad with
        "Crunchy" Poached Farm Egg,
        11–13
Salmon, Pan-Roasted Wild King or Ivory,
    103–5
Salt, 4
Salt-Roasted Bosc Pear and Roquefort
    Salad, 23–25
Salty Clear Caramel, 203–4
Sand Dabs Stuffed with Lobster, 70–71
Santa Barbara Spot Prawns, 110–11
Sauces. See also Aioli; Pesto
    Andouille Gumbo Sauce, 131, 133
    Calvados Duck Sauce, 143, 145
    Caramel Sauce, 215, 217

Cider Caramel Sauce, 198–99
Cider Sauce, 103, 105, 161, 163
Foie Gras Sauce, 146, 148
Hot Fudge Sauce, 232
Red Wine Sauce, 86, 88
Saffron Sauce, 14, 16
Spanish Sherry Sauce, 80, 84
Tartar Sauce, 234
Truffle Sauce, 193–94
Sausage
    Andouille Gumbo Sauce, 131, 133
    Porcini-Pork Sausage, 233
    Porcini-Pork Sausage Wrapped in
        Pancetta, 158–59
    Pot of Steamed Clams and Chorizo,
        121–23
Sautéed Spinach, 80, 83
Scallops
    buying, 67
    Seared Sea Scallops, 67–68
Sea bass
    California White Sea Bass Roasted
        with Olives and Basil, 96–97
    Provençal Fish Soup, 37–39
    Seared Sea Scallops, 67–68
Shaved Apple and Fennel Salad, 103,
    105
Shaved Brussels Sprouts, 161–63
Shelling Bean Salad, 67–68
Sherbet, Carrot, 208, 210
Sherry
    Asian Pear, Thyme, and Spanish
        Sherry Relish, 80, 84

    Sherry Vinegar Reduction, 76, 79
    Spanish Sherry Sauce, 80, 84
    types of, 78
    vinegar, 78
Shiitake and White Soy Tartare, 64–65
Shortcakes, Chocolate Cherry, 200–202
Shrimp and prawns
    Herb-Roasted Jumbo Prawns, 37, 39
    Paella Stock, 121, 123
    Santa Barbara Spot Prawns, 110–11
    Shrimp and Basil Beignets, 93–95
Single Corn Stock, 31–32
Soft Saffron Aioli, 14, 16
Soups
    Artichoke Soup, 41–43
    Braised Chestnut Soup, 35–36
    Cauliflower Soup with Maine Lobster,
        29
    Provençal Fish Soup, 37–39
    Roasted Ratatouille Soup with White
        Beans and Serrano Ham, 33–34
    White Corn Soup, 31–32
Spanish Sherry Sauce, 80, 84
Spicy Corn Bread Stuffing, 131–32
Spicy Red Chile Tartare, 64–65
Spinach
    Creamed Spinach, 229
    Pancetta and Baby Spinach Salad,
        106, 108
    Sautéed Spinach, 80, 83
    Veal Cheek Ravioli, 171–75

Spiny Lobster Paella, 121–23
Spring Vegetables, 98, 101
Squab, Pan-Roasted, 146–49
Squash
　Kabocha Squash Puree, 80, 83, 84
　Roasted Ratatouille Soup with White
　　Beans and Serrano Ham, 33–34
Squid
　cleaning, 56
　Pan-Seared Monterey Calamari,
　　54–56
　Squid Ink Vinaigrette, 54, 56
"Steamship" Short Ribs Bourguignon,
　185–90
Stocks
　Bacon Braising Stock, 228
　as base for sauces, 4
　Dark Chicken Stock, 230–31
　Double Corn Stock, 32
　Fish Fumet, 229–30
　Light Chicken Stock, 230
　Paella Stock, 121, 123
　Rich Beef Stock, 231
　Single Corn Stock, 31–32
Sweetbreads, Glazed, in Potato Crust,
　86–89
Sweet White Corn and Chanterelles,
　177–78
Syrup, Vanilla, 223, 225

T

Tartar Sauce, 234
Tarts
　Chocolate Tart Dough, 203–4
　Manjari Chocolate Truffle Tart, 203–4
Timbales, Bavarian, 223–25
Toasted Walnut Relish, 23, 25
Toffee
　Chocolate Toffee Crunch, 218–21
　Macadamia Nut Toffee, 218, 221
Tomatoes
　Fried Green Tomato and Crispy
　　Hama Hama Oyster "BLT,"
　　57–59
　Green Tomato Vinaigrette, 57, 59
　Heirloom Tomato Carpaccio, 93–95
　Heirloom Tomatoes, 177–79
　Mediterranean Mussels with
　　Panzanella and Arugula, 14–16
　Oven-Roasted Tomatoes, 232
　Provençal Fish Soup, 37–39
　Roasted Ratatouille Soup with White
　　Beans and Serrano Ham, 33–34
　Tomato Gratin, 106, 108
　Tomato Vinaigrette, 96–97
Trio of Tuna Tartares, 64–65
Truffles
　Black Truffle Pappardelle, 51–53
　Carpaccio of Fresh Hearts of Palm,
　　Cucumbers, and Summer
　　Truffles, 21–22
　Goat Cheese and Truffle Ravioli,
　　60–61

New Year's Eve Venison Chop
　"Rossini," 193–95
　oil, 51
　Truffle Sauce, 193–94
　varieties of, 21, 51, 60
Tuiles, Chocolate Lace, 218, 220–21
Tuna
　Jalapeño and Pepper Tartare, 64–65
　Shiitake and White Soy Tartare,
　　64–65
　Spicy Red Chile Tartare, 64–65
　Trio of Tuna Tartares, 64–65
Twice-Cooked Potatoes with Garlic
　Mousseline, 134–37

V

Vanilla
　Bavarian Timbales, 223–25
　Ice Cream Sandwiches, 223–25
　Old-Fashioned Vanilla Ice Cream,
　　200–202
　types of, 223
　Vanilla Crème Brûlée, 223–25
　Vanilla Syrup, 223, 225
　Vanilla, Vanilla, Vanilla, 223–25
Veal
　Glazed Sweetbreads in Potato Crust,
　　86–89
　Roasted Veal Tenderloin, 171–75
　Veal Cheek Ravioli, 171–75
　Veal Chops Stuffed with Porcini
　　Mushrooms and Asiago Cheese,
　　168–69
　Veal Osso Buco, 171–75
　Veal, Veal, Veal, 171–75
Venison Chop "Rossini," New Year's Eve,
　193–95
Vinaigrettes. See Salad dressings and
　vinaigrettes
Vinegar, 4, 21, 78

W

Walnuts
　Candied Nuts, 228
　Candied Walnut Ice Cream, 208, 210
　Glazed Walnuts, 134, 136–37
　Toasted Walnut Relish, 23, 25
　toasting, 234
　Walnut Caramel, 208, 211
Warm Arugula and Olive Salad with
　Glazed Walnuts, 134–37
Warm Medjool Dates Stuffed with Goat
　Cheese, 19–20
Watercress
　Potato, Bacon, and Watercress
　　Cakes, 103–4
　Shaved Apple and Fennel Salad,
　　103, 105
Whipped Cream, 206–7
White and Green Beans with Garlic
　Confit, 158–59

White Asparagus Salad with "Crunchy"
　Poached Farm Egg, 11–13
White chocolate
　White Chocolate–Banana Cream Pie,
　　206–7
　White Chocolate Pastry Cream,
　　206–7
White Corn Soup, 31–32
Whole-Apple Crisp, 198–99

Z

Zucchini
　Roasted Ratatouille Soup with White
　　Beans and Serrano Ham, 33–34